Frederick Charles Husenbeth, Henry. asn Weedall

The life of the right reverend Monsignor Weedall, D.D., Domestic Prolete of his Holiness, Pope Pius IX. and president of St. Marys College, Oscott, including incidentally The early history of Oscott College

Frederick Charles Husenbeth, Henry. asn Weedall

The life of the right reverend Monsignor Weedall, D.D., Domestic Prolete of his Holiness, Pope Pius IX. and president of St. Marys College, Oscott, including incidentally The early history of Oscott College

ISBN/EAN: 9783741158308

Manufactured in Europe, USA, Canada, Australia, Japa

Cover: Foto ©Andreas Hilbeck / pixelio.de

Manufactured and distributed by brebook publishing software (www.brebook.com)

Frederick Charles Husenbeth, Henry. asn Weedall

The life of the right reverend Monsignor Weedall, D.D., Domestic Prolete of his Holiness, Pope Pius IX. and president of St. Marys College, Oscott, including incidentally The early history of Oscott College

THE LIFE

OF

THE RIGHT REVEREND

Monsignor Weedall, D.D.,

DOMESTIC PRELATE OF HIS HOLINESS, POPE PIUS IX.;
VICAR GENERAL OF THE DIOCESE,
AND PROVOST OF THE CHAPTER, OF BIRMINGHAM;
AND
PRESIDENT OF ST. MARY'S COLLEGE, OSCOTT;

INCLUDING INCIDENTALLY
THE EARLY HISTORY OF OSCOTT COLLEGE.

BY

F. C. HUSENBETH, D.D., V.G.,
PROVOST OF NORTHAMPTON.

"*Who in his life propped up the* HOUSE, *and in his days fortified the* TEMPLE."
ECCLESIASTICUS L., 1.

LONDON:
LONGMAN, GREEN, LONGMAN, AND ROBERTS.
1860.

To the Pupils and Friends

Of St. Mary's College, Oscott,

THIS LIFE

Of the most Distinguished of her Sons,

is dedicated

By his Schoolfellow, Pupil, and Friend,

THE AUTHOR.

Cossey, February 18th, 1860.

PREFACE.

The following pages have no higher pretensions than to present a familiar history of the lamented MONSIGNOR WEEDALL. They chiefly embody and embalm the reminiscences of an old and admiring friend;—who was a boy with him at school,—a pupil under him at college,—a brother priest with him in after years,—and throughout his meritorious career, his devoted and affectionate, though humble friend. It will be perceived to be the production of one, very decidedly a

> "Laudator temporis acti
> Se puero:"

but to many it will not be on that account the less acceptable.

The author gladly avails himself of this opportunity to express his warm thanks to his old and dear friend, Canon McDonnell, who supplied him with some particulars of the early years of their mutual friend, which he could not otherwise have recorded: and to another highly esteemed friend, Provost Bagnall, who kindly permitted him to use at discretion the papers which had come into his possession, as executor of the lamented prelate deceased.

It will hardly be considered that too much space is occupied in this biography by accounts of Dr. WEEDALL's Sermons, and passages extracted from them; since it was as a preacher that he shone most brilliantly. Nothing indeed more strongly evinced the fervour of his piety, the elegant cultivation of his mind, and the superior character of his abilities, than his pulpit compositions.

But let this suffice, in a few words, for a warning to the readers. And now we must come to the narration.*

COSSEY, *February 25th*, 1860.

* 2 MACHABEES, VI., 17.

CONTENTS.

CHAPTER I.

Introductory Observations—Biography—Summary of Dr. Weedall's Career and Character—His Birth and Early Years—He is sent to School at Sedgley Park—His Character there—His Ode on Sedgley Park 1

CHAPTER II.

Removal from Sedgley Park—History of the Mission of Oscott—Commencement of an Ecclesiastical Seminary there—Beginning of the College at Oscott—Its First Church Students—Weedall's Arrival at Oscott—Other Arrivals—Humble Ceremonial in the Chapel ... 16

CHAPTER III.

The "New Government"—St. Mary's College, Oscott—Its Superiors—The "Laura" Built—Weedall's Talents—Drawback from Weakness of his Eyes—The Repository—Weedall's Excellence in Various Games—Also as a Teacher—Conferences—Prones—Chapel Services—Vestments—Organ—Choir 32

CHAPTER IV.

Mr. Weedall Studies Theology under Mr. Potts—He is Initiated in Holy Orders—Gives Catechetical Instruction to the Children in the Poor School in Birmingham—His Poetry—His Controversy with Cobbett—Is Ordained Priest—His First Mass—First Printed Sermon—Other Exercises of the Holy Ministry 53

CHAPTER V.

Mr. Weedall's Class in Rhetoric—Christmas Exhibition—His Amanuensis—Controversy in the "Orthodox Journal"—Mr. Potts Disabled by Paralysis—Changes in consequence in the College—Mr. Weedall's Occasional Priestly Duties—Sermon at St. Chad's—Events at Oscott—Exhibition Room 74

CHAPTER VI.

Mr. Weedall's Sermon at Sheffield—Decline of Mr. Quick's Health—Mr. Weedall Officiates on Sundays at Vespers—His Catechetical Lectures—Sermon at Liverpool—Death of Mr. Quick—Mr. Weedall becomes Vice-President, Professor of Theology, and Spiritual Director 91

CHAPTER VII.

Mr. Weedall as Professor of Divinity—As Spiritual Director—Death of Mr. Potts—His Funeral—Mr. Weedall's Discourse on the Occasion 104

CHAPTER VIII.

Mr. Weedall meets Dr. Parr at Dinner—Purchase of Holdford Farm—His Turn for Farming—Instance of his Affection and Kindness—Of his Moderation and Considerateness—Eloquent and Impressive Passage Introduced in one of his Homilies—Mr. Weedall as Prefect of Studies—His Editions of the Douay Grammar 113

CHAPTER IX.

Mr. Weedall made Acting President of the College—Gives up the Spiritual Care of Students and Congregation—Continues Professor of Divinity and Prefect of Studies—Death of John Payne—Mr. Weedall's Sermon at his Funeral—His Inscription for the Monument—His Extensive Reading—Consecration of Bishop Walsh—Dr. Weedall's Sermon on the Occasion—Sermon at the Opening of the Chapel at Northampton—Visit to Weston Underwood 124

CHAPTER X.

Death of Bishop Milner—Bishop Walsh leaves Oscott—Mr. Weedall President—Chosen a Canon of the English Chapter—Made Vicar General—Handsome Present brought him by a Deputation from the Catholics of Birmingham—His Sermons at the Opening of New Chapels at Wolverhampton and Nottingham—His Health seriously Impaired—Receives his Diploma of DD.—His Installation at the College—His Visit to O'Connell in Birmingham—Letter to the Editor of the "Birmingham Journal"—His Letter to the Editor of the "Catholic Journal"—His Health Improved 141

CHAPTER XI.

Dr. Weedall's Health Seriously Impaired—Retires for a little Excursion—Makes a Tour on the Continent—Mr. Foley President in his Absence—Dr. W.'s Visits to Rome and Naples—Letters on the Miracle of St. Januarius—His Return to Oscott—Sermons at the Openings of Chapels at West Bromwich and Grantham—Pastoral written by him on Collections for the District Fund—Chapel Openings at Bilston, Lichfield, and Sutton Coldfield 160

CHAPTER XII.

Necessity of a New College—The Building Commenced—Pastoral for Collections written by Dr. Weedall—His active Superintendence of the New Building—First Stone of the New Chapel Laid—Bishop Walsh's Journey to Rome—Circular of Dr. Weedall as V. G. on the New Marriage Act—Blessing of the Chapel Bell—Dr. Weedall's Address on the Occasion—Consecration and Opening of the New Chapel—Dr. Weedall's Sermon on the Day of Opening 176

CHAPTER XIII.

First Procession of Corpus Christi at the New College—Dr. Weedall's Sermon on the Occasion—Bishop Milner's Supposed Vision in Dr. Newman's Sermon—Situation of the New Building—The "Beggar's Bush"—Dr. Weedall's New Arrangements—Sermon on the Assumption—State of the Old College—Mr. Foley opens it as a Preparatory School—The Marini Library—The College associated to the London University—Presents to the College—Its Prosperity and Fair Prospects 192

CHAPTER XIV.

Dr. Weedall meets with Severe Trials—Is unexpectedly Appointed a Bishop—His Distress of Mind in consequence—Determines to go to Rome to Seek a Release from the Appointment—His Farewell Address on Leaving Oscott—Stops at Lucca—Dr. Baines' Conversation with the Pope, and Success in Dr. Weedall's Behalf—He Goes to Rome—His Letters from Rome detailing the whole Progress of His Affair—His Memorial to Propaganda 202

CHAPTER XV.

Dr. Weedall Presented to the Pope—Uncertainty of His Future Position—Offers Made to Him—Remains in Rome till the end of Spring—Returns to England—Visits Cossey and Oxburgh—Goes to Reside at Old Oscott—Is Invited to Remove to the Eastern District—Relieves and Succeeds Mr. Foley at Hampton-on-the-Hill—Undertakes the Mission at Leamington 219

CHAPTER XVI.

Dr. Weedall on the Mission at Leamington—His Difficulties, Duties, and Habits there—Sermon on Fasting—Decoration of His Chapel—His Converts—Sermon at Northampton—Sermon at Leamington on Confession—Newspaper Correspondence entailed by it—His Address to the Choir—His General Character as a Missioner ... 231

CHAPTER XVII.

Dr. Weedall's Address at the Instalment of Bishop Ullathorne—He is called to St. Chad's, Birmingham, and made Vicar General and Dean of the Cathedral—His Funeral Sermon on Bishop Walsh—He Retires to Handsworth—His Sermon at the Funeral of Lady Throckmorton—Funeral of Dr. Kirk—Dr. Weedall's Memoir of Him—Dr. Weedall appointed Provost of Birmingham—Assists at the First Council of Westminster—Accompanies Bishop Errington on his Visitation—Meets with an Accident—Death of John, Earl of Shrewsbury—Dr. Weedall's Funeral Oration over Him—Death of Earl Bertram, his Successor 247

CHAPTER XVIII.

Dr. Weedall is Reinstated as President of Oscott College—Serious Attack of Illness—Is made a Domestic Prelate of His Holiness—His Letter of Thanks to the Pope—Celebration of this Event, together with his Jubilee 266

CHAPTER XIX.

Dr. Weedall's Active Labours in the College—Exhibition at Midsummer, 1854—Festival on the Feast of St. Cecily—Proposal to Erect an Academic Hall—Dr. Weedall's Visit to the Manchester Exhibition—Dangerous Illness in Lent, 1859—Partial Recovery—Visit to Malvern—Return to Oscott—Last Sickness—Death—Funeral—Proposed Chantry to his Memory 285

CHAPTER XX.

Dr. Weedall's Personal Appearance, Physical Qualities, and Habits—Mental Qualities—Tastes—Love of Reading—Neglect of Correspondence—His Cheerfulness and Wit—His Qualities as President—Instances of Benevolence—His Talents and Peculiarities as a Preacher—His Great Virtues—Conclusion 298

Life of Monsignor Weedall.

CHAPTER I.

INTRODUCTORY OBSERVATIONS—BIOGRAPHY—SUMMARY OF DR. WEEDALL'S CAREER AND CHARACTER—HIS BIRTH AND EARLY YEARS.—HE IS SENT TO SCHOOL AT SEDGLEY PARK—HIS CHARACTER THERE—HIS ODE ON SEDGLEY PARK.

OUR FIRST desire, when we have lost an old and intimate friend, is to perpetuate his memory. Every thing that recalls him to our minds is precious; every recollection of him is affectionately cherished. He has dropped from our side, he has fallen out of our circle; but we cannot bear that he should be wholly lost to us. Hence our earliest wish is to have a record of his life; so to preserve, as best we may, those traits of his character, those incidents of his life, and those deeds of his achieving which we ourselves love to remember, and which others may be interested to know. It might, on some accounts, be better to let a certain time pass, before a biography is attempted; for some things may not be so well told soon after a friend's departure: but on the other hand, many things will vanish past recovery, if we do not hasten to preserve them; and all must be read with less and less interest, the more the time is protracted before they are given to the public. Moreover, as it has been wisely observed by Dr. Johnson, it is only those who have been familiar and intimate with a man, who can properly write his life. "Biography," he says, "is rarely well executed. They only who live "with a man, can write his life with any genuine "exactness and discrimination."* He says again: "Lives can only be written from personal know- "ledge, which is growing every day less, and in a "short time is lost for ever."† These considerations must be the writer's apology, if any be needed, for the present work appearing so early. The subject of this biography had been so long known and loved by the writer, that he needed only the impulse of esteem and affection to hasten to pay this tribute to his memory, even if other considerations had not justified the mournful, yet most grateful and soothing task.

The writer is fully aware of the truth of what our great moralist also observes, "that if the bio- "grapher writes from personal knowledge, and "makes haste to gratify the public curiosity, there is "danger lest his interest, his fear, his gratitude, or "his tenderness, overpower his fidelity, and tempt "him to conceal, if not to invent."‡ This danger it will be his study to escape, by keeping steadily in view that he is not merely to gratify friendship and

* Boswell's *Life of Johnson*, Vol. ii., Ch. xiv.
† Johnson—*Life of Addison*. ‡ Rambler, No. 60.

affection in this biography, but to discharge the public duty of not concealing the deficiencies, while he records the great merits and virtues of a distinguished ornament of the Catholic Church in this country; one of those whom Divine Providence raises up only from time to time, for his own great designs and especial purposes. For in truth it is no ordinary man who has been taken from us in the RIGHT REVEREND MONSIGNOR WEEDALL. It is just that we should *praise men of renown, and our fathers in their generation...men of great power, and endued with their wisdom...and by the strength of wisdom (instructing) the people in most holy words.** He belonged to the number of such men; and the voice of inspiration has warranted us in celebrating their praises: *Let the people show forth their wisdom, and the church declare their praise.*† Distinguished men are granted to us at times for extraordinary purposes, and fitted especially for particular undertakings. DR. WEEDALL,—for we prefer to call him by the familiar title by which he was designated to the end, notwithstanding his higher dignity of Monsignor,—seems to have been called and qualified in a remarkable manner for college life and administration; and for the especial exigencies of St. Mary's College, at Oscott. He passed more than forty years of his life at Oscott; he succeeded eminently there; while in every other position, though he was ever laborious and edifying, he seemed always in some degree out of his element. Oscott College owes

* ECCLESIASTICUS XLV., 1, 3, 4.   † IBID, v. 15.

him a deep and enduring debt of gratitude and reverence. As a student, he was brilliant and exemplary: *he shone in his days as the morning star in the midst of a cloud, and as the moon at the full.** As a professor, he was distinguished not only for his extensive erudition, but his felicitous method of imparting knowledge to his pupils. As president, his administration was marked by great wisdom and discernment; his authority was paternal, and his government characterised by firmness, ever tempered by mildness and engaging sweetness. As a priest, *as the sun when it shineth, so did he shine in the temple of God.*† And when promoted to the prelacy, he did honour to the dignity so deservedly conferred upon him: *when he put on the robe of glory, and was clothed with the perfection of power: when he went up to the holy altar he honoured the vesture of holiness.*‡ But the especial vocation of DR. WEEDALL was the building, the organisation, and the government of the new College of St. Mary, at Oscott. With that college his name is so closely identified, that it must go down to generations inseparably connected with its history, its reputation, and its distinguished position as a college and a seminary. The life of one so eminent well deserves a lasting record; its details cannot fail to attract the eager perusal of his numerous friends and admirers; while the most indifferent reader must peruse them with interest and edification.

* ECCLUS. L., 6.
† IBID L., 7.   ‡ IBID, v. 11, 12.

HENRY WEEDALL was the son of a respectable medical practitioner, who had been at Douay College with Bishop Milner. He was born in London on the 6th of September, 1788. His parents both died when he was very young. His father died of a severe nervous affection of the head and probably eyes, similar to that which his distinguished son seems to have inherited from him, and under which he suffered so much from about the age of ten to the end of his life. Of his early childhood we have no accounts; but he was surely a child of benediction, and the sweetness of his boyhood leaves no room to doubt that he was most engaging in his infancy, and first years of intelligence. Like another Samuel, he seemed born for the house of the Lord; and we can imagine his mother, like Elcana, anxious that *he* might *appear before the Lord, and might abide always there.** Doubtless she could have added with that happy mother: *I also have lent him to the Lord; all the days of his life, he shall be lent to the Lord.*† With this view he was sent to the school at Sedgley Park at the very early age of six years. He arrived there on the 11th of December, 1794. That venerable establishment had been in existence thirty-one years, and had kept steadily increasing in numbers and usefulness. It was now under the able presidency of the Rev. John Kirk, who, from having been the spiritual director, had exchanged offices with the Rev. Thomas Southworth in the preceding year; but on the express condition that Mr. Southworth should

* 1 KINGS, L, 23.   † IBID, v. 28.

remain in the establishment as vice-president and spiritual director. For the latter office Mr. Southworth was peculiarly qualified, and the exchange appeared to be greatly for the benefit of the establishment. The arrangement, however, did not long continue. Mr. Kirk went to reside with Bishop Berington as his secretary at Longbirch, and resigned the office of president, which was resumed by Mr. Southworth, in November of the year 1797.

It was then during the short presidentship of Mr. Kirk, that little WEEDALL was placed at Sedgley Park, a tender child of only six years and three months. Speaking of this event in his beautiful Memoir of Dr. Kirk, he himself describes it in these glowing terms: " It was at this happy con-
" juncture that the writer of this memoir, late in the
" year 1794, first received the benignant smiles
" and paternal cares of those most benignant and
" paternal, but firm and prudent Superiors, of whom
" his grateful memory prompts him to say with the
" Roman poet—

" ' *Animæ quales neque candidiores*
" ' *Terra tulit, neque queis me sit devinctior alter.*' " *

If he was thus benignantly received and smiled upon by these kind and holy men, he presented every attraction for their benevolence. He was a delicate child of sweet and engaging manners, placed unusually young in a school of rough boys, and thus claiming a more than ordinary share of paternal care and protection. He was patronised by the

* *Memoir of Rev. Dr. Kirk*, "Catholic Directory," 1853.

late Rev. John Jones, so long the eloquent preacher and respected missioner in London, at Warwick Street Chapel. Parlour boarders were taken at that time at Sedgley Park; Mr. Bowdon was one of them, and Mr. Jones another. The latter was very fond of little WEEDALL, took great notice of him, and patronised him for many years, indeed as long as he himself lived. WEEDALL is described by those who knew him when he first came to the school, as very little and delicate, with a sweet and engaging countenance, and very amiable manners. The writer became his schoolfellow in the latter part of his stay at Sedgley Park, and has a very distinct recollection of him at that time. He was small and stunted in his growth, but had a large and fine head, with a broad, open forehead. His eyes were light and large, but always weak. His complexion was clear and colourless; his mouth and lips formed for eloquence, evidently the *os magna locuturum*. His hair was light, and had that remarkable growth over his right temple, which is familiarly called a *calf-lick;* a rather graceful feature in the face of a child, but a troublesome accompaniment to a person grown up. He found it so for many years, especially during the time that he wore hair powder, as all priests formerly did, not being able to bring his hair to correspond on both sides of his forehead. But this peculiarity was not perceptible in the latter part of his life, after he had long taken to brushing his hair back from his forehead.

That love of neatness which distinguished DR. WEEDALL through life, was very apparent in his boyhood. His dress was always neatly arranged, and nothing slovenly was ever seen about him. His white cravat, a rare acquisition in those times among Park boys, was always clean, and tied with remarkable attention. His box, or little cupboard in the playroom, was observable above those of other boys for being nicely papered, and its contents arranged in exact order; his books in the "Study," and in the Chapel, were always carefully covered and tidily kept; his missal was the most elegant in the school, with its gilt leaves and handsome register, worked with gold thread at the top and pendants; he was in short a model of neatness in every thing. He was always cheerful and amiable, and beloved by every one. He is thus described by one of his companions still living: "He was an universal favourite with his superiors, and among the boys; blameless, gentle, amiable, and clever." He joined in every game, and generally excelled in the various sports of the playground. But his favourite game was hand ball, for which his compact little frame peculiarly fitted him. He was remarkably fond of birds; and the writer used to assist him in carrying out his cages with birds in the mornings, to hang them on the pales at the end of the " Bounds," or playground. He would come and pull your ear in the same good-natured manner which he retained all his life, and ask you to help him to carry out his cages; and every one was ready and happy to oblige him. He used to relate the loss of a favourite bird, which was killed in, or over the porch in the playroom; and said that he did not remember feeling so acute anguish on any other occasion, as he experienced on the loss of that bird. This little trait of early sensibility was surely a precious augury of that tender heart which distinguished him so remarkably through life. Afterwards at Oscott he kept a bullfinch; and he spent a good part of one Midsummer vacation in whistling to it in hopes of teaching it to sing the tune of "The Siege of Belle-Isle." In front of the pales were the boys' gardens, railed off from the playground. WEEDALL's garden was the middle one, kept in the neatest order, and always the best. On each side of the path, up the middle of his garden, he always had a thick row of the genuine old Park "Snaps" *(Antirrhinum Spurium)*, which grew finer and taller than those in any other boy's garden. He had a nice little arbour with a seat close to the pales, and this was more elegantly formed and neatly kept than any of the others.

He complained one time to two intimate companions how the grubs eat off the roots of his flowers. They took the hint, and thinking that he could well spare a lupine, pulled one up, tore away most of the root, and then replanted it. They afterwards called his attention to it: he took it up, and remarked upon it, as an illustration of what he had before told them. They laughed, and he saw what they had been doing, and laughed too in perfect good humour.

At the time when little "HARRY WEEDALL," as we always called him, first went to Sedgley Park, besides the president and spiritual director already mentioned, the following masters or teachers resided there and conducted the studies, Messrs. Joseph Harbut, John Sumner, Thomas Richmond, Thomas Daniel, and Thomas Yates. Happy was the teacher who had WEEDALL for his pupil. He was gifted with very superior abilities, and his docility and application were ever conspicuous. He was first under Mr. Harbut, who was very fond of him, and extremely kind to him. He made rapid progress in all his studies, and generally excelled. He was a good writer, and his remarkably neat and regular hand writing is well known to have remained unaltered to the end. Few indeed at the age of three score and ten can write so firm and beautiful a hand as he wrote; it never betrayed the least shaking or slovenliness. Mr. Sumner had the principal share in his education, was always proud of his pupil, and retained to the end of his life the most affectionate regard for him, omitting no opportunity of extolling his shining abilities, and fine character, exhibited through the entire course of his education at Sedgley Park. Dr. WEEDALL, on his part, ever cherished a great affection and veneration for his early instructors. He spoke with great veneration at all times of Mr. Southworth, regarding him in every sense as a father. He always expressed great gratitude and affection for Mr. Harbut, and more particularly for Mr. Sumner, who had been his English master for the principal part of his time at Sedgley Park.

It is always so gratifying to learn any little traits of character, or youthful adventures of those whom we have loved and venerated in after years, that the few anecdotes remembered of young WEEDALL, however trifling, must not be omitted. One time he was attempting, as the boys often did, to walk along the rails which separated the boys' gardens from the "bounds," when he fell astride the rail, and hurt himself considerably. He used to describe his suffering from this accident as intolerable. Another anecdote starts up to the writer's recollection of a very different character. One night in the chapel he fell asleep during prayers. At the pause made for the examination of conscience, he awoke during the silence; and either wishing to appear attentive, or imagining that he had heard the end of a prayer, he answered out loud, "Amen!"—A respectable lady at Wolverhampton, Mrs. Devey, appears to have had him in some way entrusted to her care, for he often was allowed to go to see her, and used to visit her as his early friend and benefactress, after he removed to Oscott. She presented him with his first pair of razors, one of which is still constantly used by his old friend, Canon McDonnell.

But it was in the most important duties of piety and religion, that HENRY WEEDALL was the brightest example: and was "*as the rainbow giving* "*light in the bright clouds, and as the flower of* "*roses in the days of the spring, and as the lilies* "*that are on the brink of the water, and as the* "*sweet smelling frankincense in the time of sum-* "*mer.*"* He never forgot the sublime object of

* ECCLUS. L., 8.

his vocation. He knew that it required of him thoroughly to learn himself what he humbly hoped to be commissioned one day to teach to others, and faithfully to practise those virtues which he would have to inculcate. For both objects he laboured assiduously, and in both was he eminently successful. When the writer of these lines first knew him, he was the head boy in studies of the whole school, and knelt in the first place in the chapel. He was chosen to serve at the altar, and William Wareing, afterwards Bishop of Northampton, served with him. In those primitive days, when our ceremonial was extremely simple and limited, he enjoyed a great privilege and distinction. He was that boy alluded to in the *History of Sedgley Park*, chap. viii., whose office it was to remove the priest's chair on Sundays, extinguish the candles after Vespers, and kneel in the Sanctuary at Benediction, to act as thurifer, though he held the thurible only just before the incensations, and neither wore surplice nor cassock, but only his ordinary clothes. In every way, however, this youth deserved and secured approbation and distinction. He went through his unusually long course of nine years and a half at Sedgley Park with the highest credit; the model of a student, whom all looked upon with admiration and affection; whom all his schoolfellows might well emulate; and with whose conduct all must have been edified. He had been at the Park from his tender years, and it had become his cherished home. He was now to part with many whom he loved, and from a spot to which he was strongly endeared. Like a stream separating from the parent spring, to pursue its own solitary course, he felt acutely as he lingered on the threshold of the venerable establishment; and we can imagine his farewell to have resembled what has been thus beautifully expressed:

> " Farewell, with whom to these retreats I strayed,
> By youthful sports, by youthful toils allied!
> Joyous we sojourned in this circling shade,
> And wept to find the paths of life divide."

But a sublime vocation called him, and higher destinies awaited him; and he nerved his spirits to a willing obedience to the necessity which duty imposed. He left Sedgley Park, June 11, 1804, in company with Mark John McNeal, a student, who had long kept second in the school, but had never been able to surpass WEEDALL. McNeal and WEEDALL were the only boys at the time who learned Greek. There were two more who learned Latin with them, Joseph Scott and William Frost. WEEDALL continued under Mr. Sumner in his English studies, but the Rev. Joseph Birch, who succeeded Mr. Southworth as president of Sedgley Park in 1816, was his master in Greek, Latin, and French. Though WEEDALL always kept first place both in Greek and Latin, he did not succeed so well in French. In this, Francis McDonnell, elder brother of the respected Canon of Clifton, always held the first place, and McNeal got second place quite as often as WEEDALL. However, he never dropped lower than the third place in the class, which consisted of seven boys. Mark John McNeal entered Oscott also as a church student, but left it shortly after, and became a teacher, first at Baddesley Green Academy, and afterwards at Sedgley Park. He finally became a medical practitioner at Paris, and died there August 24, 1823, aged 34. Dr. WEEDALL ever retained the warmest feelings of gratitude and affection for Sedgley Park, and gave expression to them, a few years after leaving it, in the following beautiful

ODE

ON A DISTANT PROSPECT OF SEDGLEY PARK.

Ille terrarum mihi præter omnes
Angulus ridet.   Hor.

Hail sacred spot! from noise and world retired,
    Where Sedgley's tops majestically rise!
How throbs my heart with gratitude inspired,
    Whene'er thy image meets my longing eyes.

When memory, with retrospective ken,
    Looks back on years that long have ceased to roll,
Tells me of joys I ne'er can taste again,
    And calls up all the boy within my soul.

Ah! happy scenes of innocent delight,
    Scenes of an age when every sport could please,
When with light spirits and a mind as light,
    I flutter'd through the morning of my days.

Stranger at once to jealousy and strife,
    Refined revenge and self tormenting rage,
With all the ills that pester human life,
    And damp the pleasures of maturer age.

Well might the Bard, who felt a joy like this,
  When Eton's turrets rose upon his eyes,
Urge the bold truth, " *Where ignorance is bliss,*
  'Tis sure the height of *folly to be wise.*"

For ah! too soon experience grows mature,
  And points to dangers little known before,
To Scylla's eddying gulf where Sirens lure
  In velvet song on pleasure's silken shore.

Waked into life ten thousand wild desires,
  Which erst had slumbered—might they slumber still!
Seditious rise—wide spread the glaring fires,
  A faithless beacon to mislead the will.

Oh! if my age in cloistered walls immured,
  Has haply yet escaped each latent rock,
While thousands, though more virtuously secured,
  Have felt their virtue yielding to the shock;—

Thanks to thy precepts,—venerable sage,
  Who early bent my heart to virtue's sway,
Sketch'd the rough features of a vicious age,
  Then bade me follow where thou led'st the way.

Oh! could my lays, immortal as my theme,
  On virtue's brow the fading wreath prolong,
Then should my song ennoble SOUTHWORTH's name,
  And SOUTHWORTH's name should dignify my song.

Then should oblivion, foe to absent worth,
  Pause where entombed thy mortal relics lie,
Though no proud columns load the moss-grown earth,
  " The Muse forbids the virtuous man to die."

Oscott, 1813.

CHAPTER II.

Removal from Sedgley Park—History of the Mission of Oscott—Commencement of an Ecclesiastical Seminary there—Beginning of the College at Oscott—Its First Church Students—Weedall's Arrival at Oscott—Other Arrivals—Humble Ceremonial in the Chapel.

Henry Weedall had now received a good substantial education at Sedgley Park, and had been there exactly nine years and a half, a much longer time than scholars usually remain; which is accounted for by his entering the school at so early an age. Being destined for the ecclesiastical state, he was to continue his course in another establishment, at Oscott, distant twelve miles from the Park. This removal to a college and seminary was a serious and important step in his life, as it must be in the career of every young aspirant to the sacred ministry. Hitherto he had been mixed up with a large number of boys, most of whom were intended for various trades and professions in secular life: but he had never lost sight of his own more sacred destination, nor relaxed in that ardent pursuit of piety which would prepare him to fulfil it. But he was now to be associated with at least a few ecclesiastical students, and to be more directly trained in his sublime vocation. It was in his regard like the period when the mother of Samuel carried her little son to *appear before the Lord, and abide always in the house of the Lord in Silo.* For this youth was alike destined to spend nearly the whole of his life in the house of the Lord, and within the hallowed precincts of collegiate seclusion. He, like another Samuel, was *to minister before the face of the Lord,* and *become great before the Lord.* And, like that holy prophet, it may be truly said, though in a subordinate degree, of the subject of this biography, that he *advanced and grew on, and pleased both the Lord and men.**

The college to which HENRY WEEDALL now removed, was but recently commenced. It was situated at Oscott, about five miles from Birmingham, where there had been, however, for many years, a secluded country mission. It was formerly the private property of the Rev. Andrew Bromwich, who was ordained at Lisbon, and became a confessor of the faith in the dreary times of persecution. He was tried and condemned to death in 1679, as he himself informs us in the speech which he had prepared to deliver on the scaffold, "for "the only crime of priesthood...for the conscionable "discharge of that divine calling." He was afterwards, however, reprieved, and after lying some time in prison, seems to have been forgotten, rather than actually pardoned, so that his release was permitted, or connived at. He returned to his home and property at Oscott, and took charge of the few Catholics there, and in the neighbourhood.

* 1 KINGS I. and II., *passim.*

He survived till the year 1703. His antique chair of very rude construction is still preserved. His uncle, Rev. Francis Fitter, also a Lisbon priest, succeeded him, and died in 1711, at the advanced age of 89. His successor was Rev. Philip Hickin, who died in 1735. After some other pastors, among whom were Rev. C. Fitz-Williams, Rev. James Layfield, and Rev. Joseph Barnes, the mission of Oscott was taken charge of by Rev. Pierce Parry, about the year 1752. It was very soon after this, probably in the year following, that Bishop Hornyold, who was then coadjutor to Bishop Stonor, built a new house at Oscott, contributing himself £100 towards the erection, the rest of the expense being liberally made up by the contributions of a few wealthy Catholics. This house was built with the intention of its being made the residence of the Vicars Apostolic of the Midland District, in case they should at any time be obliged to leave their actual residence at Longbirch, near Wolverhampton. Thus was raised what we should term the old house of Oscott, on the site of the former residence of the Rev. Andrew Bromwich. The top story was the chapel, extending West the whole length of the front; the altar being at the end nearest to that building, which was added about forty years later, when Oscott was first opened as a college. Soon after the year 1778, Rev. P. Parry built a new chapel, extending along the East side of the house, with a long room over it for a dormitory.

As the new house at Oscott was not actually required for the Bishop's residence, and was larger than the priest himself required, it was let to a Mrs. Johnson, who had previously kept a boarding school for young ladies, near Harvington, in Worcestershire. The writer was well acquainted subsequently with a lady who had been one of her pupils at Oscott. From her account of Mrs. Johnson, it is no way surprising that she met with little success, and so remained at Oscott but a short time. The Rev. Mr. Parry was afflicted with paralysis, which after repeated strokes quite incapacitated him; so that he was removed from Oscott in 1785. He went with Mrs. Johnson to reside at Aldridge, only about four miles distant. The Rev. Joseph Berington was then appointed to the Oscott mission, by Bishop Thomas Talbot, and came to reside there in the summer of the same year, 1785. The solitude and quietness of the place, and the small number of the congregation were favourable to his literary pursuits. He wrote most of his works at Oscott. Dr. Charles Berington was appointed coadjutor to Bishop Talbot in the following year. He stood in the relationship of third cousin to Mr. Joseph Berington, and came to reside with him at Oscott soon after his consecration, and remained there till about the year 1792. Mr. Berington took great interest in the place, and laid out the garden tastefully, planting it with shrubs, which he selected from Mr. Giffard's nursery, at Chillington, in the autumn of the same year. The house at this time remained uncoloured, and the bricks had begun to show the hues of age. It was afterwards coloured and rough-cast of á light colour. Mr. Berington with great taste had trained roses, vines, and creeping plants up the walls and round the windows. Mrs. Schimmelpenninck, then Miss Galton, a young lady, whose parents resided at Barr Hall, very near Oscott, and who often visited Mr. Berington, and his sister who lived with him, has given a vivid and generally accurate description of the place at this time. "An inclosure," she says, "of two or three acres, partly shrubbery, partly kitchen garden, and partly flower garden, surrounded the dwelling; hedges, flowers, fruits, and espaliers, all in the greatest luxuriance, yet kept in that trim order, united with elegance, which formed the especial characteristic of Mr. Berington." All this was in a few years superseded by the bare playground of the college, but even that ground was long after called the "Garden," by the older Oscotians, and particularly by the venerable subject of this biography. The house had a three sided porch in front, which remained till 1816, when Bishop Milner built the Exhibition Room and colonnades. It was then removed, and the front of the house made level and uniform. Mrs. Schimmelpenninck describes this porch, with its stone seats outside, and seats also inside. Its semi-hexagonal form afforded the convenience of a bow window above, in the room which Mr. Berington made his study and library, and which, in later times, became the bed room of the president of the college. She mentions that over the fire-place in the dining room appeared this quotation from Prov. xv., 17, in antique characters: "Melius est vocari ad olera cum charitate, quam ad vitulum saginatum cum odio."* Mr. Berington removed from Oscott in May, 1793, and became chaplain to Sir John Throckmorton, Bart., at Buckland, where he remained till his death, which occurred December 1, 1827, when he had attained the advanced age of 85.

Mr. Berington's successor at Oscott was the Rev. Anthony Clough, who came thither from Heythrop; but he died at Oscott on the 7th September following, "lamented, as he had been beloved and honoured, by all who knew him." The mission of Oscott was then supplied temporarily by the Rev. John Kirk, who went over from Sedgley Park, till the appointment of the Rev. John Bew, D.D., in the following year, 1794.

The Rev. Dr. Bew had been for several years the superior of the Seminary of St. Gregory at Paris, and engaged there in the education of ecclesiastical students. He had been obliged to abandon it, in consequence of the French Revolution. The Rev. John Kirk went over to Longbirch, while he was supplying the mission at Oscott, to see the Bishop, Dr. T. Talbot and his coadjutor, Dr. C. Berington. Walking with them in the garden, he ventured to propose to them the plan of placing Dr. Bew at Oscott, where he might educate a few students for the Church, as the breaking up of our seminaries on the continent had induced the necessity of speedily devising some means for continuing the supply of clergy for our English missions. Thus Mr. Kirk was in reality the originator of a

* *Life of Mrs. Schimmelpenninck*, 2 vols., 1858.

seminary at Oscott. It would appear, however, that the Bishops did not at once come into his view; for he observed in a letter to the present writer, that he could not say whether they had the same idea with himself, or not. They probably took time to consider so important an undertaking: but it finally met with their approval, for in the following year, 1794, Dr. Bew was appointed to Oscott, and by desire of their Lordships, Mr. Kirk accompanied him there early in the above year.

Dr. Bew began with two students professedly for the Church. These were Stephen Phillips, who came to Oscott in May, 1794, and John Holiday, who arrived there in July: but neither persevered in studying for the Church. Phillips left Oscott in July, 1796, and in 1805 eloped with the daughter of a noble lord, was married by the priest at Oxford, Rev. Charles Leslie, who died the 28th of December, 1806, and afterwards at Gretna Green. Holiday left Oscott in September, 1795, and enlisted in the army, after which he was never heard of. The first lay student at Oscott was Charles Mostyn, father of the present Lord Vaux; the next was Joseph Bowdon, who came September 3rd, 1794; for when at Oscott, he had no intention of embracing the ecclesiastical state. He left Oscott in or about the year 1795. After remaining about two years at home, he conceived an ardent desire to study for the Church, and with this view entered St. Edmund's College, at Old Hall Green, where he was ordained priest in 1805. After serving the missions of Mawley and Long Birch, he came to

Sedgley Park, as spiritual director in 1808. In 1836 he became president; and died there the 4th of December, 1844, at the age of 66. Thus the first efforts of Dr. Bew in his laudable undertaking to educate ecclesiastical students had been unsuccessful; though from no want of ability, or assiduous attention on his part. His talents and merits were justly appreciated by his ecclesiastical superiors, as will appear from the sequel.

We are now to speak of the first establishment of a college at Oscott; for what has been described was only a very humble commencement of a seminary for a few ecclesiastical students. The house itself could have accommodated only a few; but the time was come for its limits to be extended, and its character to become more elevated and conspicuous. There were several acres of land round about the house, left by the Rev. Andrew Bromwich, the founder of the mission, for the support of the pastor. Part of this land was sold, by consent of the Bishop, in Mr. Berington's time, and the purchase money invested in the French funds. This, of course, was lost in the general confiscation of property in the French Revolution. The owner of some other land close to the house at Oscott, was offended because the mission land had not been offered to him for purchase, and retaliated by building two mean cottages close to the priest's house, and placing a tinker in one of them, whose noisy occupation would be a disturbance and annoyance. Mr. Berington, however, sent his compliments and thanks to the old squire for the convenience he had thus afforded him of having his kettles mended without sending them between five and six miles to Birmingham. The property of the mission was thus reduced to a few patches of land lying here and there around the house; but this sale would never have been resorted to, if the purpose for which Oscott was destined could have been foreseen. The loss of the acres sold was long felt, and the college was most inconveniently straitened, till many years after, when more land was happily acquired by the judicious exertions of Dr. Weedall.

The Rt. Rev. Dr. Thomas Talbot, Bishop of Acon, *in partibus*, and Vicar Apostolic of the Midland District, died at Bristol, whither he had gone for his health, on the 24th of February, 1795. He was succeeded by his coadjutor, Dr. Charles Berington; under whose sanction and patronage some leading members of the Catholic nobility and gentry undertook the erection of a college and seminary at Oscott. Some of these were the Lords Petre and Stourton, Sir John Throckmorton, Mr. Hornyold, and Mr. Bernard Howard, afterwards Duke of Norfolk. Accordingly, having obtained a lease of the old house, they built a wing to it of considerable extent, but in very plain style. It comprised a refectory, playroom, study place, dormitory, and several private rooms for masters and upper students. When this building was ready for occupation, the college of Oscott was opened in the year 1796, under the presidency of the Rev. John Bew, D.D., with the Rev. Thomas Potts as vice-president. Mr. Potts was a Douay priest, who had been sent to that college with the Rev. Alban Butler, in June, 1765. He was ordained priest in June, 1778, returned to England in October, 1780, and served the mission at Brailes for the first year. He was next chaplain to F. Turvile, Esq., at Husbands Bosworth, and thence was called to become vice-president of the new college at Oscott. The result abundantly proved the wisdom of the choice; for Mr. Potts, as Dr. WEEDALL so well observed, "conducted the classical studies of "that house with a grandeur of ability peculiarly "his own, and a vigour and enthusiasm which will "long be remembered."* Thus then the new college was commenced under the conduct of two able and excellent superiors, the Rev. John Bew, D.D., and the Rev. Thomas Potts.

The terms of the new college were first advertised in the "Directory" for 1799, the pension being there stated at thirty pounds per annum. The same advertisement appeared every year, till in 1807, when it was announced that the pension was forty pounds.

It is time now to return to the subject of this biography, but the short history given of the first beginnings of Oscott will not be deemed out of place in the Life of one so long and intimately associated with the college. The first ecclesiastical students came to the new college from Sedgley Park on the Assumption, 1796. They were Robert Richmond, Francis Martyn, and Thomas Latham.

* Preface to "*A Discourse at the Funeral of the Rev. Thomas Potts,*" by the Rev. HENRY WEEDALL, p. vi.

The last, who was a youth of great promise, was not destined to complete his scholastic course; he died April 5th, 1802, sincerely and deservedly lamented. The other two, it is well known, became exemplary priests, and models of a missionary life. HENRY WEEDALL and John Mark McNeal followed these, eight years after, arriving at Oscott, from Sedgley Park, on the 11th of June, 1804. WEEDALL was then a youth of almost sixteen, of great abilities and great amiability of character; in fact, affording that promising augury of merit and distinction so fully borne out by his subsequent course, whether at college or on the mission, whether as student or superior.

This removal to Oscott was to him a most important step in life. The sublimity of his vocation now appeared before him in more imposing, if not more alarming, grandeur. He had passed from a respectable school to a regularly disciplined college, and an ecclesiastical seminary. He felt fresh animation from the aids and incentives to piety as well as study, with which he was now happily surrounded. These, however, were not without painful and trying drawbacks, from exposure to the occasional taunts and disedifying conduct of some of the lay students. But he was encouraged by superiors, and edified by those few who were ardently pursuing the same glorious course which he came to follow. In his classical studies he possessed great advantages under the tuition of Mr. Potts, a profound scholar and judicious teacher; while his happy dispositions were nurtured, and his piety cherished and wisely directed, under the spiritual guidance of Dr. Bew. Mr. Berington frequently visited Oscott after he had removed to Buckland, and.was often invited to preach to his former flock. Thus young WEEDALL had before him some excellent models of pulpit eloquence; and the sequel will show how well he profited by them.

With that strong affection for his *alma mater*, Sedgley Park, which he ever after retained, he took the earliest opportunity of visiting the "old place." The first letter which he received at Oscott had been written to him by his particular favourite among the boys at Sedgley Park, John Briggs, now Bishop of Beverley. During the first Christmas holidays of his residence at Oscott, he obtained leave to walk over to the Park, and came thither with McNeal, who had accompanied him to Oscott in the preceding month of June. The sensation among the Park boys, when these two appeared, is well remembered by the writer, who, in common with most others, could not resist the temptation to look back in the chapel to catch a hasty view of "HARRY WEEDALL" in the tribune. We were surprised to see both him and McNeal so genteelly and neatly dressed in black; and altogether so improved since they had left us.

The infant seminary of Oscott soon began to yield its fruit, and give happy promise of those blessed results which have since followed so copiously. A year and a half after WEEDALL entered the college, its first priest was ordained. This was the Rev. Francis Martyn, who received the sacred order of priesthood from Bishop Milner, at Wolverhampton, December 21st, 1805. This was a happy event for Oscott, and for the mission, and well calculated to revive the hopes of Catholics, after the destruction of our most important nurseries for the priesthood upon the Continent. It was an event, too, which our youthful student must have contemplated with no ordinary emotion; and from which he received fresh stimulus to make giant strides both in learning and virtue. Another source of encouragement was the occasional arrival of fresh students for the church. It has been already mentioned that one of the first three ecclesiastical students, Latham, had died two years before WEEDALL'S arrival; another, Robert Richmond, had been obliged to leave the college and interrupt his studies, from the weakness of his eyes, soon after our student's arrival. When, therefore, Francis Martyn was ordained, and had left Oscott January 25th, 1806, WEEDALL was left for a time the only student for the church. But it was for a short time only; for on the 26th of March, 1806, three more youths were transplanted from the nursery at Sedgley Park to continue their ecclesiastical studies at Oscott College. They were brought thither by the Rev. Joseph Birch; and were William Wareing, William Foley, and Thomas McDonnell. Foley quitted Oscott at Midsummer of the following year, and gave up studying for the church for some time. Providence however so ordered his fortunes, that he was brought back to his original purpose, and returned to Oscott, October 1st, 1817. He was ordained priest, February 25th, 1820, and after beginning the mission at Northampton, and building a chapel there in 1825, supplying the place of DR. WEEDALL as temporary president at Oscott in 1830, and having charge of a preparatory establishment at Old Oscott, and then of the mission of Hampton on the Hill, near Warwick, his health failed, and he died at the New College, at Oscott, February 11th, 1843, and was the first buried there.

The other two still happily survive. Dr. Wareing was the first Vicar Apostolic of the Eastern District; and subsequently the first Bishop of Northampton. He was, at his own earnest entreaty, released from his episcopal charge, February 11th, 1858, and retired to his present residence at East Bergholt, on the 2nd of June following, with the title of Bishop of Retimo *in partibus*. Canon McDonnell was ordained priest at Oscott, September 19th, 1817, and after a meritorious course of active and zealous labour, principally in Birmingham, undertook the care of his present flock, at Shortwood, April 1st, 1852. It was cheering and consoling to our student to be rejoined by these his former companions; and we can imagine the ardour with which all four now contended in the glorious career before them. The college, however, was still in its infancy; and though both its superiors were learned and pious men, the chapel services were of necessity conducted in a very humble and unimposing manner. Catholics had been relieved indeed from the more severe of the penal laws; but they were still subject to obloquy and persecution in many ways. They hardly dared to avow or practise their religion openly; and their clergy had only recently ventured to dress in black. Catholic priests almost all wore brown; the Rev. Joseph Berington was the first to appear in a black coat, and he was blamed by many for needlessly exposing the clergy to insult and persecution. No splendid ceremonial was as yet attempted in Catholic chapels. Dr. Bew, however, ventured, soon after WEEDALL's arrival, to have Benediction with the Blessed Sacrament; and in those who are familiar with our grand church services in these days, and who have seen DR. WEEDALL himself so often the celebrant in the imposing offices of our ritual, it will excite a smile, and an exclamation of astonishment, to be told that at the first attempt to get up Benediction at Oscott, they could procure no better incense than a little rosin, which WEEDALL, being sacristan, scraped out of some broken knife-handles in the kitchen! This he often used to relate, in illustration of the consoling progress of religion which he had witnessed, and in gratitude to God, who graciously *brought back the captivity of Sion, when we became like men comforted.**

But let not these humble beginnings be despised. There was true devotion, solid piety, and tried virtue under these plain unimposing services. Little can Catholics who live in these days conceive of the state of things even in the times which are here recorded, when we could hardly walk abroad without some insult, when we said Mass chiefly in

* Ps. cxxv., 1.

garret chapels, and in obscure localities, and were occasionally hooted and had stones thrown after us, as it has happened even to the present writer. Let it be remembered that the God of Israel was long worshipped in a tabernacle covered with skins; and that when the Jews laboured to build the holy city again, each man *with one of his hands did his work, and with the other held his sword.** Let us bless God that he has enabled us to do glorious things for his divine service in our generation; but let us also revere the memory of those admirable men by whom the foundations of our ruined temples were courageously laid again; and the great work of restoring religion in our land was steadily, though unostentatiously, pursued in defiance of great and formidable difficulties.

* 2 Esdras iv., 17.

CHAPTER III.

The "New Government"—St. Mary's College, Oscott—
Its Superiors—The "Laura" Built—Weedall's Ta-
lents—Drawback from Weakness of his Eyes—The
Repository—Weedall's Excellence in Various Games—
Also as a Teacher—Conferences—Prones—Chapel
Services—Vestments—Organ—Choir.

The first period of Oscott College has been always known as "The Old Government." It lasted exactly twelve years. Two church students completed their course under it, and were ordained priests; Mr. Martyn, already mentioned, and Mr. Robert Richmond, who received the holy order of priesthood March 14th, 1807. A number of lay students also received an excellent education under the "Old Government," one of whom is too well known and revered by the whole Catholic body to be left without special mention here, the Honble. Charles Langdale, who came to the college in the spring of 1798. Several ecclesiastics had also commenced their studies at Oscott, and pursued them with great credit, and in the true spirit of their vocation, when an important change took place in the establishment. The noblemen and gentlemen who had hitherto been the governors of the college, withdrew from its direction. Its finances were not in a sound condition. Dr. Bew understood better the management of religious and educational affairs, than the administration of temporalities. Considerable debts had been contracted, which caused anxiety and dissatisfaction in its governors. They came therefore to a resolution to offer the college to Bishop Milner, on condition of his making himself responsible for its liabilities. Dr. Milner at first hesitated at a proposal, which, though it appeared on the one hand extremely eligible, had a formidable aspect on the other, on account of its attendant difficulties. He consulted his Vicar-General, the Rev. John Perry, a man of distinguished zeal and piety, seasoned with great wisdom and discretion, and, by his advice, Dr. Milner determined to accept the offer. He became then the sole proprietor and director of the college, taking upon himself its liabilities, which, as the present writer heard at the time, did not exceed £600; but which an old and highly respected Oscott priest believes to have reached to about £900. The transfer to Bishop Milner took place in the summer of 1808 ; and thus ended the "Old Government" of Oscott College.

This was a most important period in the history of Oscott, as well as in the life of the distinguished subject of the present biography. It was likewise a momentous enterprise for the illustrious Bishop Milner. But he was not a man to shrink from any undertaking, however arduous, by which the glory of his divine Master, and the salvation of souls, could be promoted. He had meditated on the encouraging words of St. Bernard: "Non te tædeat frater, magna incipere, et inchoata tenere: perseverantia informat merita, coronat bona proposita, remunerat currentem, ducit ad bravium et portum. Hæc est qua laureantur martyres, qua virgines coronantur, *qua sacerdotes sublimantur.*"* He put his broad shoulder at once to the wheel, and entered with heroic courage upon his arduous and meritorious undertaking. He began by placing his college under that sublime patronage which has never been invoked in vain, that of the glorious Mother of God, she to whom we constantly address these petitions, "Ora pro populo, interveni pro clero:" *Pray for the people, intercede for the clergy.* It was henceforth to be called, and has been ever since known as ST. MARY'S COLLEGE.

The "New Government" began with the solemn dedication of the college, under the patronage of the Blessed Virgin Mary, on the Feast of the Assumption, 1808. It will be remembered, as a remarkable coincidence, that the old college had also been opened on the Assumption, in 1796. Bishop Milner celebrated the Mass, and delivered an animated discourse on the festival of the day. There was, however, no High Mass, nor any grand ceremonial: a piano-forte supplied the want of an organ; the respected family of the Jones' from Wolverhampton were entrusted with the musical department, and it has been amusingly

---

* Be not weary, brother, of beginning great things, and of continuing what you have begun: perseverance procures merit, crowns good resolutions, rewards him who runs, leads to the prize and the haven of salvation. It is by this that martyrs are laurelled, that virgins are crowned, *that priests are raised to a sublime elevation.*

related by one who was present, that the singing was little more than the Litany of Loretto, which they made to last out as long as possible. The dedication of the new college was thus announced in the "Directory" of the following year: "St. Mary's College, Oscott. On the late festival of the Assumption of the B. V. Mary, the Holy Sacrifice of the Mass was offered up in a solemn manner for its prosperity. It is now under the direction of the Rt. Rev. Dr. Milner." That enlightened prelate had placed it under able superiors. The Rev. Dr. Bew had withdrawn from Oscott; he went first to London, and soon after took charge of the mission at Brighton, where he remained till 1817. He died at Havant, October 25th, 1829. Dr. Milner appointed the Rev. Thomas Potts first president of St. Mary's College, who had been acting all along as vice-president with Dr. Bew. He transferred at the same time from Sedgley Park, the Rev. Thomas Walsh, who had been chaplain to his predecessor, Bishop Stapleton, and afterwards vice-president and spiritual director at Sedgley Park. A better choice for the newly-organised college of St. Mary's could not have been made, as the experience of the whole seventeen years that he remained there abundantly proved. Dr. WEEDALL himself has thus summed up his admirable career at Oscott, with eloquence and fidelity. "In the administration of the seminary he confined himself, by preference, to the spiritual department, and in the management of that he was supremely excellent. He devoted himself to the work, heart and soul. He combined the devout ascetic with the practical missionary, and laboured to bring up the young ecclesiastics, obedient, modest, humble, moderate in their views, mortified in their habits, assiduous in prayer, meditation, and spiritual reading. And though encouraging, generally, an adequate cultivation of talent, and a just application of the mind to every useful branch of education, he directed their chief attention to the science of the Saints, the theology of the heart, and to a familiar study of the Art Manual of a Priest, the art of preaching, instructing, and catechizing; the art of directing wisely in the Confessional, and of gaining souls to Christ."* With reference to their new spiritual guide, WEEDALL remarked at the time to his fellow ecclesiastical students, that their former director, Dr. Bew, did not, in his instructions in the Confessional, give them any advice peculiar to ecclesiastics, or make any allusions to their vocation; but with Mr. Walsh, the case was very different. No difference, however, was perceptible in WEEDALL, for he was always regular, pious, and exemplary, inspiring with respect even those students who were accustomed to scoff at and torment ecclesiastics.

In the first advertisement of St. Mary's College, which appeared in the "Directory" of the following year, 1809, penned by Bishop Milner, it was announced that the pension would in future be

* *Funeral Oration on Right Rev. Dr. Walsh*, by Rev. HENRY WEEDALL, D.D.

forty-two guineas. It was there also mentioned that Mr. Walsh would take care not only of the spiritual, but also of the economical concerns of the establishment. For the latter he was far less fitted than for the spiritual care of the inmates: and it was soon made over to another, a memorable superior of St. Mary's College, Mr. John Francis Quick. He was a convert, and began his studies for the church only at the age of thirty, being placed for that purpose under the able tuition of the Rev. Joseph Bowdon, then missioner at Longbirch. But now Mr. Bowdon was appointed to succeed Mr. Walsh at Sedgley Park, and Mr. Quick was at the same time removed to the new seminary of St. Mary's, at Oscott. He had only yet received Minor Orders. He was, however, soon made Procurator of the College, having in that office the charge of all its temporal concerns, which he administered for several years afterwards with the greatest care and prudence.

Thus was Oscott College remodelled, and most auspiciously initiated, under an able and efficient administration, superintended and frequently visited by the illustrious Bishop Milner. The number of students at this time was about forty-five; indeed, there was not accommodation for more than fifty, before that building was erected opposite to the old house, which was known as the "Laura," a name which was chosen for it by Mr. Quick, in allusion to those clusters of cells of holy men in the deserts, which were so called.

This building stood detached, and has since

been taken down. It consisted of three rooms on the ground floor; that nearest the road being the Procurator's office, the centre room serving as a playroom and fireroom for little boys, and the next being an infirmary, where a nurse usually sat in the day time, and employed her spare hours in doing small repairs to the boys' clothes. The staircase was at this end, and led up to two small rooms for church students or masters, and a long room known as the "Laura," and which gave its name to the whole building. This accommodated seven of the more advanced church students, who each had his little establishment of table, washing stand, chair, and bookcase, opposite or near to his bed. Above this were two other small rooms, and another long room, which was a dormitory for the younger church boys, familiarly called the "demi-gods." This was later on made into small separate rooms.

Though this is a biography of the most eminent of St. Mary's sons, and not a professed history of the college itself, it is neither possible nor desirable to let pass occasions continually presented of recording portions of its history. WEEDALL was closely identified with it in all its stages. He entered it in its infancy, he witnessed its gradual development, and was intimately connected with every step of its progress; he brought it on to maturity, he raised it to its highest splendour, and devoted to its resuscitation all the remaining strength and influence of his declining years. At this period of its inauguration as St. Mary's College, he was twenty years of age. His amiable disposition has been already commemorated; he was beloved for it at Sedgley Park, and equally so at Oscott, and in every stage of his life. He had a guileless heart, and an innocent and humble mind. If "to dread no eye, and to suspect no tongue, is the great prerogative of innocence, an exemption granted only to invariable virtue,"* he assuredly enjoyed that great prerogative. He was ever cheerful, and joined as heartily in the sports of the playground, as he applied diligently to the exercises of the "study place." His health was generally good, but his eyes were always weak. For a considerable time the state of his eyes debarred him from all reading; and he was allowed by the president, Dr. Bew, to take walks about the country. He had recourse, among other expedients, to ingenious exercises of handicraft, among which it is remembered that he carved for himself a very neat top to a walking stick. His eyes did not afford any outward evidence of weakness, except a little watery and glistening appearance; but his head seems to have been the seat of the malady, and it proved a very serious drawback, and caused him grievous suffering through life. Still he pursued his favourite game of hand ball, in defiance of the assurance of Horace, that

"Pila lippis inimicum."†

He always had to depend on others to read to him, and to write for him at his dictation; both of which services the present writer rendered him for years

* JOHNSON.   † Hand ball is bad for those who have weak eyes.

with great pleasure. Being so much with him for these offices, the writer was very anxious to procure for him any relief, and with this view he once consulted a very eminent oculist for him; who, after considering his case, advised that he should always read with his back to the light, and was of opinion that he would derive much benefit from the use of a peculiar kind of spectacles consisting of silver bowls like tea spoons, each having an opening not much larger than a pinhole in the centre, through which alone the light was to be admitted to the eye. But Mr. Weedall could not be prevailed upon to try such an experiment, alleging the odd appearance it would give him. So he laboured on the best he could; and considering the great disadvantage he suffered from this weakness of his eyes, it was always a matter of astonishment how he acquired the quantity and variety of learning which he was known to possess. His eyes certainly improved as he advanced in years; for latterly he read and wrote a great deal by daylight, though he attempted very little of either after dark; whereas in his early time, he often, for long intervals of time, could not bear to use his eyes either to read or write.

This seems the proper place to give his own painful account of his peculiar and distressing affection of the eyes and head. It is extracted from a paper in his own handwriting, written in August, 1840, to which a more especial reference will be made in the sequel.

"The disorder under which I have laboured for so many years is one of no ordinary character; not a headache, but a mischievous affection of the nerves of the head. Indeed I never found a person similarly affected. It began when I was about ten years old, and went on increasing with intensity and active mischief throughout the whole of my course. I found a difficulty in going through my humanity studies, and when I came to philosophy and divinity, it had increased to an alarming height. I could not read even for five minutes in the day; I could not even at times bear the light. I was obliged to give up entirely my course of philosophy; and the whole of my theological studies, such as they were, were learned by listening to a fellow divine, who would read me the lesson. I made up the whole as well as I could by chance snatches, just as I was able; but I had serious difficulties in taking Orders."

His talents soon became conspicuous. The students in the winter evenings established what was termed the "Repository." A box was set up in the playroom to receive literary contributions; and an editor chosen, by whom these were read up publicly once a week. WEEDALL contributed several witty and spirited pieces, both in prose and verse, some of which will be long remembered in the annals of Oscott. All of these the present writer has often seen in the author's own handwriting, and of some he has taken copies, by permission; which is mentioned here, because DR. WEEDALL somewhat shrunk from owning these lighter effusions in his graver and more dignified years. Three of them were printed many years after in the "Oscotian," a Journal written, and even printed, entirely by Oscott students; and of which a second edition with illustrations was printed in Birmingham, in three small volumes, in 1826-29.

These pieces were, "*Mrs. Thrifty*," a fragment of a comedy, the subject being the college housekeeper of the time, whose parsimony was inimitably burlesqued in that very clever composition; and "*The Ghost of a big pair of Breeches*," which, though long supposed to refer to an antiquated and well known pair of inexpressibles belonging to a certain student, are now known, from the author's own explanation a few years back, in a letter to his present biographer, to have had no individual application. Another piece was the "*Journal of a Student*," which, though Johnson declared, when admitting a similar paper into his "Idler," written by Warton, that the "Journal of the Citizen in the Spectator" had almost precluded the attempt of any future writer, abounded in very clever and original hits, and one in particular, which the temptation to record here is irresistible. The hero of the Journal has been sent up to the president to be flogged, for a practical joke in school time. A Spanish boy is sent with him to hoist. So the Journal proceeds thus: "B., a good-natured blubbering Spaniard, can't speak English. Spaniard shall cover my rear, thought I. So with a dexterous manœuvre, hoisted up spluttering Spaniard, and get flogged by *proxy*. *Cujus a me corpus*, forget how the passage runs, *sublatum*—no, that's not the word, but no matter, *sublatum est, quod contra decuit ab illo, meum.* Cicero. A good practical joke; an English flogging *done into* Spanish. B. didn't like the *translation*." It is only to be regretted that all these three clever pieces are very incorrectly given in the "Oscotian." Another of WEEDALL's contributions to the "Repository" was a Sapphic Ode on the disappearance of certain correspondents, which introduced all the parties with very ludicrous effect. There were several more of his pieces, but these were the most remarkable. The "Repository," like all similar attempts which depend on the ardour of youth, soon died away; but it was revived some years after, and during its second period of existence, in 1822, among other meritorious contributions, must be mentioned " *The Hopwas Hunt,*" by Charles Arrowsmith, a youth of great promise, intended for the church, but carried off two years later by consumption. It was a composition of singular merit and originality. In a poem of great vigour, well sustained through a hundred and twenty lines, Arrowsmith described in florid and spirited language a hunt, in which many of the college youths were sketched with inimitable drollery, and ridiculous fidelity. The writer has preserved a copy, and treasures it as it deserves. No similar poem exists: it is quite original. The "Repository" expanded finally into a regular periodical, printed by the students, as already mentioned, and entitled: "The Oscotian, or Literary Gazette of St. Mary's," which was kept up till the year 1829.

It has been mentioned above that WEEDALL excelled in all that he undertook, even in the games of the college students. Every Oscotian knows the favourite Oscott game of "Bandy." At this he played with dexterous activity; but on one occasion he received a terrible blow, or "coup," as the phrase ran, in his side, which took away his breath, and obliged him to withdraw in great pain. Skating was a favourite diversion also at Oscott, as great facilities were afforded for it by a large pond at a short distance, known by the name of "Oby's Pool," which soon froze over, being shallow and exposed. WEEDALL skated more gracefully and elegantly than any one else. He struck out to a length quite amazing, considering the shortness of his legs; and he moved on, with his arms generally folded, and his breast pushed forward like a swan majestically sailing against the stream. There was no figure or manœuvre on the ice that he could not perform, or that any other could execute better. He was also fond of bathing, and swam with the same ease and dexterity for which he was remarkable in every other exercise. Once, when standing on the bank, after just coming out of the water at "Oby's," he was alarmed by seeing an adder close to his feet; but with great presence of mind he remained quite still, and the reptile glided between his feet and got away. This pond was called "Oby's," after an old man named *Obadiah* Moore, who died in the farm house above the pool. He used before to live in that cottage, which was occupied subsequently by Isaac Horton, at the end of the "Hill," near the old college; where he used to carry on the coinage of base money, in connexion with certain accomplices in the neighbourhood. Some of them were convicted and executed, but Obadiah managed to escape. The name of this piece of water among the country people was the "*Commin Pewl,*" that is, the *Common Pool,* as it was situated on the extensive waste land of Sutton Coldfield.

WEEDALL, before he was a master, was entrusted with the charge of the boys when they went to bathe in this pool. On one occasion, when they were at the pool, one of them mischievously tried to turn one of the farmer's sheep into it. This brought out the farmer's sons in a great rage, and the wife of one of them who had been a servant at Oscott, and had there got the nickname of Patty Proud, said among other saucy things, that the boys ought to have some one to take care of them. They pointed to WEEDALL, but his diminutive size appeared to her so little satisfactory, that she answered very contemptuously: "Then you ought to be under better jurisdiction."

It was ever WEEDALL's practice to follow up the sound maxim of labouring to do all things well: so he played well in play time, upon the same principle that he applied well to learning in study time. Towards the end of the " Old Government," he had so far advanced in his studies, that he was called in to assist in teaching, and entrusted with a junior class, which he carried through to the end of Rhetoric. The possession of knowledge and the art of imparting it to others, are not always found concomitant: to learn is one thing, to teach, a faculty very different. WEEDALL did not possess the art of conveying every kind of knowledge which he possessed. It will be seen later on that he failed in adapting himself to the capacities of children, in catechetical instruction. But in classical teaching, and afterwards in theological, he was always eminently successful. He was mild and patient, and ready to make full allowance for the deficiency of genius in some pupils, not expecting all to be able to learn alike. But he would not tolerate idleness, or endure carelessness: nor did his mildness ever degenerate into weakness. Hence his authority was always respected; his manner of teaching and governing invariably secured the affection, as well as the ready submission and entire confidence of his pupils. When his class came before the dreaded examination of Mr. Potts, he often felt for them, and would help them out by a significant look or sign, unperceived by the formidable president. The writer on one of these occasions was wondering what to answer to a question in Latin Syntax, when his kind master WEEDALL held up two fingers behind the president's chair. The scholar immediately understood the sign, and was saved by answering promptly that the word exemplified the rule for the *double dative case*. MR. WEEDALL avoided, as much as possible, the use of a book, to spare his eyes. It was marvellous how he heard difficult lessons without having a book before him, or if he had one, almost without looking at it. The lessons were always said walking up and down in the playground, when the weather permitted it, which, as before mentioned, he always used to call the "Garden," from its having been such at his first coming to Oscott. There the little man was to be seen walking, or standing in the middle of his class, and carrying on the lesson with great animation and encouragement. It was not till some years after that the ecclesiastical students began to wear cassocks and clerical caps: so he appeared in a plain black coat, with grey "shorts," and white stockings, and with shoes always very nicely polished; and he usually wore for lightness, and as a protection to his eyes, a black leghorn hat with a broad brim, lined with green silk. He generally wore spectacles, though it was not till much later that he had recourse to green and blue glasses, and other contrivances to keep off glare and dust. It was his practice to exercise his pupils much in translations, analyses, imitations, and original compositions, from which they derived great advantages. The writer has preserved his own theme books, filled under Mr. Weedall in the school of Rhetoric; and it will give the reader a fair idea of the nature and amount of these exercises, to be informed that during four months, the class had done eighteen translations from Greek, Latin, and French, eight reviews or critiques, three essays, three themes, eight analyses, and one imitation of Horace, Epis. 7, 1st book, which the present writer turned upon the well known servant of the college, John Hales, and Tom Moseley, a character in the neighbourhood, in a composition of nearly a hundred lines in verse. These exercises were, of course, exclusive of the usual course of reading and construing Greek, Latin, and French authors.

But while Mr. Weedall was thus experiencing

the truth of the adage that "we learn by teaching," and increasing his own acquirements by his judicious method of imparting classical knowledge to his pupils, he was at the same time improving himself in a most important department of his own ecclesiastical studies. Mr. Walsh had no sooner entered upon his important charge, than with the ready and zealous co-operation of Mr. Quick, he established the admirable regulation for the church students to meet three times a week to hold spiritual conferences of an hour each. Here the young ecclesiastics were gradually initiated in the important function of preaching. Their first attempts commenced after they had completed the age of sixteen, or before that age, if they had reached the class of poetry. Every encouragement was afforded them, and the greatest indulgence shown to their early efforts. They were not expected to speak more than a quarter of an hour; and no notice was taken of any embarrassment, hesitation, or mistakes during the delivery of these little discourses. They were to be spoken by heart, but no matter how often the speaker got out, and was obliged to have recourse to his written paper; no one blamed or discouraged him, but at the end the superiors would often say a few words of commendation and encouragement, which had the happiest effect. Occasionally these compliments were somewhat ambiguously expressed, as when the writer had once to deliver a discourse in his turn before Dr. Milner, who on that evening presided at the Conference. The discourse was "On vain glory;" and at its conclusion the Bishop said: "Thank you, Sir; you have given us a very excellent discourse; you have only to apply it to yourself." The first of these Conferences was probably held on the 3rd of November, 1808, as Mr. Quick delivered on that day his first little sermon "On the goodness of God," and it is most likely that with that he opened the first Conference. His second, on the "*Titles by which God claims our service*," was delivered on the New Year's Day following. Both of these discourses the writer possesses in Mr. Quick's original MSS., and treasures them as precious memorials of the infancy of those Conferences, from which, for so many years, the church students of St. Mary's College derived very important benefit. Each one took his turn to deliver a short discourse, with which the Conference always began. It happened occasionally that some one was unprepared by some accidental hindrance. On one such occasion, MR. WEEDALL, without any previous preparation, gave an extempore discourse, with perfect self-possession and a ready flow of language, which was not only very edifying, but excited great admiration. But his discourses were always very superior, and the students always looked forward with particular pleasure to those nights when it would be his turn to address them. The writer has preserved an analysis of only one of these Conference discourses of Mr. WEEDALL's, which is on the duty of penance, its efficacy, and the opportunities of practising it. One remark at the end deserves to be preserved. He said "that to sum up

F

in a single sentence the whole theory and practice of penance, what was sweet must be bitter to us, and what was bitter must become sweet."

At these Conferences, after the short discourse, the rest of the hour was filled up with the discussion of some pious subject, or a lecture from that invaluable work, "*The Practice of Christian Perfection*," by Rodriguez, or occasionally by a debate on some point of controversy. In these debates Mr. WEEDALL always distinguished himself for readiness of reply, solidity of argument, and gracefulness of language and delivery. For those ecclesiastical students who were going through the course of Theology, there was a farther exercise in preaching, which was highly useful and improving. Every other Sunday one of the divines, in his turn, had to deliver a regular sermon to the entire college assembled in the study place in the evening. These sermons were called by the French name of *Prones*, and many of them were eloquent and admirable compositions, particularly those by Mr. Laken, one of whose *Prones* was considered so well calculated to benefit the students when they left college, that it was published under the title of "*An Address to Young People.*" In these *Prones*, however, no one surpassed Mr. WEEDALL. He was always listened to with breathless attention and profound interest, and here it was that he laid the foundation of that character which he ever after maintained for pulpit eloquence.

The weak state of Mr. WEEDALL's eyes, so often alluded to in these pages, occasioned delays in his promotion to Holy Orders. But in the mean time he was making the best use of every opportunity of advancing in theological science, and above all in the great science of the Saints, the way of virtue and perfection. The services in the College Chapel gradually increased in splendour and solemnity, and were conducted with more exact observance of rubrics and ceremonies. Not long after the opening of the new college, a fresh stimulus and additional means were given to the religious ceremonial by the acquisition of those splendid vestments which were so long used and admired. The Rev. Charles Blount, who died at Warwick, January 19th, 1810, left certain legacies to Bishop Milner, and among them some very rich and valuable vestments. All these the Bishop presented to his new college. There was one exceedingly admired, of brocade of a light green colour, beautifully diversified with flowers and ornaments, wrought in gold and colours; one of crimson damask, richly trimmed with silver lace; but above all, a white vestment quite covered with gold and silver embroidery of the richest character. There was also a vestment of black velvet trimmed with silver lace; another white satin vestment with galoon lace, and the cross and pillar worked with rich flowers in coloured silk; and a set of white satin dalmatics, likewise trimmed with galoon lace. These formed a valuable set of altar vestments, more precious than could be found in most of our chapels at that time. A small organ was procured and set up in the tribune, which was superseded by a more powerful one in after years. Then a choir was formed and instructed by Mr. Samuel Jones; and MR. WEEDALL joined it as a bass singer, and so continued for many years in the college choir. He had a clear flexible voice, and a correct ear, and sung with great expression and precision. Old Oscotians will remember how feelingly he used to sing the Lamentations at Tenebræ, and with what taste and spirit he would sing Webbe's fine and expressive Motette, "*Super flumina Babylonis.*" In fact, it might have been said of him, as truly as Johnson said of Goldsmith: *nihil quod tetigit, non ornavit.* He always took a part likewise in the vocal music at the Midsummer and Christmas Exhibitions. This began with a few songs and glees, and it was long before any instruments were introduced, except a piano-forte. MR. WEEDALL used to take the bass part, and distinguished himself by the great spirit and expression which he threw into those fine glees from Ossian's Poems, composed by Calcott. He was always of a cheerful turn, and always loved a little harmless joke. On one occasion Mr. Samuel Jones was practising the singers for one of these exhibitions, and they were going through with great gravity one of Calcott's fine Ossianic glees. WEEDALL had to sing the words: "Be thou on a moonbeam, O Morna!" which he gave with great power and spirit, but instead of the right words he mischievously sung out at the top of his voice: "Be thou on a *mopstick!*" So sudden and unexpected a travestie convulsed the leader and the choir, and utterly prevented all return for that day of the gravity indispensable for such a rehearsal.

CHAPTER IV.

Mr. Weedall Studies Theology under Mr. Potts—He is Initiated in Holy Orders—Gives Catechetical Instruction to the Children in the Poor School in Birmingham—His Poetry—His Controversy with Cobbett—Is Ordained Priest—His First Mass—First Printed Sermon—Other Exercises of the Holy Ministry.

"Let others," says St. Augustin, "choose for themselves an earthly and temporal inheritance for their enjoyment; my portion is the Lord: let others drink of poisonous pleasures; the portion of my chalice is the Lord!"* Such undoubtedly were the sentiments and frequently the pious aspirations of the subject of this biography. His sublime vocation he steadily kept in view; to this he directed all his studies, and from such direction he was animated exceedingly in his collegiate course. The reader has seen in Mr. Weedall's own words, in Chapter Third, that he was compelled, by the terrible nervous affection of his head and eyes, to refrain for a long time from all application to study; so that he was obliged to give up entirely the usual course of Philosophy. He ventured,

---

* "Eligant sibi alii partes quibus fruantur terrenas et temporales; portio mea Dominus est: bibant alii mortiferas voluptates; pars calicis mei Dominus est!"—S. Aug. in Ps. xv.

however, to commence his Theology by the help of a fellow-student reading the lessons to him. His professor was the president, the Rev. Thomas Potts, who had indeed been his preceptor in his earlier studies, from the time of his first coming to Oscott from Sedgley Park. He was always greatly attached to Mr. Potts, and had imbibed a great deal of his spirit and manner. Nothing used to amuse him more in after life than to repeat the grave and quaint expressions of his old and beloved professor, especially with those who could join him in such rehearsals. He had also, as an inevitable consequence, caught some of Mr. Potts' peculiar ways and phrases: for, as our great moralist observes, "it is not easy when we converse with one whose general character excites our veneration, to escape all contagion of his peculiarities, even when we do not deliberately think them worthy of our notice, and when they would have excited laughter or disgust, had they not been protected by their alliance to nobler qualities, and accidentally consorted with knowledge or with virtue."* Mr. Potts was a sound, cautious, and safe theologian; and in explaining the various opinions of divines on those questions which the Church leaves open to discussion, he fairly and candidly stated his own conclusions, but carefully abstained from pressing them upon his pupils. It was his laudable custom to employ them frequently in writing exercises on questions of Theology. Thus Mr. Weedall composed, during his course, the

* Dr. Johnson, "Rambler," No. 164.

following among other essays: *Justification by Faith;—Which is the more perfect state, that of a religious solitary, or that of a laborious missioner? —On Smuggling;—On Concupiscense;—On the Double Sense in the Psalms;—On the Christian and Jewish Sacraments;—On the Forms of Baptism and Confirmation.* Knowing how much most of his students were necessarily employed in teaching their respective classes, he studied in a manner for them, and came prepared with a store of collateral information on the lesson for the day, to supply for their inability to read much for themselves beyond the treatise of their author. The theology of Collet was the ordinary text book. This author was chosen by Bishop Milner, because, as he used to observe, although he was often rigid and starch, he was always safe.

The state of Mr. Weedall's eyes did not improve; but it would have been a grievous and unnecessary trial to keep back any longer, and he was accordingly initiated as a cleric, and received the tonsure, and the four Minor Orders, as the writer believes, in the latter part of the year 1811, when the Rev. Richard Hubbard was ordained priest, in the month of November. In the following year, 1812, on the 26th of May, he received the Holy Order of Subdeaconship, which bound him irrevocably, but by a willing tie, to the service of the Church in the sacred ministry. He received at the same time a dispensation from reciting the Divine Office, on account of his weak eyes, or rather a commutation of the Breviary for the Rosary of the

B. V. Mary, which he recited instead of the office. The following is his own account in the paper referred to in the preceding chapter :—

"I was obliged to have a dispensation from my office, by commutation for the Rosary, for three or four years after I was ordained Priest. I then began with Vespers and Complin, afterwards the Little Hours, and lastly Matins and Lauds, which last I was only able to manage at first by the help of others, until the psalms grew familiar to me."

It was customary at that time, and long afterwards, for the clergy to wear hair powder, and they usually began to wear it when they had taken the decisive step, by receiving the Subdeaconship. MR. WEEDALL accordingly put on powder at this time, and always looked extremely well and dignified in wearing it.

In the next year, 1813, he was promoted to the Holy Order of Deaconship, on the 15th of April. And now, as he drew nearer to the grand object of all his desires and pursuits, and had mounted to within one step of the holy altar, he felt the deep responsibility of his sacred character, and trembled at the near approach of the time when he should be ranked among the anointed priests of the New Law. "It is a difficult and arduous thing," says a holy writer, "to minister in the priesthood, to govern souls, and according to the word of Solomon, to cast oneself into the crowd of the people, and bind upon oneself sin to sin."* This MR. WEEDALL

---

* "Res difficile et ardua est ministrare in sacerdotio, animas regere, et juxta verbum Salomonis, mittere se in turbam populi, et alligare sibi peccata duplicia."—PETR. BLESSENSIS, *Ep.* 123.

felt very sensibly, and he therefore strove by every means to prepare himself well, and qualify himself in the best manner he could for the sacred priesthood, always trusting in the powerful grace of God to assist and strengthen him. The old chapel of St. Chad's, in Birmingham, was opened in 1809, and MR. WEEDALL found an excellent field for his initiation in the work of the holy ministry in the poor school attached to that chapel. He used to go over to Birmingham with undeviating punctuality every Sunday evening, for several years, to catechize and instruct the children in the poor schools; thereby rendering important assistance to the laborious and indefatigable missioner, the Rev. Edward Peach, while he was exercising his own talents in the work to which he was called, and acquiring valuable experience, for the time when he should be placed as a watchman on the towers of Israel.

Meantime, though writing was to him so fatiguing, he was not idle with his pen. He sent to the "*Orthodox Journal*" a poem, which appeared in the number for January, 1814, entitled: "*The Tears of Religion, a Dream,*" with the motto from Homer, Ὄναρ ἐκ Διός ἐστι. It referred to the dissensions and discussions in Ireland on the question of the Veto, and abounded in rich imagery, described in an easy flow of poetical language. The following stanzas will convey some idea of its structure and merits. They form a portion of the complaint of Religion, as personified in the dream.

"'But in civil contention, my son,
 They have soiled my rich mantle of snow,
And left me unfriended and lone
 To flounce in these tatters of woe.
In the long cherished Isle where I lay,
 Fell Discord the Apple has thrown,
To rob me, if haply she may,
 Of the *Emerald Gem* in my crown.

"'Then haste to my sons and declare
 The keen anguish that's bursting my heart!'
She ceased! then dissolving in air,
 Dropped a tear as she seemed to depart.
I awoke, for the kindling beam
 O'er my eyelids protruded the day,
As faintly the voice in my dream
 Low murmuring melted away."

H. W.

This, with the "*Ode on a Distant Prospect of Sedgley Park,*" already given, are the only pieces of poetry which Mr. Weedall published. They afford, however, sufficient ground to believe that in poetical composition, had he chosen to cultivate it, he would have as much excelled as in every other department of learning in which his talents were exercised.

Mr. Weedall was a constant reader of Cobbett's "Political Register;" and at this time he had a little brush of controversy with that versatile politician. His own words will best explain his motives for reading Cobbett, and how far he admired his writings. "I confess, Sir, that for many years I have read your publications with pleasure; and however I may have been inclined to differ with you on certain points, I have uniformly admired you, on political subjects at least, for originality of thought, strength of expression, clearness, accuracy, depth, and solidity of argument, that I do not often find in the productions of the day." But Cobbett had gone out of his way, and got out of his depth, by discussing religious questions. He maintained that if Bonaparte was the *scourge of God*, as some designated him, he was not answerable for his acts of violence and spoliation. MR. WEEDALL, under the signature of "A Constant Reader," endeavoured in a temperate and well argued letter to make him see the "difference between positively *authorising* an action, and only negatively *permitting* it: between *causing* an evil, and subsequently *converting* that evil into an instrument of good?" Cobbett inserted the letter, and attempted an answer to it, in which he paid a tribute of respect very unusual for him, to his correspondent's talents, which he professed himself "by no means inclined to underrate." But he said: "I will engage for him, that he has never given subjects of this sort that consideration of which his mind is capable. He has taken things upon trust; he has adopted notions in early life, which he has never had the leisure or the resolution critically to canvass." But his answer was full of sophistry, deficient in candour, and disgustingly irreverent to the Almighty and the Holy Scriptures. MR. WEEDALL sent a rejoinder, of which Cobbett must have felt the humiliating force; but he had not the fairness to insert it. It was a masterly defence and reconstruction of his former proposition, "That a man may, with perfect consistency, designate Bonaparte the *scourge of God*, or an active *instrument* in his hands, at the same time charging him with the *guilt* of every unjustifiable act committed in that capacity." The reader will peruse the following extracts with pleasure, and will not fail to perceive in this, Mr. WEEDALL's first appearance in print, in prose writing, the germ of that superior ability which distinguished him in his subsequent compositions:—

"I estimate not the morality of an action on any paltry grounds of party, or of country. Politics, Sir, do not enter into my ideas of right and wrong: I form them upon the eternal and immutable principles of truth, and, therefore, it matters not to me by whom the act is committed; if it be unjustifiable, I condemn it whether committed by Bonaparte or Alexander—whether by the sword of a Frenchman, or the spear of a Cossack. But I maintain, that to pretend to justify French plunder, or English plunder, or any plunder *in general*, because it was authorised in a *particular* case, and under *particular* circumstances, is both illogical and unfair."

Cobbett had maintained that the example of the people of God in the spoliation and extermination of the Madianites was a justification of French plunder, and asked why he was to look upon the Ten Commandments as any rule of conduct, unless the soldier was to be guided by the example of plunder in the case of the Madianites. To this Mr. WEEDALL replied:—

"Before a man can avail himself of this precedent of the Jews in regard of the Madianites, he must show clearly that the positive will of God authorises him to do the action. Again, Sir, give this historical fact the full force of a precept, and what does it enjoin? Why that a soldier placed *in the same circumstances* as the Jews, ought to act *in the same manner.* Turn it as you will, Sir, you can make no more of it. And what do the Commandments enjoin more than this; at least such of them as do not run in the form of a prohibition? What more than to command *certain things in certain circumstances?*......Why, Sir, upon your principle, a man must become a Jew after reading the Old Testament, and a Christian after reading the New, and be damned at last, for being a hypocrite in both......One word more, and I have done. You totally mistake my character, if you imagine that I have formed my religious creed upon trust, or adopted it from prejudice or local habits. It is indeed the creed of my childhood, but it has not continued, *for that reason,* to be the creed of the man. No sooner was my mind capable of judging, than I threw myself out of the ark in which I had been cradled, to examine its external construction, and the strength and solidity of its basis. I examined also the pretensions of others. I invariably found them unsafe and crazy; and was glad, like the wearied dove that found no place to rest its foot, to be taken back again into that ark in which I will live and die. No, Sir, not the 'creature of habit or of passion,' not biassed by any prejudice, save that of truth. I have pondered the subject deeply—I believe impartially and so satisfied am I of the truth of that creed which I have adopted by choice, as well as succeeded to by birth, that I shall fearlessly hazard my eternal salvation upon the profession of it. Can you, Sir, lay your hand upon your heart, and make the same avowal?"

The important time had now arrived when HENRY WEEDALL was to be promoted to the sacred dignity of the priesthood. It was the term of his long wishes, the object of his fervent aspirations, the goal of his brilliant course of collegiate exercise.

In one so pious, so thoughtful, so cautious, firm, and faithful as he was, it is easy to imagine with what intensity of holy animation he looked forward to this crowning consummation of all his pursuits. His life from the dawn of reason had been but one steady, uniform preparation for the great day which was now at hand, when he was to have imposed upon his shoulders indeed a heavy burthen, under which even Angels might tremble, but at the same time was to be entrusted with a ministry the most sublime and consoling that can employ the faculties of man during his sojourning upon earth. "A priest," says St. Bernard, "holds a heavenly office; he is become the Angel of the Lord of hosts; like an Angel, he is either elect, or reprobate: for wickedness found in Angels must be judged more strictly and inexorably than that which is human."* But he knew that though great was the burthen, great also was the grace of Him who would impose it; and thus while he always retained a wholesome fear, he never relinquished an humble confidence. The Almighty had great designs in his promotion, even as when he declared his intentions towards Samuel; *I will raise me up a faithful priest, who shall do according to my heart and my soul: and* I WILL BUILD HIM A FAITHFUL HOUSE,† *and he shall walk all day before my anointed.*

---

* "Sacerdos cœleste tenet officium, Angelus Domini exercituum factus est; tanquam Angelus, aut eligitur, aut reprobatur: inventa quippe in Angelis pravitas, districtius judicetur necesse est, et inexorabilius, quam humana."—S. BERNARDUS, in verba, *Ecce nos*, etc.

† 1 KINGS II., 35.

He received the Holy Order of Priesthood at an ordination held by the illustrious Bishop Milner, in his chapel at Wolverhampton, on the 6th April, 1814, it being Wednesday in Holy Week. His feelings on that memorable day may be better conceived than described. He used always to speak of it with fervour and rapture as the happiest day of his life. It had assigned him his privileged position for length of days in the sanctuary of his God, and in the sublime ministrations of the holiest character upon earth. It had taken him irrevocably from the distracting paths of the world, to the sacred seclusion of the courts of the Lord; and he was ready to say now with a holy Father: "What have we to do with fables? We have received the ministry of the altars of Christ, not a service to be paid to men."*

The first duty of a priest is to offer sacrifice, the great sacrifice of the new law, the Mass. But MR. WEEDALL was not too hasty in approaching the holy altar. It has been the practice of holy men to refrain for some time from celebrating their first Mass, from a deep sense of the awful sanctity of that action, and a wish to make a careful preparation for it. We read continually in the lives of the Saints, that they took time to prepare for their first Mass, and did not hasten to the altar the very day after their ordination, or even within a few days after it. The companions of St. Ignatius, after

---

* "Quid nobis cum fabulis? ministerium altaribus Christi, non obsequium hominibus deferendum recepimus."—S. AMBROS. *L. I. de Officiis*, c. 20.

receiving the Holy Order of Priesthood, retired to prepare themselves for several months by fasting and prayer; but the Saint himself deferred his first Mass for a whole year. If such examples can rarely be followed in a country like ours, where the fields are every where *white for the harvest*, and the services of our few labourers are so much needed; it is still desirable that a newly ordained priest should allow himself a decent interval to prepare for the most sublime of his sacred functions, and not run to the altar with indecorous precipitation. It was accordingly the laudable custom at St. Mary's College to take several days at least for immediate preparation; and MR. WEEDALL did not say his first Mass till eleven days after his ordination. It was on Low Sunday, the 17th of April, and in the College Chapel, that he first celebrated. "At the first sight of that young priest," says Mr. Digby, "who advances to the altar with joined palms and downcast eyes, to sing Mass, there are many present who cannot prevent their tears from bursting forth: it is a look of such profound humility and sweetness; such resignation and readiness to die for Christ; it is the countenance and air of a holy martyr."* All this was assuredly exemplified at the first Mass of this fervent young priest. On the Sunday following he preached his first public sermon. He chose a very appropriate text from II. Timothy iv., 5.—"*Do the work of an Evangelist fulfil thy ministry.*"

* "Mores Catholici," B. ii., ch. i.

The exordium of this, his first public Sermon, is very beautiful and apposite.

"In addressing you, my brethren, on the present occasion," he said, "I am excited by feelings of no ordinary nature. Though not unaccustomed to address a great proportion of my present audience, yet the circumstances under which I now appear being essentially different, different also are the emotions within me. Standing as I do within this consecrated spot, vested with a character in its own nature the most elevated, and entrusted with a charge which an angel might dread—the charge, the character, the place, all remind me of what I ought to be—while the conviction of my own insignificance tells me too plainly what I am not. At one time the mind is exalted and roused by the importance of the subject; at another, sunk and confounded by its own insufficiency; and in this conflict of all that is great with all that is mean; of all that is holy, with all that is unholy; are produced those emotions which I cannot describe. In standing before you on the present occasion to discharge a principal function of the ministry, these feelings operating with their full force, almost tempt me, like the prophet Jonas, to shrink from the task, and to expostulate with my God like Moses of old: *O Lord, I am not eloquent, neither heretofore, nor since thou hast spoken to thy servant; but I am slow of speech, and of a slow tongue.* (Gen. iv., 10.) But, my friends, when I consider that the operations of heaven act totally independent of the merits or demerits of man, that the humble are the means God employs in his designs of mercy,—when I reflect that the only instrument was a trumpet in the dilapidations of Jericho, and an earthen pitcher in the overthrow of the Madianites. When coming nearer to that work which particularly concerns myself, I behold twelve mean and illiterate fishermen chosen by God for the conversion of the world,—I seem satisfied that nothing is wanting on the part of man, but an humble and unreserved correspondence; and with this conviction I feel content, though not without diffidence and fear, as thou knowest, O God, to acquiesce in the injunction of the Apostle: *Do the work of an Evangelist fulfil thy ministry.*"

He considered that he could not commence his preaching with a more appropriate subject than the Word of God, first, as regards the preacher, and secondly, as regards the hearers. Accordingly, the sermon is arranged under two heads, *the qualifications of the preacher*, and *the dispositions of the hearers*. The following affecting passage shows the holy preparation which he himself had made for the sacred ministry :—

"When first I turned my mind to the consideration of this momentous choice, I received little encouragement to embrace it. I was told that it was an important, a painful, and a perilous charge; that where singly to escape was a miracle of grace, multiplied were the difficulties a hundredfold when undertaking a responsibility for others. That by identifying myself with the many, I became accountable before God for their salvation. I was forewarned of every danger and of every trial, and was bid to remember that the depths of hell were paved with those unfortunate millions who had engaged in this state without a call, or who had failed to discharge its many and important obligations. Finally, I was instructed to recommend the matter to God; and pardon me if I say that I did what every one in such a situation was bound to do. I looked out with eagerness for the star that I hoped was to guide me. I watched with anxiety its every movement,—and thou knowest, O God, how I trembled when I thought I saw it settle over the sanctuary. That tremor still agitates my frame; and long, very long, may it be ere the salutary emotion subsides within me."

Another feeling passage is very characteristic of the preacher. It is certainly most advisable to keep oneself entirely out of view in preaching; but if ever any reference to self might be allowable, it was on such an occasion, and from the lips of such a minister.

"How far my own character may affect the force of my words, I know not. Of myself I can say nothing. I am not a stranger to most of you, and my life, from my youth upwards, is before you, all *having known me from the beginning*. (Acts xxvi., 5.) If, then, the retrospect in your judgment afford matter for animadversion, I deprecate not your censures; but oh! let them be passed in the spirit of charity: have regard to the infirmity of nature, and the levity of youth, and remember that the judgment which you pass upon the faults of others, will be the measure of the judgment that will be passed upon your own. But should you be inclined to severity, let it not detract from the truths I deliver; blame the man, but not the minister; condemn me, I am content; but hurt not yourselves,—strike me, but hear me. Hear me with patience,—hear me with temper,—but above all, hear with that singleness and sincerity of mind that waits only to be convinced, immediately to practise."

Thus did this noble son of St. Mary's enter cordially and energetically upon his holy career in the sacred ministry. Though employed still in teaching classics in the college, he found frequent occasions for the exercise of clerical functions. During the ensuing Midsummer vacation, he remained at the college, and frequently officiated and preached in the chapel on Sundays. Nor was it long before a more important occasion presented itself, when he appeared before a large audience, in the old chapel, St. Peter's, Birmingham, of which the Rev. James Hawley, O. S. F., was at that time the pastor. He was requested to preach a sermon there for the benefit of the Catholic schools, which required the erection of a commodious school room. His sermon was delivered on Sunday, October 30th, 1814, and was afterwards printed " to promote the benevolent object of the institution," being the first of his published discourses. It is long and argumentative, but composed in nervous language of exciting eloquence. He first shows the proper meaning of charity.

"Charity, then, is not the mere indulgence of a benevolent feeling; not the mechanical ebullition of a sympathetic heart; not the unmeaning and capricious fling of liberality; but a steady, uniform, and well regulated concern for our neighbour, originating in views of a higher kind, and directed by motives altogether supernatural....... Ostentation is not charity, nor sensibility a virtue; and among the many whom the Gospel records to have cast their abundance into the treasury, we might be led to suspect that only one was actuated by unexceptionable motives, at least, only one received the approbation of Christ."

He proceeds to prove by an interesting chain of reasoning that " the obligation of charity is equally demonstrable from the natural, as from the divine law." He next shows that charity is our interest as well as our duty, and that even in this life, real charity is seldom unrewarded. This argument, however, he urges with caution.

" For," he continues, in a strain of eloquence which so many will recognise as peculiarly his own, " we should be careful how we are swayed by motives of temporal interest ......I know not any character so pitiful as of the man who is charitable from a motive of selfishness; who gives in order to receive, and who regulates the extent of his benevolence by the probability of a profitable return—a mere trader in human misery: he speculates in the wants of his fellow creatures, and enlarges or contracts his compassion upon the cold calculations of profit and loss. Methinks I hear such a man exclaim, while he clenches with tenacious grasp the unwilling contribution, '*What will you give me, and I will deliver*' it '*to you!*'* What will I give you? I will give you a claim upon the future mercies of the Almighty,—I will give you the benedictions of heaven, and the blessings of the poor,—I will give you the prayers of these children, in whose cause I am pleading,—and to complete the payment, will remit you to your own breast for the pure, unmixed, and exquisite raptures of self-approbation,

He proceeds to refute the usual pleas of impracticability from the increasing difficulties of the times, the wants of a numerous family, and the inadequacy of private means: and as the sermon was preached a short time after a grand Oratorio, he does not fail to press that circumstance into the cause. Having exposed the readiness with which money is expended on superfluities and luxuries, and all without a single hint about poverty or the difficulties of the times, he thus continues:—

"Oh no! these, it seems, are apologies consecrated solely to uncharitableness. You are only poor when you are to relieve distress; on these occasions it is a compliment to believe that you are so, although in other circumstances to tell you that you were poor, would be deemed a deliberate insult. But I forget myself—there are cases when distress ceases to be regarded with suspicion—when she is even welcomed with a frank and generous liberality.

* St. Matthew xxvi., 15.

But then she must employ artifice to circumvent your compassion. She must throw off her tattered rags, she must deck herself out in the gaiety of attire, and with music and song she must harmonise you into benevolence by the charms of her minstrelsy. Yes, and I verily believe, that had you this day been invited to a *concert* instead of a *sermon*, I might have had to congratulate these children that all their wants would be amply supplied."

After replying forcibly to the remaining objection from the inadequacy of private means, he proceeds finally to show that the leading cause of misery is ignorance; "ignorance of the true interests of man, and of the means to promote them." And he examines the probabilities that uninstructed minds will mistake the nature of true happiness, and pursue that vicious indulgence which generally ends in want and misery. Thus he comes directly to his appeal in behalf of the poor children, after a graphic and powerful description of the consequences which must ensue from their not being properly educated."

"Impressed in their infancy with no sentiments either of morality or religion, by parents perhaps ignorant of both, and habituated to scenes of gross sensuality, their minds very little superior to animal instinct, and their ideas of happiness seldom rising above the low gratifications of sense; their knowledge of a future state of rewards and punishments too indistinct either to elevate their hopes or restrain their licentiousness,—these children are thrust into the streets as soon as they are able to work, exposed to the multiplied dangers of the world, to the rudest assaults of temptation, and to the most detestable arts of seduction: initiated into all the horrid mysteries of vice, and familiarised to the grossest exhibitions of depravity, which if it reign in any one place with more than usual effrontery and wanton, in every varied form of nameless obscenity, it is in the streets of a large and populous town."

This brings him, finally, to the precise object of his appeal to the charity of his audience, after explaining which, he pours out one of those brilliant and pathetic perorations, for which he was always so remarkable.

" To you these children look up with asking eagerness, in the hope that you will befriend them......I am confident that if conscience be allowed to discuss their claims, these children will be supported. But if self-love be permitted to arbitrate betwixt you,—then, my children, look elsewhere for support; cast upwards those patient but disappointed looks to that heaven where dwells the common Father of the poor and the rich, and he *who heareth the young ravens when they cry*,* will devise other modes of providing for your necessities, or will teach you the art of resignation. But the time may come when, in your turn, you may rule the destinies of this very people, whom I now address in your behalf. Yes, my brethren, the day will come, when your lot will be decided by the criterion of charity. That day when the archangel shall trumpet forth the dissolution of time, and wind a blast that shall shiver creation ; when the solemn decree shall go out from the eternal throne to summon the world to judgment; and weeping, trembling man shall appear before his Redeemer to receive his final sentence; what will be the articles of impeachment? *I was hungry*, will the Judge say, *and you gave me not to eat; I was thirsty, and you gave me not to drink*, &c........But no—I am wrong—I injure you, my brethren, I read my error in your looks. God forbid that I should predict for you such a reception. Rather let me hope that the charity of this day will be recorded for your glory, and that you will stand up with confidence before the throne because *you have not*

* Job xxxviii., 41.

eaten your morsel alone, but have shared it with the fatherless; because you were the protectors of the poor, and the comforters of them that mourned."*

This eloquent sermon produced the desired effect in a very liberal collection. Nothing like it had been ever heard in Birmingham; and when published, it was eagerly bought up, and thereby the ends of charity were still further promoted.

But Mr. WEEDALL found other opportunities of exercising the sacred ministry with which he was now entrusted. The pastor of the congregation attached to the chapel at Oscott was then the Rev. Thomas Walsh, afterwards Bishop. Knowing the zeal and abilities of MR. WEEDALL, he was glad to avail himself of his willing services in instructing the poor, and occasionally visiting the sick of the congregation. The flock were scattered in various directions and at various distances from the college; and it afforded him exercise, while it gave him meritorious occupation, to go round to them. On account of his weak eyes, he could not at that time read or write by candle light; therefore he made the most of the daylight for study; and then he would sally forth in the dusk to the cottages of the poor, to give them religious instruction and consolation, and save them the fatigue of coming to Mr. Walsh, after the exhausting labours of their daily toil. It became MR. WEEDALL's habit for many years thus to take his walks in the dark, and alone, in all weathers; and he rarely walked out at any other time. If he had no special visit to make to

* Job XXIX., and XXXI.

any poor person, he would take his dark and dreary walk over the wide waste of Sutton Coldfield, or he would even sometimes go in the direction of Birmingham, as far as Aston Park wall, touch the wall with his stick, and then hasten back, making his walk full eight miles by the time that he reached home. It was during these walks that he recited his Rosary in lieu of the Divine Office, and that he planned and thought over his beautiful sermons. Thus did this admirable man find means to study and attend to his duties in teaching during the day; and when the evening came, when others looked for rest and recreation, he contrived to combine with needful exercise the meritorious works of religion and charity.

CHAPTER V.

Mr. Weedall's Class in Rhetoric—Christmas Exhibition—His Amanuensis—Controversy in the "Orthodox Journal"—Mr. Potts Disabled by Paralysis—Changes in Consequence in the College—Mr. Weedall's Occasional Priestly Duties—Sermon at St. Chad's—Events at Oscott—Exhibition Room.

It was observed in the last chapter that Mr. Weedall continued to teach in the college after he was ordained priest. At first Bishop Milner was uncertain as to the success of his undertaking, and therefore would not venture to incur the expense of hired teachers. Thus Weedall and others, as they advanced to the higher studies themselves, were employed in teaching the junior classes. But Almighty God singularly blessed the college, and it prospered, its holy Patroness watching over it; so that as various ecclesiastics flocked to it, it was rendered permanently independent of extraneous assistance. At the time of his ordination to the priesthood, Mr. Weedall was teaching a class in Rhetoric, which they finished under his tuition at the ensuing Christmas. The class was composed of the following students, Robert Throckmorton, the present worthy baronet, John

Shea, Andrew Blake, Michael and Daniel Callaghan, and the present writer. A synopsis has been already given of their exercises during the concluding half-year. At Christmas, all of them, except the two Callaghans, who were cousins, took parts in performing the tragedy of Philoctetes, in English, which was adapted from the Greek of Sophocles by the present biographer, who selected and blended the best passages from the versions of Potter and Francklin. The performance took place in the Refectory, being the first attempt at presenting an entire tragedy. The writer performed the part of Philoctetes, having borrowed an antique Flemish bow, and some Indian arrows, from the private museum of a friend, a collector of curiosities. This was the first exhibition, the harbinger of those much grander and more complete performances, which took place regularly at Christmas and Midsummer in after years. Mr. Weedall took great pains in training the performers in their several parts for weeks beforehand.

The writer was for some time the willing amanuensis of Mr. Weedall, writing out for him any thing that he wished to have copied, and often writing his sermons for him, as he dictated them, walking up and down his room. Mr. Weedall occupied at this time the middle room in the upper suite of rooms in front; but not long after he removed to a larger apartment on the opposite side, and towards the end of the passage. This was one of two adjoining rooms, called "Calefactories," from their having fire-places. It had been previously shared by three boys, and used to contain three beds; but it was afterwards fitted up as a single room for MR. WEEDALL, and made a very comfortable and respectable apartment. His amanuensis used also to read to him at stated times, usually every day. On those days when there was study in the afternoon, they met at three o'clock, and he read aloud to MR. WEEDALL *Fleury's Church History*, in French, for an hour, always walking about the roads or fields, when the weather would permit. In this manner he read to him fifteen volumes of that valuable work in the original. Besides this, he used to meet MR. WEEDALL immediately after night prayers, when he had returned from his solitary walk, and read to him for about half an hour some useful work, such as the *Lives* of *Fenelon* and *Bossuet—Reviews*, or any important publications of the day.

On one occasion, when they were returning through a field near the college, they perceived old Wiggin, the farmer, whose house was close to the college, coming up the field. MR. WEEDALL proposed to his companion to shut up Fleury, and to get into a little friendly conversation with the farmer, in the hope of enlightening him somewhat on the subject of religion. So when Wiggin came up to them, after the usual salutations, and some common-place remarks on the weather, MR. WEEDALL reminded him that his grey hairs were an admonition of his life drawing to a close, and of the necessity of each of us doing all the good in our power, to be prepared for our last end. Wiggin very coolly replied: "Why yes, we mun all dew what we con: you gentlemen mind your bewks, and stick to your larning; and we muck the fields, and get as good crops as we con. So we all dew good in our way." With this the old man walked off, perfectly satisfied that he did all the good he could in his way, and leaving us to be amused at the result of our zealous endeavour to improve him. He lived many years after this, and died in July, 1833, being about ninety years old.

Indeed it was marvellous how, with the serious impediments under which MR. WEEDALL laboured from the affection of his head and eyes, he yet managed to keep up even with the literary productions and controversies of the day. In a Catholic Magazine, published at the time, called the "*Orthodox Journal*," appeared in the number for May, 1814, a Letter from a zealous Priest, the Rev. N. Gilbert, under the initials N. G., to show that Infant Baptism is taught in Scripture. MR. WEEDALL wrote against him in the next number of the Journal, under the initials H. W., and sought to establish, 1st, that separating Scripture from Tradition, the attempt to determine the famous declaration of our Saviour to Nicodemus (St. John iii.), even to Baptism in general, would be difficult, and the result unsatisfactory; but 2ndly, that even conceding the passage to be clear as to the general necessity of Baptism, it would not be easy to show that the precept extends to Infants. His reasoning throughout he admitted to be hypothetical, and he only intended to combat the unsafe principle of resting an article of Faith upon Scripture alone. This drew forth a very long defence from N. G. He professed his object to be good, being to preserve the only authority in support of Infant Baptism which could have any weight with Protestants. He proceeded with tedious prolixity to demonstrate, as he considered, that the sense of the Scriptural passage is clear and indubitable, independently of tradition. MR. WEEDALL replied, and concluded the controversy, by a letter of moderate length, in which he professed to apprehend no danger from his own line of argument, his only object being to establish the inconsistency of Protestants in disclaiming on all points a rule of faith which in many they secretly, though unconsciously, retain. He restated the question, and repeated his reasoning in a more condensed form. He confessed himself not in the smallest degree enlightened by all the elucidation of his opponent.

"I cannot for my life," he said, "understand how a passage of Scripture can be *clear*, and yet stand in need of authority *to fix its meaning*; or how it can be absolutely determinable but to *one sense*, whilst the very act of fixing it supposes it determinable to *more*......and, therefore, I repeat, what was the original subject of dispute between us, that though the Catholic Church can clear up the difficulty, the Protestant Church cannot *satisfy* her children that Infant Baptism is taught in Scripture."

An impartial reader, after going through the letters on both sides, would probably find it difficult to determine which party had the better of the contest. It arose from a passage of Dr. Lingard's in his "*Strictures on Dr. Marsh's Comparative View*," in which he said:—

"They (the founders of the Modern Church of England) had agreed to retain Infant Baptism: it was therefore necessary to rest it on some ground. On Scripture they could not; for *it is not taught in Scripture*. On tradition they dared not; for tradition they had already rejected."

MR. WEEDALL, in the outset, observed that the writers were *Arcades ambo;* and, perhaps, after reading the whole correspondence, it may be fairly pronounced that the competitors were *Arcades tres*. It was a point quite open to discussion; but what practically beneficial result was to be obtained from victory on either side was problematical. So MR. WEEDALL even seemed to think: for, in concluding the controversy, he observed:—

"Perhaps your readers may be of opinion that more than sufficient has already been said upon the subject: they are now in possession of the arguments on both sides of the question, and from them they will form their own opinion. If they decide for me, I shall gain: if against me, I shall not lose.......It is difficult to combat as false on one ground what you believe to be true on another; for though you write not in despite of consistency, you write in despite of conviction."

At the close of the year 1815, a painful event occurred in the college, which caused some important changes in that establishment. Mr. Potts, who had presided over the college since its re-organisation by Bishop Milner, and had also taught Divinity during the same period, was suddenly seized with a fit of paralysis, on a Sunday, the last

day of the year 1815. It was very slight, but in
some degree it altered his speech at first, and soon
began to show its effects upon his mind. Shortly
after he had a second attack, which still further
debilitated him. Dr. Milner came over from
Wolverhampton, decided on relieving him from all
duty, and settled that he should remain nominally
president, retaining his rooms as usual, and enjoying the *otium cum dignitate*. From that time his fine
mind became gradually weaker; but he suffered
no pain, and was able to take his walks with little
or no inconvenience. For a short time he said
Mass, and still longer the Breviary, with the help
of some one to recite it with him, a charitable office
which often fell to the lot of the present writer;
but the Bishop was obliged to forbid him to
continue it, and desired him to say the Rosary, or
some part of it, as far as he felt able, instead. But
he grew childish, so that any little thing set him
laughing, and he was wholly incapable of any
serious occupation. It was a melancholy spectacle
to see so noble a mind completely prostrated; and
a physician from London, Dr. Hawkins, whose
sons were students at the college, having paid a
visit to St. Mary's, and seen the afflicting state of
Mr. Potts in September, 1817, was so concerned
for him, that he wrote a letter to Mr. Walsh, containing a system of diet and regimen which he felt
confident would, if rigidly followed, not only prevent further attacks, but bring him back to what he
ought to be at his age of sixty-three, whereas he was
now more like a man of eighty-five. He attributed

the paralysis to a long diseased state of the digestive organs, and laid down as most essential that Mr. Potts should take no "stimulating poisons,"—no ale, beer, wine, fermented or spirituous liquors, *on any pretence*, but drink warm water or milk, with ginger. He gave minute directions for his diet and clothing, and wished him to wash his hands in warm water, using flour of mustard with the soap, and to bathe his feet twice a week in a hot decoction of mustard and horseradish. The superiors felt grateful to Dr. Hawkins for his kind solicitude and valuable advice. They would have endeavoured to follow it exactly with Mr. Potts, but that they felt a great delicacy in interfering in any way with the treatment of his regular physician, Dr. John Johnstone, of Birmingham. Indeed, it would have been no easy matter to bring Mr. Potts to submit to the regimen prescribed by Dr. Hawkins. He was fond of some things that were very unwholesome for him, and he would have them, if at all practicable. In his state of imbecility there was no reasoning with him, and of course coercion was not likely to be attempted. So he went on in his usual way, with his appetite good, and himself free from suffering of any kind, always cheerful, always ready to laugh at any trifle; and eating, drinking, and sleeping always well. In this state he continued, with very little alteration, during the four remaining years of his life.

This lamented incapacity of Mr. Potts entailed some changes in St. Mary's College. The two important offices of President and Professor of

Theology became at once vacant, as Mr. Potts had held both. Bishop Milner accordingly proceeded to fill them, and was happily enabled to provide for both without calling in extraneous aid, which is often a hazardous experiment, and open to serious objections. He appointed Mr. Quick president; and with that readiness to "spend himself and be spent" for the benefit of the college and its students, Mr. Quick undertook to teach Divinity, as well as to fulfil the onerous duties of president. He began with the school of Divinity, January 12th, 1816, and for a short time he even superadded the teaching of a class in Philosophy. On first taking the professor's chair in the school of Theology, he very humbly disclaimed any ability to teach, but said he wished to be considered merely as the hand or index to point out the daily portion of theological studies to his pupils. He undertook more than any one person could hope to carry on without experiencing the fatal consequences of over exertion; and too soon paid the penalty by an early death.

Mr. Walsh continued, as before, vice-president and spiritual director to the house, as well as pastor of the congregation. MR. WEEDALL also went on as usual with classical teaching, but frequently preached in the College Chapel, instructed converts, and assisted Mr. Walsh in various branches of the sacred ministry. Besides these opportunities of exercising his clerical functions, he often went to supply for priests in the neighbourhood in cases of sickness or absence, as at Bloxwich, for the Rev. F. Martyn; at Lichfield, for the Rev. John Kirk;

and at Birmingham, for one or other of the respected pastors of the two chapels. Occasionally, too, he preached in the neighbouring chapels. On the Epiphany of 1816 he preached at Wolverhampton, and one who was present spoke very highly of the sermon, and said: "I stood up to see and admire."

Having preached the charity sermon already mentioned, at the old chapel in Birmingham, the year before, with signal success, in behalf of the Catholic Poor Schools, he was requested to appear again in the same meritorious cause at the new chapel of St. Chad's. This had been erected in a populous part of the town but a few years before, and opened by Bishop Milner, December 17th, 1809, when he delivered an extempore discourse, the substance of which was afterwards published. MR. WEEDALL, ever willing to exert his powers in the cause of religion and charity, delivered another admirable sermon in this chapel, on Sunday, the 31st of December, 1815, being the very day on which Mr. Potts was first visited by a stroke of paralysis.

This sermon is shorter, but more didactic than his former one preached at St. Peter's Chapel. He considered that he could adopt no line of argument more profitable and successful than to instruct his audience in the *obligation* of alms deeds, because, said he, "there is no one virtue of our age which combines more apparent compliance with less real practice." He proceeded, therefore, to "detail the theology of the question, by insisting, first, on the obligation of relieving the poor; and next, on the means we possess of complying with this obligation." By a train of elaborate reasoning, such as generally composed the body of his sermons, he worked out these two propositions. The first he established from reason, and then from revelation, pouring out a rich succession of texts from both Testaments, each text in support of some distinct branch of his argument. Having shown the *obligation*, he proceeded to prove that the *means* are the superfluities of the rich. The reader will recognise the eloquence of WEEDALL in the following energetic demolition of a too common pretence:—

"But perhaps you may say you have no superfluities —that when the provisions are completed which I have just detailed, there will remain no surplus for charity. Not in the ruinous combination of extravagance and luxury, I believe it: not on the plan of satisfying the many factitious wants that clamour around us. But, my brethren, we needs must recollect that although religion is bountiful to our real wants, it will show no indulgence to our artificial ones. If, then, we would be as careful of our souls as we too often are of our miserable gains, we must examine with rigid exactness the whole system of our expenditure; we must dare to question the justice of those demands which folly and fashion unceasingly urge; and however painful the sacrifice, we must strike off with a desperate economy every item suggested by prodigality, ambition, sensuality, or pride. Run through the whole length of your establishment, and say whether every expense is regulated by the moderation of the gospel. Does temperance, or does appetite, preside at your tables? Have vanity or extravagance no share in the purveyance? Is there no unnecessary waste? No crumbs that bestrew your floor, and no thought to collect them for the hungry orphan? Are your horses and your servants proportioned to your rank? Might no retrenchment be made in the costliness of your furniture,—none in the splendour of your dress? Might not the frequency of your excursions be diminished,—excursions more for pleasure than for profit? Do the idle and the vicious never feed upon the patrimony of the poor? Is it never hazarded at the card, or the gaming table? Never wasted at the assembly or the theatre, or thoughtlessly distributed amongst the innumerable channels of trifling, dangerous, or guilty pleasures? Unreasonably, then, do you plead you have no superfluities, till this necessary deduction be previously made."

He refutes the frequent assertion that the profusion of the rich is, after all, the best practical charity.

"My brethren,......it may be sound policy, but it is wretched morality. A scheme which is radically bad can never be sanctified in its effects; and if luxury, pride, and effeminacy be of this description, it is little to say that they are productive of accidental good......But granting that some benefit is derived to the poor from the dissemination of wealth, does it fall, think ye, where most it is due? Does it spread to the hovels of indigence, and not rather to the abodes of comparative abundance? When I see a man......overstepping the sphere of his vocation, dashing along the road to luxury and preferment, trampling down in his career the thousands who were destined to be dependent on his bounty, and smothering in embryo the finest feelings of his nature; of such a man I am tempted to believe that he has voluntarily thrown himself out of the pale of salvation, and made himself an outlaw upon the merits of his Redeemer. And pursuing him into retirement, could imagination realise its rational fancies, at his side might you see the faded forms of want, disease, and misery, pressing around the groaning table to snatch away the meats that have been purchased by their patrimony; and above might you see the broad eye of vengeance full spread on the usurper, as if to recognise in the garb that he unfurls to heaven, the mantle of some abandoned orphan. *The garment indeed is my son's, an evil wild beast hath eaten him up, a beast hath devoured Joseph.* (Gen. xxxvii., 33.)

After exposing the wants of the poor children, and stating that with the contributions of the last year, a school-room had been built for upwards of one hundred and thirty children, but that a considerable debt had been unavoidably contracted, for which further donations were needed, he thus pathetically concludes a very eloquent and moving discourse:—

"Once you heard me with indulgence, and I fain would a second time bespeak your favour......for these poor children, these little benighted wanderers, whom your own pastor has delegated to my care, whom you yourselves have consigned to my advocacy;—dear to me because they are destitute; but dearer still because the apt resemblance of my Saviour! For them I pray; for them I supplicate; I beseech you not to abandon those whom your charity has warmed into light and life. And yet it is not I that supplicate!—I but give utterance to louder prayers. It is your own nature that supplicates! It is your religion that supplicates! It is your Redeemer!—It is your God!—Oh, could animation once more revive that agonising figure; could the blood but creep one single round, and warm into articulation one faltering accent, then would the voice of Jesus Christ plead for these children, it would repeat the charge which once he made—'If you love me, *feed my lambs;*' and by another solemn transfer of his own rights, would engage in their behalf all the tenderness which your bursting hearts could testify to him.—*Whatsoever you do to the least of these little ones*, it would say, *you do it unto me.* Matt. xxv., 40."

In the Midsummer vacation of 1816, MR. WEEDALL made his first excursion on the Continent, and spent a short time in Paris with a former student of the college, Mr. George Mecham. There had been a splendid termination of the scholastic half-year by excellent speaking at the Exhibition, when Philoctetes was again performed, the principal part being taken by Thomas Green, now the worthy missioner at Madeley. Bishop Milner presided, as he constantly attended the Exhibitions, and distributed a greater number of premiums than usual, and several medals to students who were not to return. An amusing incident occurred to MR. WEEDALL during his short tour in France. He went duly provided with a testimonial of his priesthood and character from Bishop Milner. But as this was not drawn up with much formality, the sacristan of a church where he applied to say Mass, demurred about permitting him to celebrate, excusing himself on account of some impostors having lately tried to deceive him, pretending to be priests. However, as MR. WEEDALL remonstrated against his unreasonable scruples, the sacristan bethought him of an effectual test, and said to him: "Eh bien, dites moi donc *l'Orate fratres.*" MR. WEEDALL declared, that thus suddenly called upon, he had some fear of not getting through it, but he did say it correctly. Upon which the sacristan was satisfied, but observed, with an air of great self-satisfaction, " Voila ou je les attrappe ! "

In July, Mr. Wareing quitted Oscott, and went to reside at Sedgley Park, whence he supplied on Sundays the mission at Moseley Court, and taught classics at the Park during the week. At the close of that year, Mr. Benson, one of the divines, was seized on the 1st of November with typhus fever of a severe form, and shortly after, another was attacked. The first, happily, recovered; but the other, Mr. John Kirk, nephew of the Rev. John Kirk, of Lichfield, was carried off by that malignant disorder, on the 29th of December. In consequence of this infectious disease in the house, the superiors deemed it expedient to anticipate the Christmas vacation, and omit the usual examinations and exhibition. Accordingly the studies were interrupted, and the students broke up early in December, and nearly all left the college for their respective homes. By the mercy of Divine Providence, the fever spread no further: and after Christmas the college had re-assembled, with all its inmates vigourously pursuing their respective studies and duties, to make up for lost time. The want of proper accommodation for the sick in cases of infectious maladies had been severely felt in the late trying visitation; and to provide for any future emergency, a small building was shortly after erected at the top of the garden, a short distance from the house. However, it was never occupied, as the farm-house subsequently purchased afforded far more convenient means of lodging and attending patients.

It was in this year, 1816, that Bishop Milner made a noble addition to the buildings of the college, by erecting the Exhibition Room, and connecting the "Laura" with the old part of the building by an *Ambulacrum* at each end of the new erection, carried along the front of the "Laura" on one side, and before the old part of the building on the other. This large and convenient room was opened on the 25th of November, 1816, by a Lecture on the Steam Engine, delivered by the present writer. It was afterwards regularly used for Prones, Lectures, and Exhibitions. It was the scene of many admirable performances, and honoured by the frequent presence of the illustrious Milner, and many other distinguished persons, and occasionally used for divine service when the chapel was under repairs. But it was most unfortunately burnt down by an accidental fire in the night of the 25th of January, while this biography was writing. The loss to the pious community who now conduct the orphanage at the Old College is quite a calamity: but every old Oscotian will deeply grieve for the total destruction of this noble memorial of MILNER's love of Oscott, and of the many happy festive days which they have witnessed within it.

Though various changes had taken place in the offices of the college, MR. WEEDALL had continued all along to teach classics, and to exercise his sacred ministry in various ways, as occasions offered. At the Midsummer Exhibition of 1817, his class were prepared by him with great care, for a considerable time, for the performance of an English version of the tragedy of Œdipus Tyrannus, adapted, like Philoctetes, from the translations of Sophocles, by

Potter and Francklin. As the class were not strong enough for all the parts, the present writer was requested to undertake the character of Œdipus, though it was not customary for students in Divinity to speak at the Exhibitions. It was a privilege to study elocution under such a master. Being an orator of first rate talent himself, MR. WEEDALL was well qualified to direct his pupils in this important branch of education, and he spared no time or labour to render them as perfect as possible in the art of declamation, as well as in every other department of knowledge, for which they were confided to his care.

CHAPTER VI.

Mr. Weedall's Sermon at Sheffield—Decline of Mr. Quick's Health—Mr. Weedall Officiates on Sundays at Vespers—His Catechetical Lectures—Sermon at Liverpool—Death of Mr. Quick—Mr. Weedall becomes Vice-President, Professor of Theology, and Spiritual Director.

Ever ready to aid in the glorious cause of Religion and Charity, Mr. Weedall accepted an invitation to preach a sermon at Sheffield, on the 30th of April, 1818, on the anniversary of the opening of the chapel in that town; and published it afterwards for the benefit of the Catholic Sunday School there. It was his first published sermon on a subject of doctrine and controversy, and was entitled, "The Spirit and the Truth of Religion." It is worked out with great power, and is of great length: indeed too long, for if more condensed, it would have had more force and been more convincing. It is, however, a masterly performance, and has always been greatly admired. The text is from St. John iv.: *God is a spirit, and they that adore him, must adore him in spirit and in truth.* This naturally suggests the division of the sermon into its two portions; the first inculcating the duty of worshipping God with the heart and soul, and not merely with the exterior rites of religion: and the second showing the necessity of a right form of worship, that we may adore God in truth. He pursues the first part, through our respective duties to God, our neighbour, and ourselves, inculcating the obligation of performing all with a true interior spirit of religion, but at the same time attending to the authorised forms of exterior worship. He comes in the second part to the necessity of adoring God also in *truth*. Here he treats of the means provided for the preservation of the truth by the establishment of the Church, which includes those only who hold the true doctrine of Christ. That no one might mistake this Church, it is *visible* to all, and may be readily discovered by all who will be at the pains to seek for it.

"These propositions, my brethren, are of immense importance, involving, as they most assuredly do, the salvation of every individual now before me. But to you, my dear brethren of a different persuasion, whom the circumstances of the day have accidentally assembled,—to you I particularly address myself. I appeal to your own breasts on this momentous question,—what degree of security do you feel in the religious creed you have adopted? Is your security of that fearless and determined nature, that you would stake your lives and your souls on the truth of it? Or, in sober fact, does it amount only to this,—that after some care and deliberation, you have taken up with that which in your consciences you believe to be the most excellent? But such belief does not generate security; it does not exclude the possibility of at least something still more excellent. You may be right,— I pass it,—but you *may also be wrong*. The very principles of your religion, therefore, will prompt you to this enquiry.

That religion is built on *private judgment*, and private judgment, being liable to error, ought never to close its investigations till it arrive at absolute certainty."

He proceeds to point out the four marks of the true Church from the Holy Scriptures; and then observes that, having detained his audience for so unusual a time, it is not his intention to attend them in the actual application of these marks; but he will nevertheless venture to throw out a few observations that will greatly simplify the work. Here has always appeared to be a considerable defect in this sermon. The most practical and important part is of necessity hurried over and too briefly dismissed, because the first portion of the discourse has been drawn out to an unnecessary and tiresome length. What the preacher does say in his concluding pages is so fine and forcible, that it makes us doubly regret that he did not so manage the composition of the entire sermon, as to be enabled to dwell chiefly upon this part, upon which the effect of the whole was mainly to depend. The value of this too brief portion may be partly estimated by the following extracts:—

"And first, as to the mark *Unity*. Every man is not capable of examining separately the whole of the doctrines of any particular church, in order to ascertain whether the members of that church are united in the same faith; because every one is not possessed of sufficient knowledge to enable him to conduct an investigation of this nature; but every man can understand that no church can be united where there is nothing to unite; and there is nothing to unite where each member is left to the suggestions of his own fancy. Whatever church, therefore, grounds its doctrines on Scripture interpreted by private judgment, and authorises each individual to interpret for himself, and to form his own articles of faith, that church has no principle of union, and cannot, therefore, be one...... He will naturally look out for that body which...obliging all its members to rally round one acknowledged head, and to subscribe to doctrines universally received, and warranted divine, will alone present him at once with unity of faith and security of conscience. My brethren! as such a church only is one, there is only one such church."

Again, on the mark of *Apostolicity*.

"It is not then in the modern sects—and here let me premise to you, my brethren, that in making this observation, I wish not to offer the slightest disrespect to the private opinions of any individual before me—but truth obliges me to declare what I feel may be maintained against the world,—that it is not in the modern sects of Luther or of Calvin, of Cranmer or of Knox, of Whitfield or of Wesley, that we are to look for this Apostolicity either of origin or of office, to each one of whom it may be said, 'thou art' scarce fifty years old, and hast thou seen the Apostles? No, my brethren, the character will apply to that church alone, which can trace the unbroken succession of 252 bishops, from St. Peter the Prince of the Apostles, to the present illustrious and venerable Pontiff, Pius VII. You start at that name, my brethren, and all your prejudices awaken within you. What! you exclaim, refer me to the Church of Rome, that corrupt, that superstitious, that idolatrous church! Say rather, my brethren, that insulted, that calumniated, that much injured church; a church whose doctrines are admired in proportion as they are known, but which must be known before they can be admired; a church which has never shrunk from argument, because her doctrines are irrefutable; but which has never been answered but by calumny, because she is established upon truth."

The whole composition is very beautiful, and much of it, if not original, certainly worked out in his own peculiar style, and very eloquent. It produced a great impression on the audience, and no doubt caused in many conviction, as well as admiration. It will hardly be credited that this elaborate sermon was first preached by him in the humble chapel at Hopwas, near Lichfield, only 24 feet long by 12 wide, on the occasion of its being opened for divine service in 1815. But such was the zeal and energy of his fine mind, that his judgment could not always keep pace with it; for certainly this noble composition was totally out of place in a small country chapel, where not half a dozen of his audience were capable of appreciating, or even understanding it.

Mr. Quick, the president, had been accustomed always to officiate at Vespers on Sundays. But the consequence of his undertaking too many employments, and working incessantly, without allowing himself adequate rest to recruit his strength, were beginning to appear in the decline of his health. MR. WEEDALL, therefore, relieved him of this part of his labours by taking upon himself the duty of the afternoon service. On Sunday, April 19th, of this year, 1818, he commenced a course of lectures after Vespers on the catechism. He began with a beautiful discourse on the necessity of understanding and becoming thoroughly acquainted with religion. His text was: *This is eternal life, that they may know Thee, the only true God, and Jesus Christ whom Thou hast sent.* St. John xvii., 3.

He observed that he had chosen the subject, not as immediately connected with the office of the day, but as preparatory to a course of catechetical instructions which would be continued, by the Divine blessing, every Sunday at the afternoon service. He warned his hearers against two prevalent mistakes concerning religion, the first, of those who give it too much latitude, and imagine it necessary to go through a complete course of theology; and the second, of those who think they know enough when they have learned the principal mysteries of our faith, and can repeat some half dozen pages of their catechism. Both, he said, were grievously mistaken; for religion is the knowledge of God, and of our duty to him; the study of religion is the study of Jesus Christ; the desire of religion is the desire of advancing in the knowledge of him, and of his holy truths. He proceeded to prove the importance of religion. Christianity is our profession, and we are bound to understand it thoroughly, that we may exercise it faithfully. The weakness of our nature demands that we gain strength from the knowledge of religion. The danger of error and immorality renders the knowledge of religion doubly necessary. He proved this necessity also from negative arguments. The consequences of ignorance of religion are most fatal. An imperfect system of religion becomes interwoven with the moral constitution of man, and he is unable to withstand the seductions of vice, because he is not half convinced of the importance of virtue. This he exemplified by the career of a young man entering the world, and only half instructed in his religion. His faith is attacked, his virtue is attacked, his heart is ready to yield, and his head but half resolved is all that he can oppose; and when half the head is opposed to the whole heart, the struggle cannot remain long undecided.

But imagine a youth with firmer principles, well instructed and well armed. Before such an one every foe must fall; impiety will be confounded, vice repulsed, infidelity unmasked. He went on to trace the steady career of such a youth, and contrasted it with the course of him who is but ill instructed, his gradual mistrust of our holy religion, and a fatal indifference, which is but one remove from infidelity.

"But give me," said he, "a well instructed Catholic, and he shall neither be a scandal to the weak, nor a triumph to the enemies of his faith."

These catechetical lectures Mr. WEEDALL continued for two or three years. When he came to the Second Article of the Creed, he completed the connexion between that and the first, by the biblical history of the world, and of the chosen people of God, down to the coming of our divine Redeemer. This occupied a long succession of Sundays, as he gave well studied and minute narratives of every event, accompanied by such reflections and applications as arose from the subjects treated.—On one occasion, on a Sunday morning, a fire had broken out in the cottage of a poor Catholic, rather more than a mile from the college. It was a distressing scene to behold the cottage nearly burnt down, almost all the effects of its inmates consumed, and the poor wife and children houseless. Mr. Weedall had been with others from the college to see and render what assistance could be afforded to the distressed family; and in the afternoon he interrupted his usual lecture by a moving appeal in their behalf. He said that though many cases of distress had before presented themselves, he had never thought proper to allude to them in that place. But he described this as a calamity so peculiar, that he could not refrain from dwelling upon it, which he did very pathetically, and appealing to the charity of all present to contribute some little towards the relief of the sufferers. It is superfluous to add that a very liberal sum was given by the inmates of the college for the poor family, in answer to this moving and eloquent appeal.—He prepared his Sunday afternoon lectures with great care and labour; and so anxious was he to make them what he conceived they ought to be, that it frequently happened that when the whole house were assembled in the chapel at the hour of Vespers, Mr. Weedall was heard walking up and down the large dormitory above, still preparing what he had to say; and thus they were kept waiting for some time before he came down to begin Vespers.

Mr. Weedall had already advocated the cause of charity with so much eloquence and success on the occasions already dwelt upon, that it was not long before he received another urgent application for a charity sermon. This came from Liverpool, where the spacious new chapel of St. Nicholas, which is now the Catholic Cathedral Church, had been erected six years; and in this he was requested to exert his eloquence in behalf of the large poor schools instituted in that populous town. He complied, and preached the sermon on Sunday, the 2nd of August, 1818. The gentlemen at whose request it was delivered, repeatedly solicited its publication, before they could obtain the consent of the preacher, who "had no wish to obtrude himself again upon the notice of the public." The sermon is entitled: "The effects of ignorance on the character and conduct of man." The text is: *Suffer the little children to come unto me, &c.*, and after enlarging upon the interesting scene which it describes, and applying it admirably to the immediate object of his discourse, he proceeds to show that " the duties of charity are commensurate with the wants of our fellow creatures, and that the evil of ignorance is of all the most malignant and mischievous, and therefore that it is a paramount duty to rescue the poor children from its terrible effects." He illustrates this by showing, in a succession of masterly arguments, that man steps into existence ignorant of his God, ignorant of himself, ignorant of his glorious destiny, and ignorant of the means and motives for attaining it. This fills up the first portion of the sermon: the second is devoted to exhibiting the *positive* form of ignorance, as stimulating all the passions, and withdrawing every restraint. He shows that in the absence of Religion and Education the fairest edifices of God and nature will be involved in one moral conflagration.

"The source of the evil lies beyond the reach of civil correction. Statesmen may speculate in remedies, may heap laws upon laws, and invest those laws with the severest sanctions, but without the lights and the motives of religion, those sanctions will be powerless. A temporary effect may be produced, interest may be weighed against interest, self love may be thrown, as it were, on its back, and the recumbent bribed into peace, by displaying the advantages of submission; but when the persuasive is withdrawn, or when interests have exchanged their value, then will the lawless giant rise up to shake him in his strength, will burst the cords that bind him, 'as a man would break a thread of tow when it toucheth the fire,' and seizing with desperate grasp the pillars of law and of justice, will bury himself and them under the ruins of morality and order."

After powerfully pleading for the poor children, that "the little innocents" may not be "thrown upon the world in its lowest and most profligate paths, where the wonder would be, not that they should turn out very generally vicious, but that any individual amongst them should retain one single feature of its innocence;"—he thus eloquently concludes this very able discourse:—

"Pardon me if I do say that for the sake of these children I should rejoice to hear that charity had outstripped itself upon the present occasion, and that the sums which prudence had prescribed to each individual on entering this chapel as the extent of his donations, had been found insufficient for the burst of sensibility that had suddenly and overwhelmingly rushed upon his heart. Providence, I know, has been bountiful to many of you beyond the average dispensation of his favours. If, then, your tables are well supplied, if your cups overflow, O think of the homes where the table is never spread, where the cup is never filled, where *the whole head is sick, and the whole heart is sad*,* and though the present appeal is not made with a direct view to relieve misery of this description, yet that it tends indirectly and not very remotely to prevent it. And, my brethren, when that solemn hour shall arrive which we are all destined to experience, and when rank and riches and every worldly distinction shall hang suspended over the grave, then may the recollection of this day's deeds be a *help to you on your beds of sorrow, and turn all your couch for you in your sickness* ;† may it alleviate the pangs of dissolution, may it wipe off the damp dews that thicken on the brow, may it lighten the heart, and brighten the view, and transfer your hopes sweetly and quietly to another and a better world, where *the goods of the just man shall be established in the Lord, and where the assembly of the Saints shall publish his alms-deeds.*‡ In the name, &c."

It has been already mentioned that the health of the active and indefatigable president, Mr. Quick, had been impaired by his severe and unremitting labours in the college. His spirit was too ardent, he attempted too much, and thus his course was painfully short, and too soon consummated. He went during the Midsummer vacation to his native country, Devonshire, to visit his friends, and, if possible, to recruit his health; but in vain. He had scarcely returned to Oscott, when he became alarmingly ill. He bore his last sickness with the most edifying patience and resignation, and particularly desired his doctor not to give him any opiates, so that he might be in full possession of his senses, and be enabled to make a merit of his sufferings. He died on the 13th of August, 1818,

* Isaias i., 5. † Ps. xl., 4. ‡ Ecclus. xxxi., 11.

at the early age of 40. Of him it might truly be said, that *being made perfect in a short space, he fulfilled a long time.*

On MR. WEEDALL's return on that very day from preaching at Liverpool, he anxiously enquired, as he entered the house, after the health of Mr. Quick. He was answered rather abruptly that he was just dead. He was shocked and grieved exceedingly, not having heard of his being worse than usual. He covered his face with his hands, uttered a fervent exclamation, and burst into tears. To him, of course, was delegated the painful task of preaching the funeral oration at the solemn dirge, which took place in the chapel, on Monday, the 17th of August. This discourse has not been preserved; but the writer remembers that it was extremely eloquent, and full of deep feeling, and that it moved every one present to tears. Mr. Quick was buried at the parish church at Handsworth, and Dr. Milner placed a tablet to his memory in the sacristy of the college, with an inscription which he composed, in which the character of Mr. Quick is admirably summed up in these few words, "humble, meek, benevolent, mortified, indefatigable, but above all, zealous for the salvation of souls, and the glory of his divine Master."

Bishop Milner exclaimed, when he heard of Mr. Quick's death : "I have lost my right hand." He knew his value, and felt his loss most acutely. He was the life and soul of St. Mary's College;

* WISDOM IV., 13.

she owed him a debt incalculable; his loss was one extremely difficult to supply; yet it was necessary to make arrangements without delay, as the studies were now to recommence after the vacation of Midsummer. The Bishop provided the best he could for the management of the college after this sad bereavement; and by his direction, Mr. Walsh became President, and MR. WEEDALL Vice-President, Professor of Divinity, and spiritual director of the lay-students and servants. Mr. Walsh continued as before to take the spiritual direction of the ecclesiastics and of the congregation.

CHAPTER VII.

Mr. Weedall as Professor of Divinity—As Spiritual Director—Death of Mr. Potts—His Funeral—Mr. Weedall's Discourse on the Occasion.

This was an important period in the life of Mr. Weedall. He was most unexpectedly called upon to undertake at once three arduous and responsible offices. But though he had been far from desiring any one of them, he considered it his duty to accept them, in the spirit of that admirable maxim of the great St. Augustin: "Vos exhortamur, ut si quam operam vestra mater Ecclesia desideravit, nec elatione avida suscipiatis, nec blandiente desidia respuatis."* On the 28th of September, 1818, he first began with a class of divines, who had been studying two years under the lamented Mr. Quick. He opened the school with a very pleasing address to his scholars, pleasantly observing, however, in the outset, that he had not come prepared with a set speech for the occasion. The treatise which they were studying was "*De Incarnatione*," in Collet's "*Theologia Dogmatica*," in which the class had advanced to the third *Quæstio* under their

* "We exhort you that whatever work your mother the Church has desired of you, you would neither undertake with eager elation, nor refuse with flattering indolence."—St. Aug., Epist. 48, al. 81.

former professor. He prepared himself for the important duty of teaching divinity by much labour and study, and always brought to the lesson a valuable mass of collateral information from various authors. He made great use in dogmatic divinity of the sound and lucid treatises of Dr. Delahogue, the Professor of Maynooth College, which had been published a few years before; and these, with justice, he strongly recommended to his pupils. His own manner of teaching was clear and methodical, always clothed in graceful language, and always solid and satisfactory. He was apt to go into long and somewhat tedious disquisitions, but they were ever valuable, sound, and instructive. He very seldom referred to any compositions of his own; but once, when treating on the Marks of the true Church, he prefaced a short reading from his sermon, "*On the Spirit and the truth of Religion*," by observing that he thought he might more safely call attention to what he once carefully wrote, than to what he might now less carefully say.

For the explanation of the Holy Scripture, MR. WEEDALL was indefatigable in his own researches, and in directing the studies of his pupils. He was particularly fond of the learned dissertations in the "*Bible de Vence*," and Calmet; and besides the usual commentators, he would constantly refer to the most eminent French and German biblical scholars, culling out from them all that was valuable, and warning his scholars, with the greatest care, of the dangers and delusions of scepticism and rationalism in certain German critics. On those days, chiefly Saturdays, when his duties as spiritual director prevented him from attending the Divinity school, he often exercised his class in the composition of Theological exercises. The nature of these may be seen by the following titles of some of them:—*Grace and Pelagianism—The Errors of Gothescalc—Jansenius and Jansenism—Paul of Samosata—Supremacy of the Pope—The Actions and Virtues of Infidels—Systems on the Operation of Divine Grace.*

At the same time that Mr. Weedall was thus engaged in teaching divinity, he was also employed as spiritual director to the lay students, and for a short time, also, to the domestics of the college. This important office he strove to fulfil, as he did every other, in the most perfect manner. When he had to impart instruction to those prepared by education to understand his language, he was very successful; but, as already hinted in the early part of this biography, he was not so with poor children and illiterate persons. With his own mind elegant, accomplished, and amply stored with religious lore, he poured out his knowledge too learnedly for the comprehension of little ones. He seemed not to know how to lower himself to their limited capacities; and though he did not apply the hard staff of Giezi to give them spiritual life, he did not, on the other hand, like his master the prophet, measure his words by a child's slender capacity, and *put his mouth upon the child's mouth, and his eyes upon his eyes, and his hands upon his hands, and bow himself upon him,** and so accommodate his language to the child's weak understanding, till

* 4 Kings iv, 34.

the little heart grew warm, and the eyes opened to
see the precious truths of religion. Thus he once
asked a little child if some expression was "sound
theology." But his zeal was great and his efforts unremitting in the important work of leading souls to
the knowledge and practice of religion. Shining
talents and great abilities, however, are not always
the most successful; and those to whom the humble
but meritorious work is committed of instructing
the young, the poor, and the illiterate, should,
above all things, take care to speak in easy and
plain language which all can understand: for, says
the great St. Augustin: "It is better for gram-
marians to reprehend us, than for the people not to
understand us."*

The respected Mr. Potts, who had been all
along nominally president, and enjoying, as the
Bishop directed, the *otium cum dignitate*, continued
in good bodily health, and kept up with the usual
routine of each day like the rest of the college.
But his fine mind was gone, and his intellects grew
more enfeebled. No one ever had a more pleasant
decline of life, for he had felt no pain of body or
mind for the last four years, since he was first
taken. He may be said to have laughed away his
last four years; for he would laugh at any little
occurrence or saying, and some things would
regularly set him off in a fit of laughter. It was
melancholy indeed to see his powerful spirit thus
wasted; yet it was consoling to observe that he felt

---

* "Melius est ut nos reprehendant grammatici, quam ut non intelligant populi."

no humiliation, and was unconscious of any affliction. His mind had remained much in the same state till within a month of four years from his first seizure; when on the 29th of November, 1819, one of the masters going into his room found that he had fallen on the floor, and was unable to rise. He was lying there laughing, and quite amused at the oddity of his position. He was carried to his bed, and joked as they were carrying him in, saying that they had "dented" him against the jambs of the doorway. On Sunday, the 5th of December, he died in peace, but without having been at all conscious of his approaching dissolution, in the 66th year of his age. He was buried in the vault under the sacristy, which occupied the ground floor of a building recently added to the chapel, the upper part being fitted up as a little oratory for the convenience of private Masses, and serving also for the monthly devotions in honour of the Sacred Heart of Jesus. These devotions had already been in practice for many years in England; but Bishop Milner, when he obtained the approbation of the Holy See for an Association of Missionary Priests in the Midland District, which he called the *Institutio Societatis Liberæ*, in the year 1814, procured also, that certain Indulgences, already granted to the *Sodality of the Sacred Heart* in Rome, should be extended to the members of this *Societas Libera*, and also, on certain conditions, to all the faithful of his district. One condition being that the prayers be recited before an image or picture of the Sacred Heart; when the old chapel in the house was discontinued, he had a picture of our Blessed Saviour displaying his Sacred Heart, painted on glass, in the window over the altar of this new chapel, for the convenience of the associates meeting there monthly to recite the prayers. Neither the chapel nor the altar was actually dedicated in honour of the Sacred Heart: but the picture on glass was placed there to afford the convenience of fulfilling the condition of the Indulgences.

The funeral of the Rev. Thomas Potts was conducted in the most solemn manner in the college chapel. After the Office, and High Mass of Requiem, celebrated by the Rev. Thomas Walsh, the body was borne to the vault by the ecclesiastics of the college, the pall being held by ten priests who had been pupils of the deceased, and followed by Bishop Milner, as chief mourner, in his pontificals, his train borne by little John Payne, who died a few years after at the college. MR. WEEDALL, of course, was called upon to preach the funeral sermon, which the Bishop and clergy afterwards desired him to publish. It is a very eloquent specimen of pulpit eloquence. The text was striking and affecting: "*The eyes that have seen him shall see him no more; neither shall his place any more behold him......and they that have seen him shall say, where is he?*"* It led the preacher naturally to speak of the severe loss which the college had sustained, first in the imbecility, and finally in the decease of their late venerable superior. Then after a slight sketch of

* JOB XX., 7—9.

his character and virtues, introduced principally to show the strong grounds of hope for his happiness, he proceeded to apply the moral lesson inculcated on the solemn occasion, and occupied the greater portion of the discourse with striking and beautiful thoughts and admonitions on death, in language always eloquent, and often original. A few extracts will illustrate the above imperfect analysis.

"There is a rapidity in the conquests of death with which the imagination can never keep pace; there is a random in his cast which defies calculation; and even when he approaches in form, and his attack is generally, at least, though indeterminately, expected; yet the actual stroke is so terrific and appalling, that the bewildered mind cannot readily settle itself down to a persuasion that he is become to-day the victim of death, who but yesterday sat at our side.

"My brethren, if I may characterize your minds by my own, this confusion of distress is the prevailing sensation here. Not yet have we sunk into a conviction that the whole is not an illusion; and so ill-prepared are our minds for the reality, so completely was the deceased identified with this spot, so associated with all its scenes and devotional exercises, and his form and image so inextricably involved and intertwined with the whole system and machinery of the college, that though we are surrounded by all the pomp and circumstance of death, with all its demonstrations staring us in the face, we yet can scarcely reconcile ourselves to the mournful truth,— that our venerable brother is dead. He has 'passed as a vision of the night:' and verified to the letter is the passage of the scripture, 'the eyes that have seen him shall see him no more; neither shall his place any more behold him.—And they that have seen him shall say, where is he?' Where is he? Gone, my brethren,—gone to his long home,—gone for ever! That tongue is stiff, which for so many years delighted and instructed; that eye is set which beamed forth all the benignity of virtue; and cold is the heart that overflowed with a benevolence which secured for the deceased the attachment of friends, the respect of strangers, the gratitude and affection of the youth committed to his care; and, what I trust he now experiences to be a still more valuable acquisition, the prayers and benedictions of the poor.......

"I dare not imitate the presumption of worldlings, who pronounce every one to be happy who but dies with symptoms of ordinary decency. I would not pronounce of any man without a supernatural intimation that he is absolutely at rest; because, assured as we are that the judgments of God are severer than those of men, I would not deprive the dead of those helps which religion supplies, nor the living of the powerful lesson which borrows much of its force from the uncertainty of their lot. But, my brethren, if the character of an individual can supply subjects for hope; if a life of personal innocence, dedicated exclusively to promote the honour and glory of God, the moral and religious education of youth, and the general good of his neighbour; if the example he invariably displayed,—an example which we all may well regret,—of humility, of meekness, of innocent simplicity, of guileless views and unostentatious deportment; of undeviating rectitude in action, and cautious management of words; of zeal for religion, both in its doctrines and practices; of genuine piety towards God and unbounded charity towards his neighbour:—if the close of life protracted into the view of death, with all the comforts that our holy religion supplies, and all the joy and resignation it excites;—if such considerations can console the survivors, and inspire confidence as to his actual state,—then, my brethren, may we take comfort to ourselves for the lot of our departed brother, and envy 'a death precious in the sight of the Lord.'"

Showing that mortality is inherent in man, he thus eloquently expatiates:—

"The objects around us have varied, and are constantly varying. Within our own remembrance, nature has assumed a thousand different aspects. The appearances of to-day are not such as yesterday, nor will the forms of the morrow be as those of to day. Mutability is stamped upon all things. Every leaf that falls from the tree puts you and me in mind of our mortality. And, my brethren, the generations of man are mutable as these. Ages before us have passed away, and we have succeeded to them, but without any pledge for a longer continuance. The rising generation around seem to advertise us that room must be made for them; the time accordingly will come when we also must pass away with the crowd; and it will be recorded of us, if even this be recorded, that we once lived, and that we died. 'And all the days of Seth,' says the inspired historian with solemn sententiousness, 'and all the days of Seth were nine hundred and twelve years, and he—died.' 'And Noe lived nine hundred and fifty years, and he died.'"

The writer would fain convey to the reader, if he could, an idea of the impressive manner in which this passage was delivered. For himself, he can never forget it. The dignified attitude of the preacher, his brightened eye, his uplifted hand, his solemn and sepulchral tone, and his slow and clear enunciation, broken by pauses which wound up expectation and heightened effect, produced altogether a thrilling sensation in his breathless and astonished auditory. And now that *he* too has passed away, the remembrance comes down with redoubled force and applicability upon one who is still spared to pay this just tribute to his memory, and left now almost alone of his early companions: *And they that remain of the trees of his forest shall be so few, that they shall easily be numbered, and a child shall write them down.**

* Isaias x., 19.

CHAPTER VIII.

Mr. Weedall meets Dr. Parr at Dinner—Purchase of Holdford Farm—His Turn for Farming—Instance of his Affection and Kindness—Of his Moderation and Considerateness—Eloquent and Impressive Passage Introduced in one of his Homilies—Mr. Weedall as Prefect of Studies—His Editions of the Douay Grammar.

Mr. Weedall was rarely absent from the college, and seldom accepted any invitations to visit in the neighbourhood. He would occasionally go out to dine with a brother priest, and perhaps meet there two or three more of his clerical friends; and sometimes he visited his old and revered friend at Lichfield, Mr. Kirk. In Birmingham he had but few acquaintances, besides the clergy and the leading Catholics. Sometimes, however, he dined with the eminent physician, Dr. John Johnstone, who was always called in when any serious cases of illness occurred at the college. On one of these occasions he met the learned and pedantic Dr. Parr, and was placed next to him at table. Parr was unusually civil and attentive to him; for he soon saw that he had no ordinary man by his side. The conversation, however, did not turn on any deep questions, either classical or theological; but Dr. Parr in the course of it alluding to the Catholic Church, said to Mr. Weedall, in a very pleasant way: "You are the eldest son: but we have the estate." He very freely conversed with Mr. Weedall, and invited him to come and see him at Hatton. He enquired for Bishop Milner, and requested Mr. Weedall to invite him also. "Tell him," he said, "that I shall be very happy to see him, only he must not get warm, or I shall get warm too, and then the house won't hold us."

It was in the early part of the year 1820, that negociations were begun for the purchase of a desirable farm at Holdford, on the road to Birmingham, and about three miles from the college. The want of some land of their own, and the means of supplying the college with milk, butter, and other produce, without being dependent on others, and obliged to purchase, had been always felt as a serious inconvenience; and as the college increased it was a growing evil. Bishop Milner entered cordially into the project. The farm, indeed, was situated rather too far from the college; but there appeared no prospect of procuring any land nearer, and it was an opportunity not to be missed. There was also another consideration of some importance. It adjoined the property of a gentleman who owned land close to the college. There was consequently a prospect of negociating some exchange at a future day, and thus securing some land about the college, which was on every account so desirable. This exchange, moreover, was actually effected eight years after, on perfectly equitable terms.

Holdford farm was accordingly purchased for £4,215, and proved a very valuable acquisition to the college. To Mr. WEEDALL it gave a new impulse which had a very salutary effect upon his health, and afforded him both occupation and recreation for several years, which proved exceedingly beneficial. He thus alludes to these effects in the paper referred to in Chapter Third, page 40:—

"Afterwards, however, by carefully attending to my general health, having the advantage at college of horse exercise, and by the healthy occupation of looking after the farm, and the external management of the college concerns, my head and eyes grew rather better, and the eyes more serviceable."

He had always a great liking for farming pursuits, and with his many other acquirements he had, by means which no one could account for, gained an extensive knowledge of agricultural matters.

No sooner then was Holdford farm secured and entered upon, than MR. WEEDALL began to take a lively interest and practical share in its management. He went down every day when he could spare time, and the president gladly availed himself of his willingness to superintend, and gave up the entire management of the farm into his hands. An intelligent bailiff was in charge, and resided in the farm house. There was a windmill near to the farm buildings, which proved a convenient and profitable appendage. MR. WEEDALL constantly read "*Cobbett's Register*," and of course became well acquainted with his writings on matters of agriculture, and with such works as he recommended. Among these was the famous treatise of Tull *On Horsehoeing Husbandry;* which, with Cobbett's own directions for trenching, draining, and the cultivation of mangel wurzel, then much less understood than at present, Mr. Weedall found of great practical utility.

The farm became his pride as well as his pleasure; though he never, for the sake of it, neglected any of his duties in the college. He was always pleased to show his friends over it; and when visitors came, he would generally propose a walk to the farm. There was a large dog kept chained at the door of the farm house. The present writer often accompanied Mr. Weedall to the farm, and on one occasion he asked him the name of this large and fierce looking animal. Mr. Weedall told him it was called "Rose." The writer observed that so sweet a name was misapplied when given to a dog, and particularly one so formidable. To which Mr. Weedall replied, with his well known smile on uttering any little pleasantry: "O you know, it's a *dog rose!*"

The writer is exceedingly unwilling to obtrude his own insignificance into this biography; and will certainly never do it except for the purpose of exhibiting the fine qualities and virtues of his friend. There had been an Ordination in February of this year, 1820, by Bishop Milner, when Mr. Foley and the writer received the Holy Order of

Priesthood. In the summer following, the writer left Oscott, and certainly though he had other dear friends there, he parted from no one with so much regret as his beloved and early friend MR. WEEDALL. He was also much attached to the college, and could truly say, as he quitted his happy abode, and his valued friend:

> "Sad havoc time must with my memory make,
> Ere *that* or *thou* canst fade these eyes before."*

But he wishes to record the kind and affectionate behaviour of his friend on that occasion. The writer would fain have avoided bidding farewell;

> "For in that word, that fatal word,—howe'er
> We promise,—hope,—believe,—there breathes despair."†

But MR. WEEDALL expressed his regard in the most feeling terms, and his regret at the approaching separation in the accents of genuine friendship. "Well," he said, mournfully, "we must all part ere long!" and then he paused sorrowfully, and seemed much affected. When he spoke again, he expressed a strong wish that some arrangement had been made to retain his friend in the college, knowing that his inclinations had been decidedly in favour of such residence; and then came another pause, followed by other kind words of regard and affection.

> "The grief that does not speak,
> Whispers the o'erfraught heart, and bids it break."

All this was too much for the writer's sensibility,

---

* BYRON,—*Lines to his Sister*.   † DITTO,—*Corsair*. Canto I.

and he was forced to retire abruptly, with that feeling which the poet has so finely expressed:

> "Let's not unman each other: part at once:
> All farewells should be sudden when for ever,
> Else they make an eternity of moments,
> And clog the last sands of life with tears."*

How little did he then calculate that forty years after he should write his friend's biography?

It has been already observed that MR. WEEDALL would very willingly undertake to supply on a Sunday for any neighbouring priest, in case of absence, or illness. The writer had from the time of his Ordination served the mission at Stourbridge, which was then quite in its infancy, with no better chapel than two upper rooms of a mean house in a dirty court, and low neighbourhood, which were thrown together under a low gable roof. It was a rough beginning; for he had to walk the whole distance, fifteen miles from Oscott, every Saturday afternoon, and the same back the next Monday morning. On his leaving Oscott, and for a Sunday or two before he left, MR. WEEDALL very kindly went to perform the duty at Stourbridge on the Sundays and Holidays. He continued to do so for about a month, till it could be served by a priest newly ordained. It was remarked that MR. WEEDALL did not preach when he officiated at Stourbridge, but merely read from the solid and practical lessons of Mr. Gother. His motive was supposed to be a thoughtful feeling for the young priest who was to take the mission, that he might

* *Sardanapalus.* Act v.

not be urged inconveniently to preach, or expected to deliver fine sermons from his example. His moderation and considerateness in this were noticed with admiration.

He preached, however, frequently in the college chapel, and it was always a great treat when the opportunity occurred of listening to his eloquent and stirring discourses. He was always the preacher on the great festivals, and other particular days, such as Good Friday, Candlemas Day, and Ash Wednesday. He did not always give regular sermons, but occasionally homilies on the Gospel of the day, which, however, he always made very interesting. Once when thus homilising on the Twenty-third Sunday after Pentecost, after dwelling for some time on the cure of the poor woman who touched the hem of our Saviour's garment, he quite unexpectedly poured out the following magnificent passage, which absolutely electrified the whole chapel :—

"The infirmity under which this poor object laboured, is generally of a nature to induce the sufferer to conceal it carefully from the knowledge of the world; and accordingly the Holy Fathers have discovered in the case here specified a figure of a certain vice which is shameful and shall be nameless, which infects with symptomatic madness a great proportion of mankind. A vice which has been the deadliest plague to the human race since the dismal age when *all flesh had corrupted its way, and it repented God to have made man on the earth.* (Gen. vi.) A vice that perpetrates its deeds in darkness, that pollutes the body and defiles the soul, that impairs the health, that shatters the very stamina of the constitution, that emasculates the energies of the mind, and lays prostrate all the dignity, and all the virtue, and all the happiness of man. A vice that struck down the giant strength of Sampson, that converted David into the destroyer of the brave and continent Urias, that turned Solomon into an idolater, and the hoary elders of the captivity into the perjured accusers and virtual murderers of the chaste and innocent Susanna.

"It reaches from age to age, defying in its virulence the ordinary powers of eradication. It blights all the loveliness of youth, consumes the very core of manhood, and anticipates, as well as aggravates, the decrepitude of age. Other vices may be cured by the experience of their danger, by the removal of temptation, by the separation of the object; but this malignant vice, when once engrafted into the constitution of man, grows with his growth, increases with his years, and gains equal strength from disappointment as from indulgence. Even it survives the period of its own impotency, and when every other passion lies dead and blasted in the heart, it feeds upon its own polluted recollections, and triumphs in the imagination, when age has driven it back from the external senses. Yes, even at the close of life, and in the near prospect of the grave, when the pulse beats low, and the frame totters, when the head is grey and the front withered, and death has marked each limb for its own,—under the snows of winter and the chilling frosts of age, even then do the impure fires smoulder in their embers, and casting at times a deadly gleam athwart the path of repentance, but only to scare the wretch from retracing his steps, until the spark of life becoming extinct, they kindle into a demon's torch to light him down to damnation. *His bones shall be filled with the vices of his youth, and they shall sleep with him in the dust.* (Job xx., 11.)

"But I will dwell no longer upon this hated subject. 'Tis a tale of horror, and I like it not. 'Tis a mystery of iniquity that I fear to disclose. I feel the insecurity of the ground on which I tread; I know the wriggling lubricity of the monster I have handled; but the Gospel of the day suggested it to my mind, and it is a pastor's duty, not always to be avoided. Still I have only sketched its roughest strokes, that you, my beloved brethren, might see it, and loathe it, and forget it for ever."

It is impossible to describe—though the writer so well remembers it—the sensation excited by this very striking and original treatment of a subject so delicate and difficult. It was not only a masterly piece of eloquence, but it was delivered with so much animation, emphasis, and expression, that it carried away the hearers with intense interest and rapture. The preacher pronounced with great spirit and vehemence the thrilling sentence involving the dismal consummation, when the fires of the loathsome vice "*kindle into a demon's torch to light the sinner down to damnation;*" raising his right hand to its highest reach, and lowering it progressively with the sentence, till it pointed down to the infernal abyss, with deep and terrible expressiveness. After the service, the impression produced was manifested in the serious looks of the congregated groups about the playground, all talking in amazement of the striking address which they had heard.

From the time when Mr. Potts was first attacked by the afflicting malady which closed his efficiency, at the end of the year 1815, the important office of Prefect of Studies had devolved upon MR. WEEDALL. In a college this charge is of the greatest importance; indeed the whole reputation of the establishment must depend upon its being ably and assiduously sustained. MR. WEEDALL was eminently fitted for it, and discharged it, as he did every other duty, not only conscientiously, but with such ability as to give general satisfaction. Masters as well as scholars came under his direction in this department; the choice of authors, the regulation of classes, the distribution of instruction, all depended upon the judicious arrangements of the Prefect of Studies. All these had been the care of Mr. Potts from the first opening of St. Mary's College; but in Mr. WEEDALL he had a successor fully competent. Mr. Potts had, in the year 1810, revised the venerable old "*Introduction to the Latin Language*," which had been in use at Douay College for more than a century. In his new edition, he "endeavoured to render clear what was before obscure or ambiguous, to compress what was diffuse or redundant, and to substitute for the obsolete a more modern phraseology." Mr. Potts undertook this by the express desire of Dr. Milner, to whom he paid the well merited Horatian compliment in concluding his preface:—

> "Vultus ubi tuus
> Affulsit,—gratior it dies,
> Et soles melius nitent."

MR. WEEDALL prepared and published a new edition of this Grammar, as revised and improved by his learned predecessor, with the following notice prefixed, which will sufficiently explain its character:—

"The editors of the *present edition* feel confident that the merits of this Grammar will continue to be acknowledged, in the perspicuity of its general arrangement, and the solidity and comprehensiveness of its syntax. The only alteration which it presents will be found to consist in the introduction of one new rule at page 80, and in the correction of a few verbal inaccuracies or typographical errors."

The new rule referred to the regulation of tenses, when one verb governs another in the subjunctive mood. This edition of the Douay Grammar appeared in October, 1821, and a third was published in 1832.

CHAPTER IX.

Mr. Weedall made Acting President of the College—Gives up the Spiritual Care of Students and Congregation—Continues Professor of Divinity and Prefect of Studies—Death of John Payne—Mr. Weedall's Sermon at his Funeral—His Inscription for the Monument—His Extensive Reading—Consecration of Bishop Walsh—Dr. Weedall's Sermon on the Occasion—Sermon at the Opening of the Chapel at Northampton—Visit to Weston Underwood.

Mr. Weedall had filled for some time with great credit and efficiency the important offices of Professor of Divinity, Prefect of Studies, and Spiritual Director to the lay students, when, in the summer of the year 1821, he undertook the additional charge of pastor of those of the congregation who lived at some distance from the college. Those who lived near were placed under the spiritual care of the Rev. John Abbot; but Mr. Weedall, having a horse, and being fond of riding, could more easily attend to the out-lying portion of the flock, and thus combine the active duties of missionary life with that exercise which was so beneficial to his bodily health. This arrangement, however, lasted only for a short time. For after the Midsummer vacation in 1822, an important change took place in the arrangements of the college administration.

Mr. Walsh, excellent as he was in so many ways, and especially in the spiritual department, was not well qualified for the presidentship of the college, and the discipline had become considerably relaxed under his administration. He was evidently not properly aware of the state of things in the house; but he had a long conversation with MR. WEEDALL, who rectified his erroneous notions. This conversation, however, produced no further practical result, than some vague intention of calling in extraneous assistance for the prefectship. After this, Mr. Walsh consulted the Rev. William Foley, who was procurator, and who had quite determined to give him his opinion unreservedly on the first opportunity. Mr. Foley accordingly advised him to resign the active administration of the college into the hands of MR. WEEDALL, and to resume the spiritual charge, and place himself nearly in the same position as that which he occupied when Mr. Quick was president. Mr. Foley could not too much admire the humility with which that holy man listened to him, encouraging him to say whatever he judged proper, telling him to trample on his private feelings, and have only in view the welfare of the establishment. Not only did Mr. Walsh thus humbly listen, but he at once adopted Mr. Foley's advice, and proposed it directly to MR. WEEDALL. It was at first arranged that he should continue to have charge of the distant members of the congregation; but this was soon found seriously inconvenient and incompatible, and the entire congregation was placed under the care of Mr. Abbot.

Mr. Walsh now resumed the entire spiritual direction of the college, and retained the presidentship only nominally, while Mr. Weedall became the actual president. Thus had this excellent and indefatigable priest gradually ascended through his college course of now eighteen years, to the highest and most responsible office in the establishment. His elevation was a subject of joy and congratulation to the whole house; for he was, and always had been, highly respected and sincerely beloved. Mr. Walsh was equally so: but as all are not fitted for the same things, every one felt that Mr. Walsh, holy and amiable as he was, would be much more fittingly employed in the spiritual concerns of the college, and in the care of the congregation attached to the mission of Oscott. Indeed he himself was sensible of this, and thus it is freely stated of him in his funeral oration by the subject of this biography, that "in the administration of the seminary he confined himself, by preference, to the spiritual department, and in the management of that he was supremely excellent." It was therefore in no way disparaging to the merits of Mr. Walsh, that it was thought more desirable that Mr. Weedall should relieve him of the temporal and scholastic administration of St. Mary's College.

In entering upon the important duties of the presidentship, Mr. Weedall proceeded, no doubt, in the spirit of that exquisite motto of the Abbot of St. Gertrude, at Louvain, *Præsim ut prosim:* which may be freely translated, "May I preside for the benefit of others." A mind like his must have been fully conscious of the arduous duties now imposed upon him, and equally of the assiduous care required of him. He had well considered the spirit which ought to animate him in the government of such an establishment, and had studied the admirable admonition of St. Bernard: "Erudimini qui judicatis terram, discite subditorum matres vos esse debere, non dominos: studete magis amari, quam metui; et si interdum severitate opus est, paterna sit, non tyrannica."* This, indeed, characterises most accurately the whole course of his government, to the very close of his college life, which was also the end of his existence on earth. His presidentship was marked throughout by the absence of all harshness and imperiousness; he was mild and considerate, but at the same time firm and consistent. He knew that the stability of his government would be far better secured by kindness, than by severity. He had learned that lesson of wisdom even from a Pagan moralist:

" Errat longe
Qui imperium credat esse gravius aut stabilius,
Vi quod fit, quam illud quod amicitiæ adjungitur."†
TERENTIUS.

Accordingly he gave himself to his new office with the best of dispositions, and with every qualification which it required. As he was now to be

---

* "Receive instruction, ye who judge the earth, learn that you ought to be the mothers, not the lords of those under you; study rather to be loved than feared; and if sometimes there is need of severity, let it be paternal, not tyraunical." S. BERNARD, in *Cantic*. Serm. 23.

† The following may give some idea of these lines in English:—
"Much does he err, who thinks more firm his sway
To make by force, than by affection's way."

the general superior of the house, he resigned the spiritual charge of the lay students into the able hands of Mr. Walsh; and as his duties to the college would now require his continued presence and attention, he gave up to Mr. Abbot the share he had hitherto had of the congregation. He continued, however, to teach Divinity, and to act as Prefect of Studies. The college prospered, and all went on with a new spirit and fresh energy under his excellent administration.

Among the boys at this time at the college was a very amiable and pious student, John Payne. He had come to Oscott when nine years old, and after a short course, in the latter part of which he gave great edification, was carried off by a malignant fever at the early age of fourteen, on the 11th of September, 1824. He died at the farmhouse at Holdford, whither he had been removed to secure the college from the danger of infection. His death caused a great sensation in the college, and Mr. Weedall preached a beautiful and affecting sermon at his funeral in the chapel. The reader will not be displeased at the copious extracts which follow, as they will develope the virtues of the youth, while they exhibit the eloquence of the preacher. From the text, Wisdom iv., 11, et seq.: *He was taken away lest wickedness should alter his understanding, or deceit beguile his soul, &c.* Mr. Weedall naturally began with some observations on the mysterious and impenetrable ways of Divine Providence, and then continued:—

"Of these his unsearchable ways few are found so completely to baffle enquiry as those which regulate to each one the duration of life, the time and the manner in which we are summoned respectively to quit it, which conceal the reasons why the child is summoned before the parent, the healthy before the weak. Why, of the *two men labouring in the field*, or of the *two women grinding at the mill, the one is taken, and the other is left*. (St. Matthew xxiv., 40.) And how it comes to pass that whilst age and infirmity are tottering through the city, or sinking at the gate in every variety of decrepitude, that *behold* it is *a young man* that is *carried out, the only son of his mother*, and *she a widow*." (St. Luke vii., 12.)

This allusion was the more felt and admired, as it applied precisely both to the lamented youth and his widowed mother.

"But for our moral improvement we are at liberty to conjecture; and in the mournful case before us...your feelings will concur with mine, that a happier as well as more probable solution cannot be found than what the words of my text supply. *He was taken away, lest wickedness should alter his understanding, and deceit beguile his soul. For the bewitching of vanity obscureth good things, and the wandering of concupiscence overturneth the innocent mind.*

"Of this witchery of vanity, spoken of by the wise man, which is no other than the temptations and dangerous pleasures of life, the authority, the example, and the corrupt maxims of the world; of the influences it possesses, and the power it exercises to subvert good principles, and to debauch the minds of the innocent and inexperienced, our young friend before us was deeply persuaded. And hence, on a recent occasion, as I have learned to my own great edification, and as you, my brethren, will hear with similar sentiments, when before this very altar he received the Holy Sacrament of Confirmation, he prayed in the artless fervour of his soul that God would permit him to die in his love and for his love."

To secure this, as far as he could, he had resolved to devote himself to God in the priestly state, and the preacher thus describes the means he took to prepare himself for it:—

"The time of vacation, so fatal to the virtuous resolutions of so many amongst you, was to him a time of more than ordinary carefulness, vigilance, and strict observance of his religious duties; yet not an observance of merely essential duties. He was convinced, as we all should be, that virtue will soon decline, if not supported by the wholesome discipline of mortification and self-denial. Accordingly you will hear with pleasure, and I hope with profit too, that our little friend pursued a system of painful privation, which denoted a soul more than ordinarily imbued with the spirit of penance.".........

"In the possession of such sentiments, and in the practice of the little silent virtues just described, this good child edified his friends and sanctified this very last vacation; and so far from lingering on its term, and regretting its expiration, though he left so much behind to occasion regret, he purposely hastened his return to college, that he might gratify a pious wish of receiving here the Holy Communion, on the Feast of the Assumption of our Blessed Lady.

"With all this, however, he seems to have had a presumption of a dissolution not very remote; and it is a remarkable fact that he expressed an opinion to this effect on a very late occasion to his mother, and to some confidential friends.

After expatiating on the happy lot of the deceased, and showing how enviable it should appear to all present, the preacher proceeds in this animated strain:—

"Oh! it is good to commune with the dead. They whisper the accents of encouragement, or burst on the ear in thunder. To the just man they say, *be justified still;* and to the sinner, *Wo, wo to you, ye ungodly men, who have forsaken the law of the Most High. In malediction, when you die, shall your portion be.* (Ecclus. xli., 11.)......

"On other occasions, when we speak to you of death, you deem it at a distance, and when we announce to you its recent victims, they are either unknown to you, or unseen. But here death sits before you. It has laid low your friend, your companion, the associate of your studies, your amusements, your general pursuits; one who a few days ago was kneeling at that bench which his coffin has now displaced, and who possessed as fair a claim to life as the healthiest among you.

"When we speak to you of death, you conceive it of the aged, the infirm: and seek shelter from thought under the embrace of youth. But take the dimension of that coffin! 'Tis not a roomy tenement. Read the age on that escutcheon! 'Tis below the average of your years. Therefore death is no respecter of the young. *To-day for me, to-morrow for thee!*

"When we speak to you of death, you feebly incline to virtue; but either procrastination deadens your efforts, or fancied obstacles discourage. Oh! if he who now lies before you had been so affected; if he had deferred to give his heart thus early to the Lord who made him; if he had thought to taste the pleasures of sin for a time, and then to give a filthy remnant to his Maker; if he had hastened to crop the wild flowers of youth, and like the foolish man in the Scripture, to be *crowned with roses before they wither;* if he had thought to abandon God, lest he should be abandoned by the world, and to scoff at religion, lest he should be scoffed at as religious; if he had undervalued piety because it is unfashionable, and had neglected salvation from a foolish and cowardly apprehension that it would be ultimately unattainable; my God! how dismal would his lot be now! How wretched his soul; how utterly and irrecoverably lost!"

This saintly youth was buried in the same vault under the sacristy where the remains of Mr. Potts were deposited. It was resolved to erect a tablet of white marble to his memory in the chapel, the expense of which should be defrayed entirely by his schoolfellows. The design for it was made by one among them, George Goold, who was a very clever draughtsman. It is simple, but very significant; a tablet in good taste, surmounted by a small graceful urn, at the foot of which is a lily half expanded, snapped off, and drooping over the tablet. Some of the superiors suggested appropriate inscriptions; but there was but one master spirit who could have conceived anything so beautiful and expressive as the following composition, and that was MR. WEEDALL.

A. XP. Q.
Jacet infra
Quod mortale habuit
Joannes Chrysostomus Payne
Hujus collegii egregium decus
Brevis annorum senescebat virtutibus
Ingenio pietate pudore
Insignis
Gratus ille suis dilectus et Deo
Quem ita tenerrimo redamabat affectu
Ut integra valetudine
Dissolvi vellet quo plenius amaret
Voti feliciter compos
III Id. Sep. M.DCCC.XXIV.
Vixit annos XIV.M.VIII.
Mœreutes condiscipuli
H. M. P. CC.*

* If this inscription had been composed in English, it might perhaps have been thus expressed and arranged:—

Christ, the Alpha and Omega.
Below lie
The mortal remains of
John Chrysostom Payne.
A distinguished ornament of this college:
Young in years, he grew old in virtues.
For talents, piety, and purity
Admirable.
Cherished by his companions, and beloved by God:
Whom he loved in return with so tender affection
That in perfect health
He desired to be dissolved, that he might more fully love Him.
He happily obtained his desire,
On the 11th of September, M.DCCC.XXIV.
He lived 14 years and 8 months.
His sorrowing fellow students
Erected this monument.

An engraving of this monumental tablet appeared afterwards beneath a portrait of this virtuous youth, from a full length drawing of him in the possession of MR. WEEDALL. He is there represented as an acolyth in cassock and surplice, coming out of the sanctuary of the college chapel, and bringing away the cruets from the altar. It is to be regretted, however, that the likeness is not good. It is a pleasing countenance, but it does not convey the peculiar traits and expression of John Payne. The mouth particularly is sadly distorted; he had a small and well formed mouth, and not thick lips. His forehead was broad, and his face fair, and somewhat freckled.

It has always been a subject of astonishment to all who knew MR. WEEDALL how he managed, with the continued drawback of that severe affection of his head and eyes, to acquire so much knowledge on almost every subject. If he could lay hold of any one to read to him, he was always eager to avail himself of the opportunity; if he could economise a little eyesight, he would read as long as he could endure it by daylight. He was always seen with some book under his arm, or in his hand. He contrived to keep pace with the literature of the day. Besides reading for his school of theology, he managed to acquire a good knowledge of other books in various departments of science and literature. If he took a walk with a companion, he was sure to bring forth some useful and interesting paper in a Review, or a newspaper, which he would propose to have read as they walked along. Many an article in the *Edinburgh* and *Quarterly Reviews*, in the *Morning Chronicle*, and the *Dublin Evening Post*, has the present writer read to him, as they went to bathe at the famous Rounton Well, or in Perry River, or when taking a healthy walk over Sutton Coldfield, or going together to the Holdford Farm. He was always fond of reading Cobbett's *Political Register;* for though he took no decided part in politics, he admired the manly and original style, and powerful reasoning of that extraordinary writer. At this period, moreover, Cobbett had warmly taken up the cause of Catholic Emancipation, which there can be no doubt that he indirectly promoted by the papers in his *Register*, and particularly by his *History of the Protestant Reformation in England*, which greatly aided in dissipating prejudice in the public, and thus disposing the multitude favourably towards the Catholic cause. However unprincipled Cobbett was as a public writer, it is impossible, with any justice, to refuse the tribute of admiration and gratitude to him for his strong and unanswerable arguments for Catholicity, framed with so much originality, and expressed in language so clear and forcible in many papers of his *Register*. Among others may be instanced, "To the Hampshire Parsons,"—"To the Bishop of Winchester,"—"To the King, on the prosecution of Mr. O'Connell, and the necessity of repealing the laws by which the Church is established in Ireland,"—"To the Freeholders of Ireland," all which clever compositions of Cobbett's appeared about this time.

On one occasion, Mr. WEEDALL brought into the writer's room a number of the *Register*, containing a very striking article on the Catholic religion as well as emancipation; and though he brought it evidently to have it read to him, he was so delighted with it that he began to read it aloud himself, and went on some way, forgetting in his admiration of the paper, the inconvenience he must have felt in attempting to read it.

Bishop Milner, feeling his health declining, had chosen the Rev. Thomas Walsh for his coadjutor. He was consecrated by his lordship on the 1st of May, 1825, at Wolverhampton, as Bishop of Cambysopolis *in partibus*. The other three Vicars Apostolic assisted, with their coadjutors, Dr. Poynter and Dr. Bramston, of the London District; Dr. Smith and Dr. Penswick, of the Northern; and Dr. Collingridge and Dr. Baines, of the Western. Since the dreary days of the subversion of her hierarchy in this country, England had never witnessed such an assemblage of Bishops on any occasion. Dr. WEEDALL was the preacher, and for even months beforehand, he prepared a most elaborate sermon for the occasion. The subject was the "Authority of the Church;" and he thus introduced it:—

"On this awful and interesting occasion, unknown in this edifice wherein we are congregated, unwitnessed before by the majority amongst us, and unexampled in this country since the days of her regular hierarchy:—when the representatives of our ancient and illustrious church are assembled to give effect to the canonical appointment of our venerated Pontiff, Pope Leo the Twelfth,—these passages of St. Paul in his Epistle to the Ephesians (iv., 11, 12, 13,) seem to involve a subject most suitable to be presented to your consideration. They display the groundwork of the Christian Church;—the scheme and purpose of the Divine Architect in the magnificent erection; the materials of which it is composed; the foundation stone; the columns that support its fair proportions: its strength, its solidity, its indestructibility:—spacious and vast for the congregation of nations, as the Prophet Micheas had described its prospective grandeur."

He quotes Micheas iv., 1, 2; and after showing how the Apostle, in the text from the Ephesians as above, propounds the general structure and particular design of the Church, he thus eloquently proceeds:—

"Were the records of this design as scanty and obscure as they are frequent and intelligible, yet a very little reflection would convince us, my brethren, that Jesus Christ, being the truth of God, and truth being essentially one,—*singleness* would be the character of his doctrines, and *unity* the modification of his church. For, in the moral devastation of his nature, man was as depraved in intellect, as corrupted in heart, as ignorant of the truths of religion, as he was destitute of the reality of holiness; as misled and misinformed, as deeply and deadly criminal. He needed an instructor as much as a Redeemer: one who would retrace the road to happiness, and provide the means of attaining it, at the same time that he repurchased for him life and immortality. In this state of utter destitution, therefore, Jesus appeared among men, *the way, the truth, and the life;* and whilst, by the blood of his cross, he paid the price of our redemption, by his doctrines and precepts, he taught us the conditions of its application. He prescribed the extent of submission which the understanding was to make to his revealed doctrines, as exactly as he measured the obedience which the will was to pay to his commandments. He left not these matters to the arrangements of men. Caprice was not to qualify; interest was not to control; the feeble lights of human knowledge were not to twinkle amidst the awful obscurity of his revelations. But as they were given, so they were destined to continue, and so to be received; and he who should interpose to *add to*, or to *take from*, would do it under check of the heaviest responsibility."

He proceeds to his professed enquiry: "Which of all the denominations of Christians takes the surest way for knowing, and for teaching the truths of Christ and his Gospel." He tries the various claims of *private judgment*, the authority of *a particular teacher*, of *a local, or national church;* or finally of *some authority still greater and safer*. The discourse was very long, and worked out with the greatest labour and attention; and was certainly a masterpiece of close and cogent argumentation.

Dr. Weedall had still to study a good deal for his class of divines; for he continued to teach three days in the week, taking the dogmatical divinity, while Dr. Walsh, on the alternate days, carried on the class in moral divinity. At the Christmas of 1825, he gave up the professorship of theology to the Rev. John Abbot.

The Rev. William Foley had left Oscott 22nd October, 1823, having been appointed by Bishop Milner to the then infant mission of Northampton, including occasional duty at the barracks at Weedon. There was no chapel yet in that important county town. Mr. Foley at first took a small house, the sixth below the wall of St. Peter's churchyard, on

Black Lion Hill; and here he fitted up an upper room which served for a chapel, till having purchased a piece of land some way out of the town on the road to Kingsthorpe, he was enabled, by various contributions, headed by the Bishop's name for £500, and his own for £100, the whole amount of his little savings, to erect the present house, and the old chapel adjoining. This chapel was ready for use in the autumn of 1825, and on Tuesday, the 25th of October, it was opened with as much solemnity as could in those days be attained, by the Rt. Rev. Dr. Bramston, Bishop of Usula, and coadjutor to Bishop Poynter, in the London District, the present writer assisting and arranging the ceremonial. Bishop Bramston was invited to sing the Mass, chiefly on account of his connexion with that neighbourhood, being a native of Oundle, and his family being well known in the county; and Bishop Milner readily gave permission for him to officiate in his district.

Mr. Foley naturally requested his old friend WEEDALL to preach the opening sermon on this interesting occasion, and he very willingly consented. He rode on horseback all the way from Oscott, and reached Northampton on the Monday evening. The next day he delivered to a large and highly respectable audience, among whom were many Protestants, a very eloquent, impressive, and appropriate discourse "*On Prayer*." The sermon made a great impression, and was exceedingly admired and praised by many sensible Protestants who heard it, as well as by the Catholics, among

whom were Rev. Dr. Fletcher, Rev. T. M. Mc
Donnell, Rev. M. Trovell, Rev. Mr. Malvoisin,
Lady Throckmorton, Robert Throckmorton, Esq.,
the present baronet, and his sister. The next day
MR. WEEDALL was invited by Lady Throckmorton
to pay a visit to Weston Underwood, about fourteen miles from Northampton, where Sir George
resided, and which, being an invalid, he could
never leave.

The Bishop who had officiated, Dr. Bramston,
went also to Weston Underwood the next day, and
took the present writer with him in a post-chaise.
On the way, he spoke in the highest terms of admiration of MR. WEEDALL's sermon. He particularly
praised the elegance of the language, and the
gracefulness of the delivery; but he shrewdly
remarked how particular the little man was in his
choice of words, shown by his often going back for
the exact word, when he had not at first given it.
This was indeed his frequent practice, and his
fastidiousness in this respect sometimes produced
an effect somewhat unpleasing. MR. WEEDALL
having never been at Northampton before, was
desirous of seeing all that he could; and Mr. Foley
took him to the Infirmary and the Jail, which was
kept in admirable order by an intelligent governor,
who was always very friendly and accommodating
to Mr. Foley. MR. WEEDALL indeed delayed so
long setting out for Weston, that when the dinner
hour came, he had not yet arrived. This was very
embarrassing in a house which he was visiting for
the first time. The company, however, sat down to

dinner, and when it was half over, MR. WEEDALL was at length announced. Sir George Throckmorton sent word to him to come in as he was, without ceremony, and he accordingly entered and took his place, booted and splashed, at the table. Bishop Bramston, so well known for loving a joke, after a little while, said to him very archly: "Well, MR. WEEDALL, how did you like Newport Pagnell? I always thought it a pretty little town." "Newport Pagnell, my Lord," said WEEDALL, "did I pass through such a place? I'm not aware that I did." The company began to titter, when Dr. Bramston rejoined: "Why I supposed you had lost your way, and gone on to Newport Pagnell, as you were so late." That town was about three miles farther on the road: but the facetious bishop supposed nothing of the kind: he only wanted to give MR. WEEDALL a rub for arriving so late, on his first visit to a strange house. MR. WEEDALL evidently felt the rebuke, and it must be owned that it was not altogether undeserved.

CHAPTER X.

Death of Bishop Milner—Bishop Walsh Leaves Oscott—Mr. Weedall President—Chosen a Canon of the English Chapter—Made Vicar General—Handsome Present brought him by a Deputation from the Catholics of Birmingham—His Sermons at the Opening of New Chapels at Wolverhampton and Nottingham—His Health seriously Impaired—Receives his Diploma of D.D.—His Installation at the College—His Visit to O'Connell in Birmingham—Letter to the Editor of the "Birmingham Journal"—His Letter to the Editor of the "Catholic Journal"—His Health Improved.

The year 1826 was marked by the severe and irreparable loss of the illustrious Bishop Milner, who died at his residence, Giffard House, Wolverhampton, on the 19th of April, at the age of seventy-three. He was the founder of St. Mary's College, he had watched over it with paternal care and solicitude, he frequently visited the college; and never seemed so happy as when seated there in the midst of its superiors and professors. This event, of course, entailed the removal of Dr. Walsh from Oscott, as he now became charged with the care of the Midland District, as Vicar Apostolic. Shortly after Dr. Milner's death, he left the college, and took up his residence at Wolverhampton. Mr.

WEEDALL then became absolute president, with Mr. Abbot as Vice-President. He left his old room, the "calefactory," and took possession of the two apartments always occupied by the president. It may be here remarked as a general feature of his character, that though exceedingly fond of neatness, he had never any love of finery. Everything in his rooms was plain and ordinary; and he seemed never to desire anything rich or costly. If he had any such articles, they were presents, in a manner forced upon him by friends, or parents full of respect and gratitude towards him as the guardian of their children. He seemed to have imbibed the true spirit of those fine maxims of St. Isidore: "Sacerdoti pro opibus, est virtutis ornamentum; pro voluptate, castitas; pro luxu, frugalitas; pro lætitia, eorum quibus præest ad virtutem incrementum."* He was at the same time remarkably careful of everything that he possessed; his books, his clothes, his furniture, were preserved with a care which often appeared to others too far pursued and superfluous. But this attention was evidence of an orderly and careful mind, which embraced everything in its comprehensive solicitude.

MR. WEEDALL was now become extensively known in the Catholic body, and certainly whereever known he was highly respected. All indeed appeared anxious to testify their high estimate

* The riches of a priest are the ornament of virtue; his pleasure is chastity; his luxury, frugality; his joy, the increase in virtue of those over whom he presides. ST. ISIDORE, *B*. 3, *Ep*. 354.

of his merits. A proof of this occurred in a notice which he received from the Secretary of the ancient Chapter of England, who was at that time the Rev. Francis Tuite, that he had been elected a member of that honourable body, on the 8th of May, 1827. He was requested to say whether he would accept or decline the proffered dignity, with the intimation that the capitulars, from the high esteem they had conceived for him, fervently hoped that he would signify his acceptance. He knew that the Chapter of England was an ancient and venerable institution, and had numbered among its members many prelates and eminent ecclesiastics, including the late Bishop Milner. His actual bishop, Dr. Walsh, was also a member. Mr. WEEDALL fully appreciated the honour of being a member of that respectable body, and at once signified to the secretary his acceptance. The second English bishop after the subversion of the Catholic religion in England, Dr. Smith, was appointed at the nomination of the Chapter; and after his death, Pope Alexander VII. expressly ordered that the Chapter should govern till another bishop should be appointed; and it did actually govern for the space of thirty years, till the appointment of Bishop Leyburn in 1685. The Chapter, according to the instruments of its erection and confirmation, was to continue only until there should be several Bishops and Chapters in England; and accordingly it ceased to exist on the establishment of the new Chapters, consequent upon the restoration of the hierarchy in England. But it was an enviable distinction to have been a member of a body so ancient, important, and venerable.

On the 10th of May in this year, 1827, was solemnly opened the new chapel at Walsall, built by the Rev. Francis Martyn. Bishop Walsh sung the High Mass, and about thirty priests knelt round the sanctuary. Mr. Weedall preached the sermon, a very eloquent and well argued discourse on the Sacrifice of the Mass. He was fortunate enough to rivet the attention of his audience on a subject not very attractive to Protestants, of whom there were many present; he was listened to with fixed attention and great satisfaction. Indeed a finer argumentative composition could not be conceived. The proofs came in a steady continuous stream with irresistible force, and were urged upon the mind in language eloquent, impressive, and eloquent even to precision. The text was: *Christ, our pasch, is sacrificed.* (1 Cor. v., 7.)

In the ensuing Midsummer vacation, Mr. Weedall made a little excursion, and came for the first time into Norfolk, where he paid a visit to his friend, the present writer, at Cossey. He enjoyed this visit very much, though it was but of short duration.

In February of the following year, 1828, Bishop Walsh signified to the writer that he considered it highly proper that there should be a Vicar General, whose authority should extend over the entire Midland District, and that it was his intention to appoint Mr. Weedall to that office; a measure, he observed, which he had good reason to believe would be grateful to the clergy and district in general. He added that he purposed to give MR. WEEDALL such assistance as might enable him to preach oftener in public, and should concert with him measures to obtain a better succession of ecclesiastics. The appointment was accordingly made on the 14th of June following; and MR. WEEDALL was made Vicar General of the whole District, but without prejudice to the jurisdiction previously exercised by the two Grand Vicars, Rev. Robert Beeston for Lincolnshire, and Rev. F. C. Husenbeth for Norfolk and Suffolk, which they were to exercise as before. In his letter of appointment, Bishop Walsh commended highly and justly MR. WEEDALL's great virtues, no less than his learning and experience. His health, however, at this time suffered considerably from his arduous labours, and naturally anxious and sensitive temperament. It was arranged in February that the Rev. George Morgan should remain at the college for the express purpose of assisting him, as his health was delicate, and unequal to his heavy duties.

MR. WEEDALL had so often advocated the cause of religion and charity by preaching in the chapels at Birmingham, that the two pastors, with the Catholics of both congregations, were anxious to testify their respect and gratitude to him by some handsome present. The Rev. Messrs. Peach and McDonnell, with John Hardman, Esq., accordingly went as a deputation to him to Oscott, and presented him with the works of Bossuet, and his life by Bausset, handsomely bound, in 47 volumes.

This took place on the 15th of April, 1828. The present was accompanied with an address, which was read by Rev. Edward Peach, of St. Chad's chapel. MR. WEEDALL returned an answer in warm terms of gratitude, in which occurred the following humble sentiments expressed in his own graceful and peculiar language:—

"To an humble individual like myself, who counts but few incidents in an uneventful life, the transaction of this day comes clothed in a character of importance, and excites in his breast feelings of deep and more than common interest.

"It would have been my glory, as it has always been my intention, *that, in preaching the gospel, I should deliver that gospel without charge.* (1 Cor. ix., 18.) But your liberality, gentlemen, is so munificent, and so far exceeds the merit of its object, that, whilst it exhausts my gratitude, it lays ground for serious apprehension, lest my very humble efforts may be pronounced to *have already received their reward*, when they come to be considered in that awful court, where the purest claims will be rigorously sifted, and the most indefatigable labourer must be content to rank, at best, but as an unprofitable servant."

On the 8th of May, 1828, the new chapel which Bishop Milner had commenced at Wolverhampton, but did not live to finish, was opened with great solemnity. No preacher could have been selected so adequate to the task of addressing the crowded assemblage as MR. WEEDALL, and he delivered on this occasion his fine sermon on Prayer, which, as already recorded, he had preached at the opening of the chapel at Northampton three years before. But he opened it with a new and striking exordium, which the reader will peruse with admiration. The text was the promise of the Almighty to King Solomon, to hear the prayers which should be offered in his glorious temple. (2 Paral. vii., 12, 14, 16.) After which the preacher thus proceeded:—

"My Christian brethren:—

"No scene can be displayed more appropriate, and no subject be presented more suitable to the occasion which has this day called us together, than that which is opened out in the solemn and interesting passage which I have just repeated to you. It is connected with a description of the most magnificent erection that man ever raised to his Maker; on which were exhausted all the resources of costly labour, of exquisite skill, of a vast and unsparing treasury—around which the most tumultuous interests had been excited, and on which seemed rivetted in fixed attention the gaze of Heaven and of earth. Amidst all the pomp and splendour which blazes throughout the description, we are reminded, however, of the primary and practical object for which so much wealth had been expended. Elevated upon the brazen scaffold in the sight of assembled Israel, King Solomon spread out his hands and thus prayed to the God of David his father: *Building I have built a house for thy dwelling, to be thy most firm throne for ever.* (3 Kings viii., 13.) *Now then, O Lord God of Israel, fulfil to thy servant David my father whatsoever thou hast promised him, and let thy word be established which thou hast spoken. Is it credible that God should dwell with men on the earth? If heaven, and the heaven of heavens do not contain thee, how much less this house which I have built? But to this end only is it made, that thou mayest regard the prayer of thy servant, and his supplication, O Lord, my God; and mayest hear the prayers which thy servant poureth out before thee. That thou mayest open thy eyes upon this house day and night, upon the place wherein thou hast promised that thy name should be called upon.—Whosoever shall pray in this place, hear thou from thy dwelling place, that is, from heaven, and show mercy.—Forgive the sins of thy servants, and of thy people Israel, and teach them the good way in which they may walk. Let thine eyes, I beseech thee, be open, and let thy ears be attentive to the prayer that is made in this place.* (2 Paral. vi., 16, et seq.)

"*And the Lord appeared to him, and said: I have heard thy prayer, and have chosen this place to myself for a house of sacrifice. If I shut up heaven, and there fall no rain, or if I give orders, and command the locust to devour the land; if I send pestilence among my people; and my people, upon whom my name is called, being converted, shall make supplication to me, and seek out my face, and do penance for their most wicked ways, then will I hear from heaven, and forgive their sins, and will heal their land. My eye also shall be open, and my ears attentive to the prayer of him that shall pray in this place. For I have chosen and have sanctified this place, that my name may be there for ever, and my eyes and my heart may remain there perpetually.* (2 Paral. vii., 12, 14, 16.)

"Thus was ratified the solemn compact between God and his people. The object of this grand erection was distinctly avowed by its religious founder; and the terms of the foundation as distinctly recognised and accepted by the Almighty. *The majesty of the Lord filled the temple,* and it was deputed thenceforward to be the *house of prayer.*

"My brethren, we vie not in splendour with the Jewish temple; we expect not, we need not a divine manifestation. But we claim, and we justly claim, a large benefit in that solemn negociation. An Apostle has told us that *whatever things have been written, have been written for our instruction: that through patience and the comfort of the Scriptures, we might have hope.* (Rom. xv., 4.) Now whoever has but superficially examined those Scriptures, will have remarked that of the many practical duties therein detailed, there are none so frequently insisted upon,— none, to the observance of which are attached such splendid assurances of mercy as the duty of prayer."

This solemn opening having taken place on the day after the annual meeting of the clergy held at Sedgley Park, there were no less than fifty priests present in the chapel, forty of whom knelt round the rails of the sanctuary. After the service, the clergy were gathered in groups about the bishop's garden, and all were loud in admiration of the eloquent discourse which they had heard. The Rev. James Simkiss, who had so long known the eloquent preacher, exclaimed to those around him, in his well known sharp and laconic manner: "Fine sermon! clever little man! make him a bishop!"

It was no wonder that with such eloquence, such zeal, and so much kind heartedness, MR. WEEDALL should have been so frequently engaged to preach on occasions similar to the above. The Rev. William Willson, now Bishop of Hobarton, had been ordained priest in December, 1824, and placed on the mission at Nottingham. He found there a poor chapel, 36 feet by 20, and not even a change of vestments. On the 28th of April, 1827, he laid the first stone of a new chapel, measuring outside 87 feet by 41, which was completed in the following year, and opened July 23rd, by Bishop Walsh, who celebrated High Mass, with Rev. John Gascoyne as deacon, and Rev. F. Daniel, S.J., as subdeacon. About ten other priests added solemnity to the ceremonial, and the chapel was crowded by a highly respectable congregation. Mr. Willson invited his intimate friend MR. WEEDALL to preach the opening sermon. It was within the week of the

Ninth Sunday after Pentecost, and he choose the subject of that Sunday's Gospel, Our Saviour's weeping over Jerusalem, from which he took occasion to deliver a powerful and affecting sermon *On the Substraction of Grace,* arranged under three heads: I.—That this substraction is the ordinary punishment of the abuse of grace: II.—That this punishment is strictly just: and III.—That it should warn us not to trifle with the graces of Heaven. A few extracts from this splendid sermon will give some idea of the power and eloquence of the preacher. It has been considered by good judges even as the best of his sermons. The fine vein of theology pervading the practical instruction, gives it a very high value.

"Alas! my brethren, the principle is exemplified in the very origin of man. Man himself was but the substitute for those rebellious angels, whose defection is said to have wasted one third of heaven. And descending in his history, we see Noe selected as a child of grace, and saved from the mass of infidelity. We see Abraham called out to be the father of the faithful. We see Jacob made heir to the lineal blessing which by birth belonged to Esau, but which had been bartered away by that miserable man; and the children of Jacob constituted a chosen nation to illustrate for a season the special mercies of the Almighty. We see Saul repudiated, and David anointed; as in the new law St. Mathias is elected into the sacred college, to fill up the place of Judas, who had fallen from his high dignity *that he might go to his own place,* as the sacred penman emphatically expresses it."......

"Were more examples wanting,......how might I refer you to the country so dear to us all; once an island of Saints, when religion flourished in primitive purity and fervour; when virtue formed the brightest gem in the regal diadem, and piety was the most valuable ornament of the throne; but now become a prey to religious discord, a nest of infidelity, and a mere babel of sectarism. Yes, when I look around me, and behold those sacred edifices, raised by the piety of our Catholic ancestors for the honour of God, and the celebration of his worship; those consecrated piles, whose venerable fronts, though disfigured by time and innovation, still bear marks of the golden age of Catholicity, and attest the religion of the country by which they were raised, I smite my breast as I draw the gloomy contrast between what they now are and what they have been; and I involuntarily exclaim with the plaintive Jeremias, *How hath the Lord covered with obscurity the daughter of Sion in his wrath!*"......

Where so many beautiful and striking passages occur, it is difficult to select; but the following concise exposure and refutation of the horrid Calvinistic doctrine of reprobation pre-eminently deserves extraction.

"Away, then, with that monstrous theology, which would make the Almighty the direct author of his creature's reprobation; that mischievous doctrine that some men have been predestined to gratuitous damnation. Such a doctrine is repugnant to the best feelings of piety; it conflicts with every idea we can form of a *just* God, that he would *originate* the misery of his creatures. It is repugnant, as I have shown to the whole tenor of the Scriptures, which uniformly represent the Almighty, as *desiring not the death of sinners, but rather that they be converted and live;* (Ezech. xxxiii., 11;) as *dealing patiently for their sakes, not willing that any should perish.* (2 Peter iii., 9.) *Who will have all men to be saved, and to come to the knowledge of the truth;* (1 Tim. ii., 4;) and who consequently will grant every necessary grace for those desired purposes. Oh yes; he has placed salvation within the reach of every one. To all he allows a sufficiency of grace, but indemnity for the abuse of that grace he has promised to no one. This is true Catholic doctrine; and I am sure it is reasonable doctrine to connect the happiness or misery of man with the use or abuse of his own free will. Not the sour doctrine of the Predestinarian, who consigns certain souls to antecedent and irremediable destruction,—not the unnatural doctrine of the Antinomian, who works the clumsy machinery of what he misnames justifying faith, and saving faith, which, by the way, is not the gospel faith, which consists in a belief of Christ's doctrines, his mysteries and promises, and from the due influence of all which, aided by grace, arises real justification in the soul; but a certain constrained and forcible belief of one single abstract point that a man's sins have been, and are, without any assignable cause, absolutely and certainly remitted. A proposition which the gospel nowhere encourages us to entertain; a proposition which was never embodied in any ancient creed; a process of enthusiasm which supersedes the necessity of all the salutary dispositions of the heart; which reduces salvation to a mere labour of the head; determining the future happiness of a man by the heat of his imagination; and pronouncing him one of the elect, if he can be so fortunate as to persuade himself that he is so. All this may be a good test of fanaticism, but it is no test of virtue; it may mark the degree of heat in a feverish brain, but I am sure it cannot establish the purity of the heart."

On the Sunday following, which was the tenth after Pentecost, he preached again in the afternoon, and gave a most beautiful and practical discourse on the Gospel of the Sunday, the Parable of the Pharisee and the Publican.

It was expedient indeed for MR. WEEDALL to have the relaxation which these occasional excursions afforded him, for his health was evidently impaired and endangered by overwhelming business. In the latter part of the year there were very distressing accounts of his health, and it was considered to be in a very precarious state. In the month of January of the following year, 1829, his able medical advisers Drs. John Johnstone and De Lys both gave their opinion very decidedly that if he were not relieved from the constant strain upon his mental powers, there was great danger of his becoming deranged. He had always suffered from great drowsiness in the evenings, and this had much increased; but when he went to bed he often passed sleepless nights. With all this afflicting state of health, however, he looked nearly as well as usual, though a little less full in the face. He was cheerful, alert, full of schemes, and plans, and hopes for the future. He had succeeded beyond his expectations in making the exchange of land alluded to in Chapter Eighth, giving acre for acre of the land at the Holdford farm, for land adjoining the college at Oscott. Mr. Gough, of Perry Barr, with whom the negociation was conducted, expressed himself highly delighted with MR. WEEDALL.

Every one, in fact, concurred in testifying esteem and respect for him, and was anxious to do him honour. His ecclesiastical superior, Bishop Walsh, considered it eminently due to him to be distinguished by the degree of Doctor of Divinity, and he petitioned Pope Leo XII. to confer upon him that dignity, in consideration of his having for many years held the presidentship of the episcopal seminary of St. Mary's, Oscott, as likewise having filled the chair of Professor of Theology, and proved himself by his virtues and learning, no less than by his zeal for gaining souls, truly worthy of that honour. The petition was presented to his Holiness on the 26th of January, 1829; and the Pope at once granted the petition, and wrote the following rescript himself on the back of the paper:—

"Die 27th Jan., 1829.

"Annuimus pro gratia juxta petita, et necessarias facultates oratori tribuimus ad effectum de quo in precibus.

"Leo PP. XII."

This, however, was nearly the last act of that Pontiff, for on the 10th of February he breathed his last. The year 1829 was the memorable year of Catholic Emancipation. Mr. O'Connell, accompanied by the Rev. Mr. Doyle, and Messrs. Purcel O'Gorman, Steele, O'Gorman Mahon, Dillon, Bellew, and others, passed through Birmingham on their way to London, on the 10th of February. They were waited upon there by DR. WEEDALL and the Rev. J. Gascoyne, from Oscott, and the Rev. T. M. McDonnell, and Dr. De Lys, of Birmingham. This mark of attention greatly affected Mr. O'Connell, and gave him particular gratification. The interview, however, was alluded to in very insulting terms in a paragraph in the *Birmingham Journal*, in juxta-position with another, containing very calumnious reflections on the Catholic clergy. These attacks called forth a manly and pungent defence from DR. WEEDALL, in a letter to the Editor, from which the following extract will amuse the reader :—

"The interview (with O'Connell) was, and is considered by me an honour, and a subject of self-gratulation. Therefore I cannot possibly take offence at being represented as having, in company with some estimable friends, paid my respects to Mr. O'Connell, or, in the *mock-heroic of the piece*, 'attended at the levee of the M.P.' But I cannot read with precisely the same indifference, the gross and clumsy insinuations which are thrown out against that gentleman and his party; insinuations which outrage good taste and feeling as palpably as they violate truth. 'All the party,' says the *exact* narrator, '*were armed with pistols*, which they displayed, as if for the purpose of intimidation; judging from their looks we would rather not meet such a banditti-looking crew on a lonely road.' On this point, indeed, the Editor of *The Birmingham Journal* may make himself perfectly easy. I will undertake to assure him that the 'banditti-looking crew' will never cross his path, either in courtesy or hostility. But should, perchance, his evil destiny ever bring him into unexpected contact, either in by-way or in high-way, I will just whisper in his ear the ground of his complete security. The 'banditti-looking crew' are shrewd, calculating fellows, and[they reckon the value of the shot before they expend their powder. Consequently the Birmingham Journalist is quite safe."

The letter elicited a lame apology from the Editor.

When the Doctor's cap was formally presented to the Rev. Henry Weedall by Bishop Walsh, on the 25th of March, the ceremony was preceded by a *Requiem* for his late Holiness, which cast a gloom over what otherwise would have been an occasion of general joy and congratulation in the college. The installation took place in the college chapel, and Dr. Weedall, after receiving the ring, cap, and gown of a D.D. from the hands of the Bishop, spoke as follows, evidently much affected:—

"It is incumbent on me, my Lord, to acknowledge with gratitude this testimony of approbation from the Holy See, and the particular kindness with which your Lordship has promoted the business. At the same time I am impelled to add that I acknowledge it with confusion. I feel that the duties and responsibilities of the priesthood—themselves sufficiently weighty—are multiplied in number and measure by this additional honour conferred upon me; and I am confounded by the reflection that my capabilities are very inadequate to this increase of obligation. There is nothing, indeed, which I can recognise in the compliment of this day, beyond the kind partialities of two venerated superiors, and the amiable interest which his late Holiness condescended to take in the dignity and success of our ecclesiastical establishments. The mention of that revered Pontiff awakens sorrow in every heart, and throws a damp over the ceremony of the day. Religion mourns over his early grave, and the premature event which has saddened us all, reminds me, in an especial manner, that fresh and fragrant as might have been my simple garland under other circumstances, it is now but the cypress wreath that preaches of mortality. May he rest in peace! And in the prayer of the Church, may he who was the representative of Christ upon earth, be associated to the company of his holy pontiffs in heaven! As for myself I can only say that my services and my life are dedicated to the church. My vows to her are without repentance; and although the bonds are stronger by which I am now engaged to her service, my affections are the same: *Si oblitus fuero tui Jerusalem, oblivioni detur dextera mea.*" (Ps. cxxxvi., 5.)

About forty gentlemen afterwards sat down to an excellent dinner provided at the college. Bishop Walsh, from the chair, proposed the health of the new D.D., and DR. WEEDALL returned thanks in another feeling and graceful speech, in the course of which he said :—

"I disclaim, gentlemen, any proper pretensions to the honour I have this day received. I am but a *theologus* in divinity, if I may be allowed to coin a diminutive. And I believe, gentlemen, that I am specially privileged to deal in *diminutives*. (This happy allusion to his own diminutive stature greatly amused the company.)......But *he* is the Doctor in Divinity,* who, thoroughly imbued with the truths of the gospel and the maxims of morality, is skilful in applying those truths and maxims to the ever varying practice of the mission......who must be conversant, therefore, with the human heart. Who must have trod its labyrinths; have studied its errors; have become familiar with its duties. Who must be able, consequently, to resolve its perplexities, and to supply light and guidance along the dubious paths of salvation. (Cheers.) Here is the true doctor; and many such doctors I recognise around me, to whom I should be happy to resign my nominal dignity."

The festivities were extended to the students, who had a liberal feast in the refectory. DR. WEEDALL and the parlour guests paid them a visit; and the worthy president on his appearance was greeted with loud acclamations. Of course his health was immediately proposed amid loud cheering, and the toast was given in an eloquent speech by Mr. Morgan O'Connell, a nephew of the great Liberator. DR. WEEDALL returned thanks in glowing terms in a speech turning most ingeniously upon the respective relations of president

* As he spoke this, he turned significantly towards the Rev. T. M. McDonnell.

P

and students, and ending in these beautiful and impressive words :—

"May you be happy in the possession of prudence, piety, and ability. May the avenues to fair fame, as far as they open, be crowded with young Catholic aspirants fit to contend for every honourable distinction. (Great applause.) And when, at last, you shall have gained the summit of your hopes, may you have the consolation to reflect that your recommendation with man was your *fidelity to God;* and that every point was carried without a sacrifice of moral integrity, or the compromise of a single principle of your religion." (Vehement cheering.)

The *Catholic Journal* had been established in the preceding year to promote the cause of Emancipation by new, vigorous, and extensive exertion and agitation. But as the day of deliverance dawned, it was announced in glowing and grateful language by the Editor, M. Quin, Esq., that it would cease with the number for March 15th, 1829. "Our task," he said, "is done, our mission is accomplished, and we retire. Our Journal shall forthwith cease; it shall go, amongst the other peace-offerings, a sacrifice to the Temple of Concord....the dignified course is this—the Journal was the effect of our persecution; with that persecution it shall cease." This announcement called forth numerous appeals, remonstrances, and exhortations, and among them one which the Editor printed as from a "distinguished professor of a distinguished Catholic college, who, we regret, has deprived us of the benefit which we should derive from the appearance of his name in the catalogue of our supporters." It came from Dr. Weedall, who in the latter part of it wrote in his own elegant and unique style, as follows:—

"Even for the good of the Catholic *cause*, allow me to remark, your retirement is rather premature. After the storm is past, there will be for a considerable time a swell upon the waters, and we shall require the head and hand of a judicious pilot to direct our little skiff aright."

The Editor, however, declared that his conviction of the policy of extinguishing the Journal remained the same, and it was accordingly discontinued.

Dr. Weedall's health had happily improved, and when Midsummer arrived, the annual exhibition was conducted with great spirit and ability, and elicited the warmest applause. It was pronounced by competent judges the best and most numerously countenanced of any that had preceded it. The company were more select, and Lord and Lady Stafford had come from London purposely to honour it with their presence.—The exchange of land, already mentioned, had enabled Dr. Weedall to enlarge the "bounds" or playground by the addition of that piece of ground previously known as the "Green," an advantage very little hoped for a few years before. This was not only a great acquisition to the boys, but it enabled the superiors to ensure a more complete system of discipline. After the vacation, the college was completely crowded with students; and Dr. Weedall's health was much better.

CHAPTER XI.

Dr. Weedall's Health Seriously Impaired—Retires for a little Excursion—Makes a Tour on the Continent—Mr. Foley President in his Absence—Dr. Weedall's Visits to Rome and Naples—Letters on the Miracle of St. Januarius—His Return to Oscott—Sermons at the Openings of Chapels at West Bromwich and Grantham—Pastoral Written by him on Collections for the District Fund—Chapel Openings at Bilston, Lichfield, and Sutton Coldfield.

The year 1830 opened gloomily for Oscott. Dr. Weedall's health had indeed been growing better, but his overwhelming labours, augmented as they were by the steady increase of inmates in the college, had made sad havoc again upon his head, and undermined his energies so fearfully, that it was declared by his medical attendants imperatively necessary, for saving his valuable life, that he should be at once relieved from all application, and should go away for a time, for recreation and convalescence. Accordingly, in the early part of the year, the Bishop came over to Oscott, and settled that Dr. Weedall should retire from his duties altogether for some time; and the Vice-President, the Rev. John Abbot, was temporarily charged with the office of President. Every one was edified by the cheerful readiness with which Dr. Weedall resigned every thing unreservedly into the hands of MR. ABBOT. But he was always a pattern of humility, and gained more real respectability from his cultivation of this virtue, so rare in men of great ability, than he would have done by adherence to his own will and tenacity in maintaining his exalted position; for

> "We rise in glory as we sink in pride:
> Where boasting ends, there dignity begins."
> YOUNG.

DR. WEEDALL immediately set out on a little excursion. He spent a few days early in March at Sedgley Park, where it was plainly perceived that his malady was in great measure brought on by over anxiety and a temperament too susceptible, which made him suffer under every trial more than most men would. He spent between two and three months away from the college, in visiting his friends in various places, with evident benefit to his health. He returned to Oscott in May, so much improved in health that he much wished to remain there. He resumed his office of President; but the Bishop did not consider that he had taken sufficient relaxation to ensure a continuance of health, and judged it expedient for him to make an excursion on the Continent, and stay away even for a couple of years. Mr. Denis Shine Lawlor, who had been particularly favoured by DR. WEEDALL while a student in the college, and had left it two years before, was going at this time on a lengthened tour on the Continent. On his way to London, in

May, 1830, he called at Oscott, where he found Dr. Weedall in a very nervous state, and his physicians and friends anxious to induce him to try a change of air, and allow himself some repose and variety. He was very unwilling to yield to these solicitations, till Mr. Lawlor offered himself to be his companion to Rome. It was arranged that Dr. Weedall should join Mr. Lawlor on the Rhine, who preceded him, made a tour in Holland, and awaited his arrival at the Island of Nonnenwerth, on the Rhine, where the old convent had been fitted up as an hotel.

The college at this time was full to overflowing. The Midsummer Exhibition took place as usual, went off exceedingly well, and was honoured with a numerous attendance of select company. After the distribution of prizes at its conclusion, Dr. Weedall rose, and begged that after saying so much for others, he might be permitted to say a few words for himself. The speech he proceeded to make was apparently not written, but flowed in very feeling accents from the fulness of his heart. The writer was present, and heard it with painful emotion. The worthy president alluded to his long connexion with the establishment, which by desire of his superior he was now about to quit, for the benefit of his health, impaired by his ardent devotedness to its interests.

"You have seen," he said, "the moss covering the wall of some old and venerable edifice; you have seen the ivy mantling and clinging to some antique tower or some aged tree; you have, perhaps, attempted to strip them away, and you have found how tenaciously they adhered, and how hard it was to sever them. In these you have seen the images of his case who now addresses you; and from them you may gain some idea of what I feel in being obliged to separate from this place, to which I have adhered for so many years with devoted constancy and affection."

The writer professes only to report the substance of what was said, as his memory retains it; he cannot pretend to give it in the glowing language of the able speaker, nor can he convey an adequate idea of the deep feeling with which it was slowly and emphatically delivered. DR. WEEDALL, in taking leave of his hearers, carefully observed that it was only for a time, and he hoped but for a short time; and ended his most affecting address by wishing prosperity and peace to the establishment in the words of the Church, *Pax huic domni, et omnibus habitantibus in ea!* Loud plaudits drowned the last words, but the president remained standing till the applause had subsided, and then calmly finished by giving the same in English, which he pronounced with great emotion, *Peace be to this house, and to all that dwell therein!*

The presidentship of St. Mary's College was confided during the absence of DR. WEEDALL to his friend the Rev. William Foley, who broke up his little preparatory establishment at Northampton, and repaired to Oscott in the middle of July. He had not sought this arrangement, and it cost him a great deal to leave Northampton, where he had now resided seven years, which as a mission he had absolutely created, and for which he had with great exertion built a convenient chapel and ample priest's house. His last letter from this place was written to the writer of these lines. "Open it carefully," he wrote, "for my heart is folded in it." He took with him to Oscott eight of the boys who had been under his care at Northampton, one of whom was Francis Amherst, destined to return thither twenty-eight years afterwards, to reside again in the same house as Bishop of the See of Northampton.

Dr. Weedall left St. Mary's College in June, and proceeded on his continental tour. He landed at Rotterdam, but by some mistake did not stop at Nonnenwerth. He was recognised, however, by Mr. Lawlor as the steamboat passed the island, and joined by him the next day at Coblentz. They stopped a day at St. Goar and another at Bingen. At Mentz they passed four or five days very delightfully, as they were pleased to say, at the house of some connexions of the writer. Thence they proceeded to Strasbourg, where they were domiciled with the illustrious Bishop Trevern. By an introduction from his lordship, they were received by a very interesting friend of his, who inhabited an old castle, situated in a picturesque defile, about three miles from Basle. They went thence to Schaffhausen, and made a pedestrian tour through the Oberland: visited the famous convent of Einsiedlen, and ascended Mount Rigi. From Thun, Dr. Weedall wrote to his present biographer a very interesting account of his travels. They crossed Mount Simplon, ascended the colossal statue of St. Charles, near the Lake Major, visited Arona, Turin, Milan, Genoa, and Florence. Italy and Rome were, of course, the grand attractions, and DR. WEEDALL had been eager to enjoy their glories.

> "Fair Italy!
> Thou art the garden of the world, the home
> Of all art yields, and nature can decree;
> Even in thy desert, what is like to thee?
> Thy very weeds are beautiful, thy waste
> More rich than other climes' fertility;
> Thy wreck a glory, and thy ruin graced
> With an immaculate charm which cannot be defaced."
> *Childe Harold's Pilgrimage. Canto IV.*

They did not, however, reach Rome till the 31st of October. DR. WEEDALL took up his residence near the English College, but in a very comfortless apartment. It would be saying little to record that he was delighted with the Eternal City. To a mind, pious, cultivated, and elevated like his it was perfect rapture to be there. It was his practice to read first in Alban Butler's *Lives of Saints*, or other works, the histories of the primitive martyrs: and then to sally forth and verify the actual scenes of their triumphs and martyrdom. Thus he enjoyed the glorious churches which bear their names, and contain their relics, the mighty and imposing ruins, the everlasting Colosseum, and especially the Catacombs. His letters from Rome gave glowing descriptions of these interesting objects, and of the pleasure and edification which he derived from them. He especially remarked upon the air of religion, which was every where breathed in Rome, how all was connected with religion, and how beautifully every incident and act had reference to it. His health soon began to improve: his mind was relieved of that "daily solicitude" which had so long oppressed it; and every scene around him now inspired pleasure and animation.

The short pontificate of Pope Pius VIII., of one year and eight months, was concluded by his holy death on the 30th of November in this year, 1830. DR. WEEDALL took his part in preaching a series of English sermons, which were delivered in the Church of *Santa Maria de Miracoli*, and made a beautiful allusion to this event in one of these sermons in Advent, from which the reader will peruse with pleasure the following extract:—

"Death indeed has been dealing in "the high place:" he has struck the dome of the Christian Capitol; and at a single blow, aimed with a double purpose, he has levelled in the dust the Pontiff and the Prince! *A voice hath been heard on high, lamentation and mourning and weeping.* (Jer. xxi., 15.) Rome and her senate, not less than the Church and her children, have mourned the loss of a common father; and the city has witnessed an entire population thronging around the holy altars to supplicate the God of mercies in behalf of the departed soul. We take comfort in the hope that these suffrages have been either heard or anticipated; and that he, who was the representative of Jesus Christ upon the earth, has been associated to the company of his holy predecessors in heaven. In this consoling view of the subject, we may see matter of congratulation as well as of condolence. The victory of death is the triumph of religion. And on the very tomb of her

Pontiff, the Church, "as a giant," will be seen to "refresh her race," and renew her ancient charter of immortality. Thus whilst kings and dynasties tumble around her, and earthly thrones totter in the upheaving of nations, she heeds not the volcano that spreads desolation abroad; but safe on that *rock*, on which her divine architect placed her, she smiles at the "Gentiles' rage, and the vain devices of the people;" and as fast as her chiefs drop into the grave, she beholds another length added to that chain of apostolical succession, the first link of which descended from heaven, and the last link of which shall be rivetted there. These, my brethren, are topics of profitable reflection; but they have probably suggested themselves as forcibly to your minds, as they produced, I acknowledge, a deep impression upon mine. Moreover, it is not my province to dwell upon them *officially;* I glance only at the passing arguments of our common mortality to remind each one here present to "take order to his own house," and to exhort you more earnestly with the Baptist in the Gospel: "to prepare the way of the Lord, and make straight his paths."

He wrote a very amusing letter to the Editor of the *Catholic Magazine*, who was his old and valued friend, Rev. T. M. McDonnell, which appeared in the April number of that periodical, and which is too rich to be withheld from the reader:—

"The Romans appear uniformly to be pleased with and attached to their Government. Rome is at this time, leaving the noise of the Carnival, the quietest place in Europe. I wonder that the English papers have not fabricated a conspiracy out of a good practical joke that was played by some wags upon the Cardinals towards the close of the Conclave. I suppose the fellows thought that if there was no Pope there would be no Carnival, and were therefore desirous of hastening their deliberations. They accordingly contrived to lay in some part of the premises two large fire balls with a train so calculated as to burn half an hour before explosion. About half-past nine at night these balls burst with a tremendous explosion. The Cardinals were all roused. The alarm bell rung, the drums beat to arms, troopers buckled on their cuirasses, Swiss guards sallied forth in slashed woollens and red stockings. There you might see the Knave of Clubs, the King of Hearts, and, the Jack of Trumps trotting through the courts and purlieus of the Palace, feeling with one hand if their heads were on their shoulders, and grasping their halberds with the other, to strike down the villainous Guy Fawkes with his lanthorn and matches. They found, however, no Guy Fawkes; but they found the smoking tinder, that indicated squibs and crackers. Whereat they being satisfied, and having taken due cognisance of the same, the senator and all his men, having marched up the hill, marched back again!! And so ends my epic and my letter."

Soon after the election of Pope Gregory XVI., which took place on the Feast of the Purification of the B. V. Mary, the revolutionary spirit began to appear in Italy, first at Modena, then at Bologna, and next at Petaro and Sinigaglia, which drew forth an early proclamation from the new Pope on the 9th of February. This revolutionary movement originated in a few of the higher classes, and the lawyers, but

"Some watchword for the fight
Must vindicate the wrong, and warp the right,
Religion—freedom—vengeance—what you will,
A word's enough to raise mankind to kill;
Some factious phrase by cunning caught and spread,
That guilt may reign, and wolves and worms be fed!"
Lara. Canto II.

Dr. Weedall naturally began to feel uneasy at the state of affairs, and if his mind was not at ease, his health was not likely to mend, but to be further endangered. Mr. Foley, therefore, wrote to him to invite him to return. But in a short time the revolutionary movements were at an end, and lawful authority was restored in the Papal States. Meantime, Dr. Weedall made a journey to Naples, principally with a view to witness the prodigy of the liquefaction of the sacred blood of St. Januarius, which, to use his own words, "has been the subject of such idle declamation among Protestant travellers, and of unworthy subterfuge with many Catholic writers." He was present on the feast of the translation of the relics of St. Januarius, which is kept on the first Sunday of May. He was in the sanctuary, and so close to the sacred phial, that he could not have seen it more distinctly if he had held it in his own hand. He witnessed the liquefaction of the sacred blood in the evening before the feast, again on the morning of the feast, and a third time on the next day, Monday. The reader must be referred to Dr. Weedall's beautiful letter, which appeared in the July number of the *Catholic Magazine* for a long and circumstantial account of all the particulars of these prodigies, which he witnessed, and which he there details in the clearest manner, and supports with the strongest arguments.

Nevertheless his admirable letter was destined to be the subject of " unworthy subterfuge" from a Catholic writer of great learning and distinction, who raised objections to it in a letter in the same Magazine, signed H. Y., and suggested the possibility of its being a mere physical occurrence in accordance with the known laws of nature. This brought forth other writers on both sides, and the controversy was kept up in several numbers of the Magazine, which Dr. Weedall had no opportunity of seeing till his return to England. As soon after that, however, as he could find leisure, he wrote a very long argumentative letter in the number for March, 1832, answering clearly and carefully all the difficulties which the several opponents had suggested, and supporting his answers with abundant testimonies from most valuable authorities. Whoever is desirous of sifting this question thoroughly, will find it very temperately argued, and learnedly treated, in this elegant and elaborate letter of Dr. Weedall.

At the end of August, 1831, Mr. Foley left Oscott, and returned to his mission at Northampton. The Rev. Robert Richmond acted as President in the interval before the return of Dr. Weedall, who arrived on the 18th of November, in renovated health, and good spirits, and resumed his presidentship to the great joy of the whole college. He was now forty-three years old, in the prime of life, and much better in health than he had been for several years. Still it must not be inferred that he was entirely free from his chronic and constitutional ailments; but he was in comparative ease with regard to them. He resumed his former habits with his wonted energy and activity, and what time he could spare from the internal administration of the college, he devoted as before to the care of the farm, thereby combining useful occupation with necessary exercise and relaxation.

The college was again blessed with his eloquent and impressive preaching; and with his usual zeal and readiness to oblige any of his clerical friends, he preached on particular occasions in the neighbourhood. Thus he delivered one of his most powerful and convincing sermons, *On the Catholic Church as the infallible guide to truth and salvation*, at the opening of the new chapel at West Bromwich, November 21st, 1832. This edifice had been raised at the expense of the Hon. and Rev. George Spencer, who was appointed to the pastoral care of this infant mission. DR. WEEDALL'S sermon had been first preached at the consecration of Bishop Walsh in 1825, as mentioned in Chapter Ninth, where some extracts and an account of its contents have been given.

On the 1st of May, in the following year, 1833, the new Catholic Church at Grantham was opened, which had been built at the sole expense of the Rev. T. P. Tempest. On this occasion, DR. WEEDALL delivered a very fine argumentative discourse to a numerous and respectable congregation, on the mystery of the Blessed Trinity. He had preached this first at Oscott, in the year of his ordination to the priesthood, and also later on at Stafford, on occasion of the opening of a new organ. It is a noble composition, worthy of its profound and mysterious subject; and any attempt to analyse it here would only do injustice to its impressive character and masterly eloquence.

On Sunday, the 25th of August, 1833, a pastoral was read in all the churches and chapels of the Midland District from the Bishop, Dr. Walsh, showing the necessity of collections for the extension of our holy religion and the support of its ministers. As it is known to have been written by Dr. WEEDALL, at the request and in the name of the Bishop, it claims a notice in this biography. It is an admirable example of his elegant, concise, and persuasive style. After acknowledging with gratitude the impulse given to religion by Dr. Milner, and the cordial co-operation of the clergy and laity in the good work, the pastoral proceeds:—

"We do not announce to you, beloved children, that these several sources are dried up. On the contrary, we believe that they will continue to flow as they have usually flowed. But streamlets cannot saturate a desert; neither can the benevolence of comparatively a few individuals supply the increasing wants of increasing congregations; neither would it be reasonable to calculate upon it; as unreasonable to expect it from the rich alone, as it would be unjust to look for it from the poor alone..........

"But...beloved children, we must remodel our system, and adopt some plan of contribution which shall be both more efficient and less invidious than the one which has usually been adopted. We cannot sufficiently express to you the grief of our hearts to see our beloved clergy forced to quit their rising flocks for weeks and months to roam over the country in search of means to erect a house, a school, a chapel; encountering difficulties unsuited to their habits, rebukes ill-befitting their character, impairing their health, returning, perhaps, with just sufficient to commit them to the work, and not sufficient to clear the undertaking, the seeds of bitterness thus thickly sown, and many years of their valuable lives oppressed with pecuniary embarrassments, anxiety, and secular trouble."

The pastoral then developes a plan for monthly collections, which was found easy and practical, and very effective; and which would always be steadily productive of immense advantage, if pursued regularly and perseveringly. Thus were the talents of DR. WEEDALL turned to profit in a variety of ways, as well by his own zeal and ingenuity, as by the judicious requisition of his ecclesiastical superior.

The reader will not be wearied with the records of so many openings of chapels, because they afford opportunities of exhibiting various examples of that pulpit eloquence for which the subject of this biography was so distinguished. On the 11th of September, 1834, was opened the chapel of the Holy Trinity, at Bilston, which owed its erection mainly to the awful scourge of cholera, which had depopulated whole streets in that densely crowded town, and had been followed by numerous conversions, in consequence of the heroic self-devotion of the Catholic clergy of the neighbourhood, who zealously gave their labours among the sick and dying at the hazard of their lives. The consequence was that money was liberally subscribed, and a spacious chapel speedily erected, of which the zealous and respected Rev. Thomas Sing, now Canon of Nottingham, was the pastor. DR. WEEDALL preached at the opening his beautiful sermon

On the substraction of Grace, which he had delivered at the Nottingham opening already described, but he prefaced it with this new and somewhat startling exordium:—

"*And some saying of the temple, that it was adorned with goodly stones and gifts, he said: These things which you see, the days will come, in which there shall not be left a stone upon a stone that shall not be thrown down.* St. Luke xxi., 5, 6.

"These may seem melancholy words with which to greet you on this joyful occasion, and they would really be melancholy words, if their applicability were literally and clearly established. But my meaning is not so. I stand forth no prophet of evil. Rather I prognosticate from this eventful day the accession of glory to God, of peace and charity and good will to men. When I refer to the second temple therefore, I refer to it not as the parallel of our own, either in its goodly form, or its doleful destiny. Our little unpretending edifice has been raised by exertions too pure and holy, and will be served, I am sure, by a zeal too ardent and too devoted, that I should predict its speedy dissolution. Rather may I predict, if I rightly read the augury, that as long as its perishable materials may be calculated to endure, so long will it stand the guide of the wandering Christian, the light to the erring soul, the asylum of the wayfaring penitent, the comfort of the poor man when he has none to befriend him, the balm and refreshment of many a bleeding heart.

"Then why have I commenced in a tone of sadness, and why have I selected the painful scene which the words of my text represent? It is because I consider this building as a building of mercy, because I consider these days as days of visitation, days in which graces indeed are offered to many, but in which also by many those graces will be rejected; and hence, my beloved brethren, as the rejection of grace forms a fearful infidelity, and involves a possibility of that grace being never again presented, I have thought it by no means inappropriate to the object of our meeting to lay before you this most mysterious and most awful feature in the supernatural economy of God's providence, namely,—the distribution and substraction of grace."

On September 23rd, on occasion of the re-opening of the chapel at Lichfield, enlarged and renewed in the Gothic style by great exertions on the part of the Rev. John Kirk, so long its respected pastor, DR. WEEDALL sung the High Mass, *coram pontifice*, the Rt. Rev. Dr. Walsh attending, with about twenty priests, and a lucid, argumentative, and pathetic sermon being preached by the Rev. T. M. McDonnell on the Real Presence and the Mass.

In the following week, on the 21st of October, DR. WEEDALL preached at the opening of the new chapel of the Holy Trinity at Sutton Coldfield, near the college. He delivered the grand sermon on the mystery of the Blessed Trinity, which he had preached at Grantham, of which mention has been made in the present Chapter.

CHAPTER XII.

Necessity of a New College—The Building Commenced—Pastoral for Collections Written by Dr. Weedall—His Active Superintendence of the New Building—First Stone of the New Chapel Laid—Bishop Walsh's Journey to Rome—Circular of Dr. Weedall as V. G. on the New Marriage Act—Blessing of the Chapel Bell—Dr. Weedall's Address on the Occasion—Consecration and Opening of the New Chapel—Dr. Weedall's Sermon on the Day of Opening.

The reader will remember that Dr. Weedall, when installed as Doctor of Divinity, protested fervently that his services and his life were dedicated to the Church. He was now called upon to devote them in a way more decided than ever. The college under his able presidentship had gone on steadily increasing in numbers and reputation; and it had become quite necessary to provide more extensive accommodation for its members, as well as increased means for the developement of the various branches of religious and secular education. The first idea entertained was to purchase some large mansion sufficiently commodious, with a certain quantity of land attached. With this view Dr. Weedall and Mr. Foley had actually gone together to examine a house and estate in Leicestershire, which had long been offered for sale. It would have been difficult, however, to find any building suitable for a large collegiate establishment, which had not been built for some such purpose; and, therefore, it was considered more desirable to build, if possible, a new college. It happened most opportunely that a farm was for sale at this time on Sutton Coldfield, only two miles from the college. This was purchased, and steps were immediately taken to procure contributions for erecting a new college on a scale not merely proportioned to the actual wants of the existing establishment, but calculated for its future developement and expansion.

The Rev. Jno. Kirk, of Lichfield, who well understood the requisites for a college and seminary, and took the most lively interest in the establishment at Oscott, had, in concert with Mr. Potter, an architect at Lichfield, prepared a regular plan for the erection of a new college. He brought this to Oscott, and so powerfully urged its suitableness, that the Bishop and Dr. WEEDALL, with the other superiors, were induced to adopt his plan, and the project was at once set on foot with the Bishop's authority. This was early in the year 1835; when a statement was extensively circulated by the Bishop, detailing the reasons for the proposed new building, and explaining the plan for its erection. The indispensable necessity for a new college had been represented to the clergy by Bishop Walsh, at their annual meeting at Sedgley Park, and by them received very cordially. Contributions soon began to flow in from all quarters, and the building was commenced under the happiest auspices. So much was the want of accommodation felt at the old college, that the works of the new building were pushed forward with the greatest energy and activity. Thus by the month of October, the edifice had proceeded as far as the top of the oriel window in the centre tower; one side of the quadrangle had its timbers up for the roof, and the other was ready.

The Lenten Pastoral of the year following, 1836, was written in the Bishop's name by Dr. Weedall, and was chiefly an earnest appeal to the faithful in behalf of the new college. The following extract will be read with interest:—

"To that admirable bishop, the late Right Rev. Dr. Milner, to his energy, influence, charity, and zeal, we are indebted for the only seminary we at present possess. Small as it is, and unequal to the growing wants of the district, you know, beloved children, how efficient it has generally been in the cause of religion, and how many indefatigable missioners it has sent forth among you. We trust that the spirit of its founder is still upon it; that his piety animates its members, and that there lives within its enclosure a precious germ, which, when transplanted to a more favourable spot, will develope its latent virtues, and fill the land with holy pastors, to feed and extend the fold of Christ.

"But then our hopes rest on its removal. This, policy and prudence suggest, and religion demands. It is too straitened in its present position to answer the purposes of its original destination; and though in another character the house may be made serviceable to religion, it is impossible to continue it any longer as the Seminary of the District. We earnestly therefore commend our new undertaking to your pious benevolence. But in making this appeal, beloved children, we deprecate the odium which often unjustly attaches to such applications. We fain would hope that the ground on which we stand is too high to be subject to unworthy imputation. In a work of such magnitude, and of such vast importance to religion, great means are assuredly required. But we do not look for assistance commensurate with the entire undertaking; nor do we ask anything from others until we have heavily taxed our own resources, and brought up the building to that point, when the possibility of completing it becomes as obvious, as its utility and necessity have long been clear."

The collections proved highly satisfactory; but a very large sum was requisite for so great an undertaking, and therefore applications were perseveringly made in all directions for aid, which, it is gratifying to record, were in general very liberally answered. DR. WEEDALL gave himself heart and soul to the building. He knew the vastness and the importance of the undertaking, and how much its success must depend upon his own untiring superintendence. He was every day on the spot, examining the works, looking after the workmen, directing and advising, and leaving no part of the edifice deprived of his careful attention. He took great delight in conducting his friends over the building: it was amusing to see how nimbly he trotted about, and with what agility and self-possession he would step over the rafters, where his visitors often could not venture to walk at all. He had grown perfectly familiar with ladders and narrow timbers, and felt no dizziness, nor sense of danger. He understood the most minute details of the extensive erection; and he explained them, and adverted to the progress made, with artistic precision and perfect enthusiasm. Those who have at any time been engaged in large buildings, and know how much such works depend for proper execution on constant supervision, will best appreciate all this devoted attention on the part of Dr. WEEDALL, and understand how much the new college was indebted to his care, and zeal, and assiduity.

In the spring of 1836, the building was so far advanced, that it was time to commence the chapel of the new college. Accordingly the first stone of it was laid with great solemnity, and strictly in accordance with the form prescribed in the ritual, by Bishop Walsh on the 28th of April. He was attended by about thirty priests, and the Rev. T. M. McDonnell, by desire of the Bishop, delivered a very beautiful and appropriate address on the occasion, from Apocalypse xxi., 3 : *I heard a great voice from the throne, saying: Behold the tabernacle of God with men, and he shall dwell with them.*

For want of sufficient accommodation in the old college, it was resolved this year to hold the Midsummer Exhibition in a room of the new building which was intended for the library. The experiment, it was considered, would also serve to augment the interest felt in the advancement of the new edifice. The library was accordingly fitted up temporarily with windows for the occasion, and decorated very tastefully with laurels and floral devices. The day was unfortunately one of almost incessant rain; but the company nevertheless was very numerous, nearly 200; the attendance, no doubt, being increased by the novelty of the occasion.

In the following year, 1837, Bishop Walsh left England in April, in company with Bishop Griffiths, the Vicar Apostolic of the London District, on a journey to Rome. DR. WEEDALL in the meantime had charge of the District, as Vicar General, and in that character issued, on the 22nd of June, an important document in consequence of the New Act of Parliament legalising Catholic Marriages under certain regulations. In the absence of any particular instructions from the Bishop, but "knowing sufficiently his general sentiments," as he observed, he adopted as the rule for the Midland District, "the judicious views and regulations" of Dr. Baines, the Vicar Apostolic of the Western District, and these he set forth officially in a circular letter to the clergy of the Midland District. The regulations need not here be repeated, as they have long been familiarly known and acted upon; but it may be well to note the following injunctions as of great consequence:— *First*, that the declarations required to be made by the parties at their marriage must be made *after* the essential forms of the ritual have been gone through; and *Secondly*, that the clergy are desired strongly to discourage the practice of being married in Protestant churches, and are directed to refuse the Catholic rite to any who have unnecessarily done so, as, indeed, after the new Act of Parliament, it can seldom or never be necessary. These regulations, thus authoritatively promulgated, became obligatory throughout the Midland District.

The old college was now most inconveniently crowded, so that it became necessary to put up beds in the Exhibition Room. The Exhibition at Midsummer was held, as in the preceding year, in a room in the new building prepared for the occasion, on the 20th of June, and rather more crowded with company than was desirable or agreeable. It had been hoped that the new college might be entered upon in the ensuing August, after the vacation; but this was found impracticable, and expectation now rested upon October. However, as it usually happens in similar cases, this hope was also disappointed, and the building could not be got ready for occupation till the next year, 1838.

On the 18th of the April following, the solemn ceremony took place of blessing the great bell for the college chapel, and Dr. Weedall delivered a most interesting discourse on the occasion, explanatory of the "doctrine and meaning of the Catholic Church in consecrating bells for her solemn service," on the 18th of that month. In the course of it he said:—

"In proportion as our eventful building approaches to completion, does religion claim it as her own, and consecrate it, with all its appurtenances, to her holy and immortal purposes. She fixed her seal upon its portal as it rose out of the earth.
RELIGIONI AC BONIS ARTIBUS.

"She watered its trenches with her holy lustrations, and impressed the sign of faith on its corner stone. She now invites us to another beautiful office fraught with lofty meaning, and thrilling devotion, in the solemn benediction of that instrument which will constitute a main feature, and perform an important part in the sacred worship of Almighty God, and will bespeak the assiduous attendance and devotion of all the inmates of the college.

* * * * * *

"The Bell has long been considered by the Church, in point of *material*, as the noblest herald in her service, as the trumpet to summon her children to their holy duties, to admonish them to lift up their hearts to God, to bow down their heads, to adore his awful mysteries, to bless his holy name, to implore his help in their necessities, and to pray for the living and the dead. In the sublime language of her Liturgy, which the Bishop will recite in her name, she prays that ' He who stilled by his voice the troubled sea, would vouchsafe to rise up to the help of his people; that he would shed upon this instrument the dews of his grace, that he would give a virtue to its sound that should scare away the enemy, and strengthen the faith of his Christian people. That as David's harp drew down the holy spirit, and as the thunder of the Lord thundered on the adversaries when Samuel offered up the holocaust of the Lamb, so when the sound of this metal shall move upon the air, that troops of Angels may form around the Church, and guard her believing children with an everlasting protection.' These are the benefits, spiritual and temporal, which the Church prays for and hopes to receive, not from the Bell itself, not from the *sounding Brass*, or *tinkling Cymbal*, but, on occasion of its use, from Him who employs the humblest instruments in the performance of his greatest mercies.

* * * * * *

"And this, dear Christians, and you my respected brethren and beloved friends who are to form the future inmates of this establishment, this is the great lesson which the Bell is intended frequently to preach to us.—It will break in upon our occupations, whether serious or gay, whether lawful or unlawful.—Like the voice of Christ to Martha, it will remind us of the inutility of much that we are doing, perhaps even of its sinfulness.—It will discourse, wisely and forcibly, of the value of the soul, and of the importance of attending to its salvation; of the shortness of time and the awful length of eternity.—It will sound like the solemn warnings of the last trumpet, and teach us to prepare whilst preparation is practicable. It will entone the Angelical Salutation three times each day, and bid us bend our heads, and humble our hearts in the adoration of the adorable mystery of the Incarnation. It will regulate a variety of duties, as its ancient inscription purports,

  Laudo Deum verum. Plebem voco. Congrego Clerum.
  Defunctos ploro. Pestem fugo. Festa decoro.

It will summon us to prayer, morning and evening; it will notify in deeper tones the celebration of the awful mysteries. It will remind us of the duty of praying for the dead, it will encourage us to pray in seasons of danger, it will multiply its admonitions on our holy sabbaths, and give a cheerful solemnity to the days consecrated to a more particular worship. And oh! if a good God shall vouchsafe to listen to the prayers of the Church, and to give his additional blessing to that which will, this day, be solemnly invoked, how may we hope to see piety increase and religion flourish amongst us. Prayer and praise drawn sweetly from the mouths of children,—seeds of virtue planted and sheltered,—virtuous habits formed,—grovelling minds detached from vice, and holy thoughts engendered,—hearts disengaged from earthly things and carried forward in advance to heaven, *until we enter the sanctuary of God, and understand concerning our latter end.*

"These lessons are involved in the present ceremony, and these are the blessings which the Church implores. May these lessons be impressed, and these blessings imparted. In the name of the Father, and of the Son, and of the Holy Ghost. Amen."

At length all was ready for the consecration and solemn opening of the chapel of the new college. On Tuesday, the 29th of May, 1838, the long and mysterious ceremony of consecration began at about seven o'clock in the morning, and it was only ten minutes to three in the afternoon when the High Mass and ceremonial was concluded. Bishop Walsh consecrated the chapel, and, after a most fatiguing ceremonial of upwards of seven hours duration, that good patient man quietly owned that his back wanted a little ease!

The great day, however, was the following Thursday, May 31st, when the chapel was opened with a very grand and imposing ceremonial. Bishop Walsh celebrated a pontifical High Mass, with DR. WEEDALL as assistant priest, the Rev. John Moore as deacon, and Rev. J. Nickolds as subdeacon. Bishop Briggs, of the Northern District, and Bishop Baines, of the Western, were present in pontificals, and added dignity and splendour to the ceremonial. There were about 90 priests present, of whom 68 walked in the procession, in surplices and clerical caps. There were about 550 persons in the body of the chapel. On such an occasion, no preacher could have been thought of but DR. WEEDALL; and he delivered a most beautiful discourse *On the origin, object, and influence of ecclesiastical seminaries,* from which the following passages cannot fail to delight the reader.

"Then rose up the chief of the fathers of Juda and Benjamin, and the priests, and the Levites, and every one whose spirit God had raised up, to go up to build the temple of the Lord which was in Jerusalem. And the children of Israel, the priests, and the Levites, and the rest of the children of the captivity, kept the dedication of the house of God with joy. For the Lord had made them joyful, and had turned the heart of the king to them, that he should help their hands in the work of the house of the Lord the God of Israel.—Esdras, c. i., v. 5, and c. vi., v.v. 16, 22.

"My lords, my respected brethren, beloved Christians, and friends in Jesus Christ.

"Let it not be deemed that I attach undue importance to the circumstances under which we this day assemble, if I claim for myself and for many here about me a more than ordinary share of that deep feeling and exuberance of gladness which ran through the hearts of happy Juda on the joyful occasion to which my text refers. Neither let me be considered as dealing too freely with holy thoughts and divine suggestions, if I venture to see something more than human counsels and worldly considerations in the origin, and progress, and completion of this ecclesiastical establishment; and if I attribute its success, a success beyond our humble expectations, to a divine blessing manifested, not obscurely nor scantily, towards a work which has been undertaken exclusively for His glory; and if I assimilate the general joy of this day to that recorded of Juda and Benjamin, when *the priests stood in their ornaments with trumpets, and the Levites, the sons of Asaph, with cymbals.......And they sang together hymns and praises to the Lord, because he is good, because his mercy endureth for ever towards Israel.......And the people shouted with a great shout ......and the voice was heard afar off. For the Lord had made them joyful, and had turned the heart of the king to them, that he should help their hands in the work of the house of the Lord the God of Israel.*[*]

[*] 1 Esdras, c. III., v. 10, et seq.

CHAPTER TWELFTH.

"And truly, my brethren, this day will form a joyful epoch in the history of our little Church. Just emerging from a bondage more protracted than was that of Juda, a bondage in the land of our nativity, which gave a goodly Church to desolation, but refined her purer elements, and whilst it transferred her inheritance to aliens, invigorated the faith of her children, and transmitted holy martyrs and confessors to heaven; just emerging from such a period on which the eye can look back with tranquility, because it can recognise a wholesome dispensation of Divine Providence acting upon human ignorance, which we fain would, in part, believe to have been excusable: just emerging from such a period, the timid members of our ancient Church have as yet but ventured to steal abroad by night *through the gate of the valley and the gate of the fountain*, to explore *the desolate sepulchres of their fathers*, and *to view the wall of Jerusalem which was broken down, and the gates which were consumed by fire*.* Scarcely have they yet assumed the noble bearing of Juda's illustrious leader, and encouraged one another in the words of Nehemias——*Come let us build up the walls of Jerusalem, and let us be no longer a reproach.......For the hand of our God is good with us.......He helpeth us, and we are his servants.*†

"But this feeling is propagating amongst us. A feeling of *sympathy* in the abject state of the Church of our Fathers, and of *shame* that it contrasts so unfavourably with the ease and affluence which Catholics have been given to enjoy. And may not we without offence indulge the joyous emotion, and felicitate ourselves and the Catholics of this district, on the humble portion of good which the divine blessing has enabled us to achieve, and the impulse which this building is calculated to give to our holy Religion, a Religion which is identified with all that is venerable and ancient in the country; with all that is true in faith and morals; with all that is sound in principle and politics; with all that is beautiful in art, and science, and

* 2 ESDRAS, c. II., v. 13.   † IB., c. II., v. 17.

philosophy; with all that is honourable, and just, and becoming in the ethics of life; with all that supports the social system, and prepares the soul for an eternal one; which works out pre-eminently the glory of God, and peace, and charity, and good-will to men."

After this brilliant exordium, followed by a striking application of the text to the circumstances of the removal of the college to the new building, the preacher proceeds thus eloquently to detail the peculiar objects of the Seminary:—

"Now this place is destined to become the well-spring of Catholicity, the cradle of faith and ecclesiastical discipline. And if piety has presided at its foundation, and Religion been proclaimed predominant; if knowledge and science have enlisted as her handmaids, and taste and judgment have contributed their counsels; if a system has been planned, and that system be hereafter pursued, which shall give the highest cultivation to the mind, the utmost skill in science and literature, yet so as to make all subservient to piety, and the wholesome discipline of the heart; if its moral atmosphere be kept as pure as the air of Heaven which invests it; and the frivolity and dissipation of life be as carefully excluded from its precincts as the world itself is shut out from its peaceful solitude;—if, whilst its halls and its cloisters invite to study, its liveliest interests and importance be made to concentrate in its Chapel;— if the solemn service of the Church be performed with dignity, and her beautiful ceremonies illustrated by precision, modesty, and devotion,—if humility and poverty of spirit characterise its inmates, and their only riches consist in the splendour of God's house, and in the adornment of their own souls by virtue and learning,—then will you acknowledge that we shall have raised a building calculated to work a marvellous effect upon Catholicity in this district; then will the character of the priest be exalted, and his efficiency be extended in the land;—then will

Catholic education be placed upon its proper basis, religion will be diffused, and the blessings of the true faith widely disseminated around us. Then *glorious things* may be *said of thee*, as of Sion the *city of God. Gloriosa dicta sunt de te, civitas Dei.* That *this man, and that that man were born in her. Homo et homo natus est in ea, et ipse fundavit eam altissimus.* And that a residence in thee may be a diffusion of general joy. *Sicut latantium omnium habitatio in te.**

He thus briefly, but graphically concentrates the primitive preparation for the Christian ministry :—

"For the first three hundred years of her eventful career, no systematic preparation, indeed, could be made for the sacred ministry. Her theology was *to die*, rather than *to dispute*. Her seminaries were the solitude of the desert, the catacombs, the caverns of the earth. The mere profession of christianity was evidence of sincerity. Priests and bishops were either confessors or martyrs, and saint and christian were convertible terms."

After dwelling with nervous eloquence on the training of the Apostles by our Lord himself, the institution first of *Regular Clerks,* and then of ecclesiastical Seminaries, he thus feelingly alludes to that established by St. Gregory the Great :—

"With special veneration, both as Catholics and as Englishmen, should we commemorate the Seminary established in his own palace by that illustrious patrician and pontiff, St. Gregory the Great, to whose pious sympathy and unwearied zeal our Saxon ancestors were indebted for their christianity, and with christianity, for their civilisation, happiness, and glory. With what enthusiastic gratitude does the Catholic pilgrim, when he ascends in Rome the Monte Celio, where stood the noble mansion of the Apostle of England,—whose venerable figure is warmly

* Ps. LXXXVI.

pourtrayed over our altar to be a perpetual memorial of his zeal, and of our obligations,—with what enthusiasm as he ascends, does he kiss the steps and sacred threshold over which have trod the feet of those holy men who came forth, at his bidding, to carry hither the glad tidings of salvation,—a St. Augustine, a St. Mellitus, a St. Justus, a St. Lawrence, a St. Paulinus;—and how earnestly, though feebly, when that happiness was mine, did I pray that our own Seminary might propagate such men to revive the piety and religion of our misguided countrymen."

He goes on in a sustained flow of rich imagery and felicitous expression, to show the importance of Ecclesiastical Seminaries; detailing their obligations, maxims, and advantages; and thus concludes his brilliant oration:—

"The best wishes of the Church will be realised, the expectations of the best friends of religion will be fulfilled, Catholicity will revive and re-blossom in our District, and we may live to see accomplished the warm wishes of the holy Abbot of Clairvaux, *Quis mihi det videre Ecclesiam Dei mei in diebus meis, sicut in diebus antiquis!* Who will give me to see our English Church, renovated as in the days of old, the days of her faith and fervour! May God give us to see it in our generation; may he give to our beloved Bishop to see it, before his eyes grow dim, *before the silver cord is broken, and the dust return to its earth.** May He grant this grace to his aged clergy, and this consolation to his chosen people! From the throne of his sanctuary *may He look down and see, and visit this vineyard and perfect the same which his right hand hath planted!*† He has brought it out of *Egypt a young and a tender one,* may he make it the vineyard of his election! May he train up within it the choicest vines, may he water them with his abundant graces, and deposit within these walls so largely of his

* ECCLE. XII., 6.   † Ps. LXXIX., 15.

spirit, that we may see the utmost fulfilment of his recorded promise, *Sacerdotes ejus induam salutari, et sancti ejus exultatione exultabunt*,* when all her priests shall be clothed with sanctity, and the faithful, under their guidance, shall multiply and rejoice. In the name of the Father, and of the Son, and of the Holy Ghost. Amen."

On the Saturday following, being the 2nd of June, and Whitsun Eve, the whole of the college buildings were solemnly blessed and sprinkled with Holy Water, with fervent invocations of the Divine favour and protection upon their future inmates and undertakings, preparatory to the occupation of the house, which was now gradually proceeded with.

* Ps. cxxxi., 16.

CHAPTER XIII.

FIRST PROCESSION OF CORPUS CHRISTI AT THE NEW COLLEGE—DR. WEEDALL'S SERMON ON THE OCCASION—BISHOP MILNER'S SUPPOSED VISION IN DR. NEWMAN'S SERMON—SITUATION OF THE NEW BUILDING—THE "BEGGAR'S BUSH"—DR. WEEDALL'S NEW ARRANGEMENTS—SERMON ON THE ASSUMPTION—STATE OF THE OLD COLLEGE—MR. FOLEY OPENS IT AS A PREPARATORY SCHOOL—THE MARINI LIBRARY—THE COLLEGE ASSOCIATED TO THE LONDON UNIVERSITY—PRESENTS TO THE COLLEGE—ITS PROSPERITY AND FAIR PROSPECTS.

THE new College of St. Mary was now opened and entered; and eager to offer the tribute of grateful hearts for the accomplishment of the great work, the festival of Corpus Christi, which occurred a fortnight after the opening, was celebrated with the utmost splendour which all the resources of the college could command, and with a magnificent procession of the adorable Sacrament. DR. WEEDALL, always ready, and always equal to every occasion, however important, delivered another splendid sermon on the festival and procession of this great solemnity, which he thus beautifully introduced:—

"*Is it a credible thing that God should dwell with men on the earth?*" 2 Par. vi., 18.

"My Christian brethren,

"The more than usual length of the peculiar ceremony of this day, and our general state of unpreparedness will forbid me to say much to you, on this otherwise splendid occasion. But if it is inconvenient to say much, it is unnecessary also. For I address myself to those who will enter into the spirit of my text, who will share in the humble astonishment and grateful admiration of King Solomon, when he poured out his enraptured soul in the newly erected sanctuary of his God. *Is it then a credible thing that God should dwell with men on the earth?* We ask it not in incredulity, we ask it not in diffidence, but we ask it in the language of humble expostulation, in the deep conviction of our great unworthiness. If Solomon felt it a condescension which man could not adequately acknowledge, that the great God of Heaven should consent to dwell with men, and to manifest his presence in the temple he had just completed, how warm should be our devotion, how deep our gratitude, how intense our feelings in meditating upon the wonderful mystery which occupies the Church this day. In contemplating the nearer approach, the more familiar union, the permanent residence, the sweet accessibility which our God and Redeemer accomplishes amongst us this day by a concentration of all his mercies and wonders in the adorable Sacrament of the Altar.—*Memoriam fecit mirabilium suorum misericors et miserator Dominus, escam dedit timentibus se.* Ps. cx., 4.

"If the throne of his glory stands encircled in heaven by myriads and myriads of blessed spirits, whose felicity it is to fall prostrate before Him, to cast their crowns and their sceptres at his feet, how assiduously should we crowd around the throne of his mercy, which faith proclaims this day on the Catholic altar, and consecrate our hearts and our voices in one united chorus of *benediction, and honour, and glory, and power to Him who sitteth on the throne and to the Lamb. For the Lamb that was slain is worthy to receive power, divinity, and wisdom, and strength, and honour, and glory, and benediction, for ever and ever.* Amen.

It was an auspicious day for St. Mary's College, when she was established in the new and spacious edifice erected with so much labour, and by the willing contributions and active exertions of so many of her loving children, friends, and admirers. It was a grand day of satisfaction to him, whose mind had principally planned it, whose eye and hand had directed and aided its progress, and to whose unwearied energies the new edifice was chiefly indebted for its present state of completeness. But what would have been the joy of its first founder, the illustrious MILNER, had he been living, to witness this splendid consummation of his own humble commencement! Beautifully did Dr. Newman trace out for him an imaginary vision, in his exquisite Sermon before the assembled Fathers, holding in this very college chapel the first Provincial Council in England, since the subversion of the Church of our forefathers three centuries before:—

"What would have been the feelings of that venerable man, the champion of God's ark in an evil time, could *he* have lived to see this day? It is almost presumptuous for one who knew him not, to draw pictures about him, and his thoughts, and his friends, some of whom are even here present; yet am I wrong in fancying that a day such as this, in which we stand, would have seemed to him a dream, or if he prophesied of it, to his hearers nothing but a mockery? Say that one time, rapt in spirit, he had reached forward to the future, and that his mortal eye had wandered from that lowly chapel in the valley which had been for centuries in the possession of Catholics, to the neighbouring height, then waste and solitary. And let him say to those about him,—' I see a bleak mount, looking upon an open country, over against that huge town, to whose inhabitants Catholicism is of so little account. I see the ground marked out, and an ample enclosure made; and plantations are rising there, clothing and circling in the space. And there on that high spot, far from the haunts of men, yet in the very centre of the island, a large edifice, or rather pile of edifices, appears, with many fronts and courts, and long cloisters and corridors, and story upon story.' And there it rises under the invocation of the same sweet and powerful Name, which has been our strength and consolation in the valley."

Go, reader, and pursue the thrilling continuation in the published sermon, which goes on to picture the truly grand and marvellous fact of a Provincial Synod held in all its gorgeous splendour and overpowering solemnity in this very college, built on what in MILNER's days, and long after, was but a wide and dreary waste. There was hardly for miles round a human habitation; neither was there a tree to be seen, save one old unshapen thorn, commonly called the "Beggar's bush," which just served as a forlorn landmark to the traveller on his weary track across the lonely waste of Sutton Coldfield. That venerable old thorn, still stands close by the college, a marked monument of those early times, of which the few surviving old Oscotians fondly cherish the remembrance. How often have we walked to that solitary tree, and stood gazing from it over the wide waste around us; or, perhaps, taken bow and arrows thither, and shot at its aged trunk as our target! DR. WEEDALL was fond of directing his walks to that wild and dreary scene; and it will gratify the worthy and venerable author of that sermon to know that, after its delivery, DR. WEEDALL came up to his present biographer and asked him if he was not delighted with "Dr. Milner's vision," speaking of it himself with great admiration.

Dr. WEEDALL had no sooner seen the members of the college settled in their new buildings, than he proceeded to make those judicious arrangements which improved the discipline, increased the comfort, and, at the same time, secured the efficiency of the entire establishment. His own burthens had only been augmented by the transition to the new edifice. He had a larger family to regulate and provide for, and far more extensive and numerous departments to superintend. The staff of professors was of course greater, as the number of students had multiplied, and in every part of the establishment offices and duties were extended, and cares and responsibilities seriously augmented. But his spirits were buoyant, and his courage equal to the weightier charge; and though a martyr to his chronic maladies, he held on with energy and perseverance marvellous and indomitable.

He preached in the chapel of the new college, on the Feast of the Assumption of the Blessed Virgin Mary, one of his finest sermons, and in the course of it thus briefly, but sweetly, alluded to the college, happily dedicated under her holy patronage:—

"And we, beloved brethren, and inmates of this House, we are particularly dedicated to the Blessed Virgin by special obligations. Our college is called St. Mary's College. We are called Priests of St. Mary's,—Ecclesiastics of St. Mary's,—

Students of St. Mary's. Let us be zealous clients and faithful imitators of Mary." As before, he found occasional relief and recreation in going out to preach, or perform some clerical duties at a distance. Thus, on the 6th of February, in the year following, 1839, he sung the High Mass at the opening of a new Gothic chapel at Solihull, near Birmingham, designed by Mr. Pugin; on which occasion an excellent sermon was delivered by the Rev. T. M. McDonnell, of St. Peter's, Birmingham.

The old college was now deserted, and it became a question, not easy to solve, to what purpose it might be best applied. DR. WEEDALL was anxious on the subject, often went to look about the place, and had such repairs done as were necessary. After various plans and suggestions, it was determined to make it a preparatory school, in connexion with the new college; and the Rev. Wm. Foley being appointed to the mission there, removed his young pupils from Northampton to the old college, and came, for the fourth time, to reside at Oscott. He arrived February 8th, 1839, and brought with him four boys. It was natural to suppose that he would find the house emptied of furniture, and not in the best state of cleanliness, after being almost untenanted for seven months. His own account of it will amuse those who knew his peculiar vein of droll description:—

"I have said that my present home is a rough one, and so it is. I am annoyed by noisy, dirty workmen, some in the house, others out; everything—doors, locks, floors, carpets, pots, pans, gridirons, coalhods, &c., all out of order or wanting. The oven was split, and so we get our bread from the Great Hotel on the Hill; we have no casks, and so get our beer from the same. I, indeed, and most of my four boys, drink water, but some want beer, and thus I am forced to look out for that real *superfluity*. The chapel is in a sad state, and I have begun an Herculean clearance. The congregation is reduced by Sutton and the New College to a small body. I counted about thirty grown up people last Sunday, and a person whom I engaged to count two Sundays before, reckoned thirty-two adults and thirty-three children, as the poor school is still kept up. I find one alb, and that a cotton one, one surplice, and that with tawdry Jew looking frills. The vestments correspond, and so does the priest, and so do the people. I am working double tides to rectify affairs, and for three weeks have done something."

With one on the spot so active and orderly as Mr. Foley, all however was soon put into good repair, and made clean and comfortable.

The new college filled rapidly, so that at this time, February, 1839, there were 135 students, exclusive of divines. This was almost double the average number which used to be reckoned in the old college. Bishop Walsh had purchased at Rome the valuable Marini Library, and on the 28th of October he formally made a present of it to the new college. The room intended for the Exhibitions was specially fitted up to receive it; and it was resolved to call it after the venerable donor, the "Walshian" Library, a name certainly more complimentary than euphonious.

By Her Majesty's warrant of the 18th February, 1840, St. Mary's College was admitted, with Ushaw and Stonyhurst Colleges, to the privileges of the University of London; and Dr. WEEDALL issued a circular explanatory of the advantages to be derived, and exhorting parents who wished their children to avail themselves of them, to give early notice of such wishes, that the students might be directed in their studies accordingly. In acknowledgment of the royal favour, Dr. WEEDALL presented to Her Majesty, through the Marquis of Normanby, an impression in gold of the prize medal of the college, which the Queen received very graciously, and with the expression of her entire approbation of the elegant gold medal.

Meantime the new college was receiving presents from various quarters, and becoming rapidly a repository of valuable and curious works of art, and specimens of antique carvings and furniture of mediæval patterns. The munificent John, Earl of Shrewsbury, presented a large and valuable collection of 200 pictures, besides various articles of Gothic furniture, and carved figures of saints and sacred subjects. The new college was already almost as much crowded as the old one had been before. The masters were obliged to leave the refectory, and to take their meals in a separate room; and every available space was made into bed rooms.

Thus then were realised the best hopes of the sons of St. Mary's, and of her many friends and admirers scattered over the kingdom. Thus had Dr. WEEDALL accomplished a work which had long been also the ardent object of his aspirations and exertions. For to him was the merit of the successful erection and establishment of the new college pre-eminently due. It was the wonder of all who knew him, and knew how much he suffered from constitutional maladies, how he could have carried through, and splendidly completed, a work so vast in extent, so complicated in detail, and so difficult of execution. But it was done; the fancied vision of the illustrious MILNER was no "baseless fabric;" it had been fully realised, and become an accomplished fact; and St. Mary's College towered on her proud eminence, a landmark for miles around, and a stately monument of learning and piety, of science and religion. DR. WEEDALL might well hope to repose after his herculean labours, and enjoy their fruits. He might well congratulate himself on the prospect of watching the growth, and promoting the prosperity of this colony, which, under the Divine guidance and protection, he had so prosperously established in their new and enviable locality. He might well, in his dedication Sermon, make the prayer of the Psalmist his own, with reference to St. Mary's College:—

"*Vineam de Ægypto transtulisti:...et plantasti eam......*

"*Deus virtutum convertere : respice de cœlo, et vide, et visita vineam istam.*

"*Et perfice eam, quam plantavit dextera tua :............*

"*Fiat manus tua super virum dexteræ tua : et super filium hominis, quem confirmasti tibi.*

"Thou hast brought a vineyard out of Egypt.......and planted it............

"Turn again, O God of Hosts, look down from heaven and see and visit this vineyard. And perfect the same, which thy right hand hath planted............

CHAPTER THIRTEENTH.

"Let thy hand be upon the man of thy right hand; and upon the son of man, whom thou hast confirmed for thyself."*

Under his mild and judicious government, the new house prospered and flourished; it was already nearly as full of students as it had the means of accommodating, and one heard on every side, and from every reporter, that all went well at the new college. The beloved and respected president had built himself an airy nest, and was tranquilly reposing in it; but, alas! it was doomed to be in his regard only another verification of the well-known line—

"Sic vos, non vobis, nidificatis aves!"†

How truly did Dr. Newman say in his Funeral Oration: "His was an unselfish spirit, which laboured, *and then let others enter into his labours.*"

* PSALM LXXIX., 9, 15, 16, 18.

† This line may be thus rendered in English:—
Thus birds, you build your nests with curious care,
Not for yourselves: *they fall to others' share.*

CHAPTER XIV.

Dr. Weedall Meets with Severe Trials—Is Unexpectedly Appointed a Bishop—His Distress of Mind in Consequence—Determines to go to Rome to Seek a Release from the Appointment—His Farewell Address on Leaving Oscott—Stops at Lucca—Dr. Baines' Conversation with the Pope, and Success in Dr. Weedall's Behalf—He Goes to Rome—His Letters from Rome Detailing the Whole Progress of His Affair—His Memorial to Propaganda.

"Ceux qui n'ont jamais souffert," says the judicious Fenelon, " ne savent rien; ils ne connoissent ni les biens, ni les maux; ils ignorent les hommes, ils ignorent eux memes."* But so far from being a stranger to suffering, the subject of this biography had been all his life familiar with it. He had never been entirely free from torture in his head and eyes, and there had been long periods in his life when he laboured under acute pain and misery from these affections, and also from another chronic malady which was a source of continued suffering, more or less severe, and which proved fatal in the end. If to these bodily afflictions are added the severe mental anxiety and care induced

* Those who have never suffered, know nothing; they are acquainted with neither good nor evil; they are ignorant of men, they are ignorant of themselves.

by the heavy responsibility of his difficult charge, and the incessant labour inseparable from it; and if we take also into account all the solicitude, and perplexity, and arduous exertion superadded for the last years by the difficult and multifarious work incurred in the erection of the new college, we shall be tempted to think that this good man had already endured a larger portion of trials than falls to the lot of most men. But his cup was not yet full; *for God is the Judge. One he putteth down, and another he lifteth up. For in the hand of the Lord there is a cup of strong wine full of mixture.** *His servant* was *holy*, but he was to be *sanctified still*.† The gold was yet to be cast again into the crucible, that it might come forth still more purified and refined; *for gold and silver are tried in the fire, but acceptable men in the furnace of humiliation*.‡

On a sudden, then, when he beheld his grand work accomplished, and had begun to enjoy some rest from his labours, he was obliged to part from his beloved Oscott, and bid a long farewell to the spot where he had lived and laboured for six and thirty years. A greater trial could hardly be imagined. At the age of fifty-two, with all his habits formed and rooted by long experience in a college life, after all that he had done for Oscott, after all his labours and sufferings for its welfare, when he had long toiled to nurture it and foster its growth, when he had seen it gradually advance

---

* PSALM LXXIV., 8, 9. † APOCALYPSE XXII., 11.
‡ ECCLUS. II., 5.

with alternate joy and anxiety, when he had been its child first, and then its father and protector, and had at last brought it triumphantly to completion and stability, and begun to enjoy that satisfaction and repose in it which he so eminently deserved, he was required to part at once from the home of his heart, his own beloved creation and long cherished abode. He suddenly received notice from the Holy See of his nomination as Bishop of Abydos *in partibus*, and Vicar Apostolic of the new Northern District of England; for out of the four old Districts there were now to be formed eight. At the same time, the Vice-President of the college, the Rev. William Wareing, was named Bishop of Ariopolis, and Vicar Apostolic of the new Eastern District.

This announcement came upon poor DR. WEEDALL like a thunder clap: he had never had the least idea or intimation of it. As a station of honour, he had no ambition for it; as a charge of responsibility, he shrunk from it; as a post of difficulty and anxiety, he felt quite unequal to it. Well did Dr. Newman say in his funeral oration:—

"His heart was in his old work, and on his old scene of action, and his excellent judgment told him that to begin life over again in a new sphere at the age of fifty-two, was neither desirable in itself nor suited to him........ He understood also, as all his friends would understand, that his calling was for a college life........What should *he* do, with his graceful attainments, his delicate sensitiveness, his modest and unassuming simplicity, in the rude world, amid duties which, though they involved far higher ecclesiastical dignity and spiritual privilege, were intended for men of commanding minds, and of force as well as firmness of character?......If there was any one who ought not to be transplanted, and was too useful in his present place to need it, it was the heavenly minded priest of whom I am speaking."*

It was a mystery to Dr. WEEDALL how it could have been brought about: for not the least rumour had preceded it, nor did even the Bishop, Dr. Walsh, know that any such appointment was contemplated. The other three knew as little. For one of them writing to another said, "I hope these appointments may not be correct....I should have been very sorry to have been suspected of having any hand in them." The new bishops were appointed on the 11th of May, and on the 26th, the official notices were received by Bishop Walsh, DR. WEEDALL, and Mr. Wareing. These are Bishop Walsh's own words:—

"You could not have been more astounded than I was at the appointment of my much valued friend, DR. WEEDALL, which quite overwhelmed him. I had not the least expectation of it, as I had expressly written to Propaganda, when his name amongst others was sent to me and to the other Vicars Apostolic for our respective opinions on the qualifications, &c., of the individuals proposed, that, although in other respects I considered him worthy of the episcopacy, I was decidedly of opinion that his delicate state of health would quite unfit him for the responsibility of the sacred office."

* Sermon at the Funeral of the Right Rev. H. Weedall, D.D., by J. H. Newman, D.D., of the Oratory.

The following letter from Dr. Weedall himself to the present writer will best express his own feelings. It is dated June 1st, 1840:—

"My Dear Husenbeth,

"Your letter has renewed all my affliction, which for the last few days has been most intense. I assure you I had not the *slightest suspicion* of any such event, or of the *merest possibility* of it. This announcement has been to me like the stroke of death. Even Dr. Walsh did not know of it. But it is announced under such circumstances, that my friends here will not suffer me to think that any protest ought to be made, or would be accepted. I know not what to say, or what to do. I send you the only letters I have yet received. I fear it is too late to do any thing. Pray for me, dear Husenbeth. I require a miracle of grace and support."

To understand this, it must be observed that in the letters announcing the appointment to Bishop Walsh, his lordship was ordered to make no opposition, and to enjoin obedience to the elect, and it was declared that no excuse on account of health, or of any other supposed obstacle whatever would be admitted. But what was still more extraordinary was that in one of the two letters sent for perusal to the present writer by Dr. Weedall, as intimated in the above letter, and which came to him as a private and friendly communication from an English Monsignor at Rome, not connected with the English college, he was told that this letter was written by the express command of His Holiness, to signify to Dr. Weedall that he required him, in virtue of holy obedience, to accept the mitre, and that he would admit of no excuse.

At the same time the prelate himself strongly exhorted him to offer no opposition to what was manifestly the holy will of God. *The reader is requested to bear this letter in remembrance*, on account of what will be related later on in its proper place.

No wonder that with all this solemn warning and threatening, poor DR. WEEDALL should have been bewildered and frightened, and at a loss what course to pursue. He was, as a distinguished ecclesiastic wrote, "quite heartbroken at his appointment. They will hear no excuse at Rome; he must leave his beloved Oscott, about which he has been so anxious, and in which all his affections seem centred, alas! never to return. There is one feature in the business striking, that both president and vice-president of Oscott are elected; you see the reason, it is obvious; *sed transeat!*" To add to his perplexity, it soon reached him that the clergy of his proposed District were exerting themselves to get his appointment changed, feeling aggrieved that a stranger and an invalid should be placed over them. They were anything but inviting to him. They even signified to him in substance that they considered his appointment injudicious, though they did not blame him for it; and that if it were persisted in, they should indeed endeavour to behave to him with due respect, but that he would have a troublesome life among them. But he was eager to assure every one that his nomination was wholly unexpected. He went to an old and intimate friend, a priest in the neighbourhood, and assured him with great distress of mind that the promotion had not only never been sought by him, but was decidedly contrary to his wishes.

Fortunately he determined to set off without delay for Rome, and learn on the spot the true state of the matter, and whether it was really so hopeless to petition for a release from a burthen which he had so much reason to dread and deprecate. Before he went, his portrait was painted by Herbert, who produced an excellent likeness of him, but the colouring of the face is of a dark and purplish hue, giving the unpleasant idea of extreme cold. Dr. Weedall received an address from the inmates of St. Mary's before his departure, to which he returned an answer very feeling, and, at the same time, very significant. He spoke of his long connexion with the college, dating almost from its very commencement; he alluded very humbly to his labours in the old college, and more recently in erecting and organising the new; but he added that though, like Moses, he had led them through the toils and perils of the desert, and brought them at length to the promised land, yet, like Moses, he was not permitted to enjoy it; he was not worthy of so great a blessing; it was given him only to see the desirable land, but another, like Josue, would be called to lead them to the peaceful possession and enjoyment of it; for him it was enough to see it, to invoke blessings upon all who should dwell in it, and to die in peace.

Every one was deeply affected at this paternal and pathetic address; every one felt deeply for the affliction of their old and beloved superior, and for the loss which themselves were to sustain. For whatever might be the result of his journey to Rome, one thing was certainly intended, and he, poor man, must have understood it, *he was no more to be the president of St. Mary's College.* On the 22nd of June, with a full heart and an anxious mind, DR. WEEDALL bid farewell to his dear college, and was accompanied by his friend Dr. Wareing to the railway station. Lord Dormer's little son, the Hon. John Dormer, at that time one of Mr. Foley's boys at the old college, was to have gone to Italy, where his noble father was residing, under Mr. Foley's charge; but he gave him up willingly to DR. WEEDALL's care, who was to take him on to Lucca. DR. WEEDALL announced his departure in an affectionate letter to the present writer two days before he left Oscott, in which he said he hoped by putting himself into closer communication with certain influential persons at Rome, he might still avert the heavy calamity from falling upon him. He requested letters to be addressed to him at Lucca.

In the meantime he found a most kind and valuable friend at Rome to plead his cause at the fountain head. The Right Rev. Dr. Baines was then in Rome, and was invited in the latter part of July to go out to Castel Gandolfo, where the Pope was staying by the advice of his physicians, on a special visit to his Holiness. He went accordingly on Sunday, the 19th of July; and as the Bishop himself described it, "nothing could exceed the kindness and condescension of his Holiness, who laid aside all formality, and treated me as a friend." They were alone, and after dinner, the Pope without any ceremony invited Dr. Baines to sit and talk with him, perfectly at his ease. They sat on a sofa, one at each end, and conversed with as much familiarity as two ordinary gentlemen. The Pope observed that as he had been some days away from Rome, he should like to know what arrivals there had been in his absence. Dr. Baines replied that he had not heard of any in particular, but that DR. WEEDALL was expected to arrive soon. "DR. WEEDALL!" said the Pope, "who is DR. WEEDALL?" Dr. Baines answered that his Holiness would perhaps recollect seeing him in Rome ten years before; but that he was also one of the newly appointed Vicars Apostolic for England. The Pope then said he remembered his name, and asked what he was coming to Rome for. Dr. Baines gladly seized the opportunity of explaining to his Holiness that he was coming to petition to be relieved from his appointment; but was under so much apprehension of being refused, that he could hardly summon courage to come on to Rome. The Pope asked on what grounds he wished to be released; and the Bishop told his Holiness that it was on account of the very delicate state of his health, and particularly his head, which was so bad, that he feared he should sink under the charge proposed for him. The Pope said: "Well, those are reasons to be duly weighed and considered: but why does he feel so much apprehension?" "Because," said Dr. Baines, "he has been given to understand that your Holiness has laid a special command upon him to accept the charge, and that you will listen to no excuse." "O no," said the Pope, "nothing more has been sent to him than is sent usually to bishops when appointed: of course when a bishop is nominated, it is always desired that he should accept his appointment, but no special command has been given in his case; let him draw up a proper statement of his reasons, and they shall receive due attention." This was sufficient encouragement; and Dr. Baines did not dwell farther upon the subject. But he lost no time in writing to Dr. Weedall to convey to him this consoling intelligence. He also thus expressed himself on the result of his interview with the Pope, in a letter to England: "I have settled Dr. Weedall's business, if he only come on to Rome."

When the reader compares these words of the Pope himself with the extraordinary letter sent to Dr. Weedall as above mentioned, by a certain Monsignor, he will perhaps be tempted to doubt the accuracy of the above relation; but he may fully rely upon its truth, as the writer received it word for word from the lips of Dr. Baines himself: and as will be presently seen, Dr. Baines wrote the same to Dr. Weedall. He had proceeded as far as Lucca, and was hesitating whether he should go on to Rome, or not, when on the 26th of July, he received three letters from Rome, and he wrote immediately to his friend, as follows:—

"Bagni di Lucca, Feast of St. Anne, 1840.
"MY DEAR HUSENBETH,

"I have only within this hour received three letters from Rome, and I send to you in the first place, though I shall write by this same post to Oscott, the news that these letters encourage me, and strongly urge me to go forward to Rome, suggesting reasons to hope that my applications will be attended to. Dr. Baines, whose kindness to me in this affair is beyond all gratitude, tells me that his Holiness assured him that he had not given *positive orders* for the new VV. AA. elect to accept the charge. Nothing more than is usual in cases of this kind. And that he was not aware that I had difficulties on the score of health, to which, his Holiness admits, attention ought to be paid. So that I already feel better and lighter by these communications. For I assure you that the very shadow of a mitre has made my head sorely to ache. However I am writing only on the leaves of hope. An uplifting of the wind may disperse them. So without metaphor, but in reality, continue for me your good prayers. Let me hear from you again, and send me all the news to Rome."

Thus relieved and encouraged, he hastened on to the Eternal City, and his own beautiful letter to the writer will best explain the whole of what transpired in his regard, and cannot fail to be read with intense interest and gratification:—

"Rome, Monte Citorio, 7th October, 1840.
"MY DEAR HUSENBETH,

"It was not the least part of my solicitude during my long and tedious illness that I was putting your patience and friendship to so severe a test, whilst I myself had no resource but to trust to some stray report, which I hoped would reach you, as it appears actually to have done, and which should at once explain and vindicate my silence.... — Now let me explain the state of my own affair....I remained at Lucca with Lord Dormer until I received letters encouraging me and advising me by all means to come on to Rome. I did so, and I found in the first place that my affair was perfectly an *open* affair. That his Holiness had never authorised, much less enjoined the strong language which had *tongue-tied* Dr. Walsh, and had made me long demur whether in taking the measure which I meditated, I might not be resisting the will of God. This latter I resolved not to do when I clearly saw my way, but I felt that no one in Rome could know the actual state of my health, and hence I thought it a conscientious duty to explain it to the authorities there. I met at Propaganda with the greatest kindness, but at the same time with the greatest reluctance on the part both of Cardinal Franzoni and of Monsignor Cadolini to relieve me from an appointment on which they had set their hearts, which had actually been gazetted in the new Roman Directory, and from which my improved appearance, owing to the air and baths of Lucca, offered no very obvious grounds for exemption.

"However, as I felt that my claims to exemption were not *superficial* ones, and totally independent of certain slight variations, I begged permission of his Eminence,— the Holy Father still being in the country,—to be allowed to state my reasons in a memorial, to which, of course, whatever his intentions might be, his Eminence could not object. The Pope had previously intimated to me, both through Monsignor Acton and Dr. Baines, that I need not be uneasy, that I was perfectly at liberty to make any canonical objections I might wish to urge, and assuring me that they should be attended to. I accordingly drew up a short memorial of the actual state of my health, alluding also to causes and their progress for some years back, got it translated into Italian, and two copies written out, one of which was presented to his Holiness, the other to Propaganda. All this I fortunately did a few days before I fell ill.

"The matter rested here for a *considerable time*, as the intervals here are always very long between the various stages of public or private business. Meanwhile I got *one tolerably good fever* and a terrific dysentery. As soon as I recovered a little, I wrote a letter to Cardinal Franzoni, or rather got my good friend Dr. Baggs to write it for me, begging to know whether I might consider myself as officially released. His Holiness was still at Castel Gandolfo. There I was sure to find a kind and considerate judgment. But I was unwilling to do any thing that might seem to be irregular, and not quite in accordance with the most profound respect which I felt for, and the most complete deference which I wished to pay to, the holy and venerable man, the Cardinal Prefect of Propaganda. I accordingly waited upon his Eminence, and restated the substance of my letter. I found his Eminence quite as unwilling as ever to release me from the appointment. Kind in the extreme, pious, saintly, and his wishes and prayers all seeming to concentrate in one object, the conversion of England. I entered respectfully into all his wishes, but I ventured to ask, 'has your Eminence read the memorial which I took the liberty of presenting some time ago?' 'Why no,' said the Cardinal, 'it is amongst my papers:' and turned the conversation to something else. But I was not surprised. He is too old to pay much attention to public business. But I knew that others had read it. I knew that the Pope had read it. I have some reason to think that they took a medical opinion on the case, which I rather invited, in order that there might be ground for their receding without any compromise of either the dignity or authority of Propaganda.*

---

* The following extract from a letter from the Right Rev. Dr. Baines, dated Frescati, 14th September, 1840, will throw further light upon the tedious delay to which poor DR. WEEDALL was subjected: "One thing I have accomplished. I have procured the liberation of DR. WEEDALL... Notwithstanding the declared consent of the Pope for his being released, the Propaganda hung back, and wanted not to give their sanction. They

"Here, however, was a second or a third stage, and *another interval*, of which of course I took advantage to *get through another stout fever* at Mr. Englefield's beautiful villa, near Frascati. This was of much longer duration. I was to have gone with Dr. Baines to be introduced to the Pope at Castel Gandolfo, but was confined to my bed. His Holiness, however, sent me a most fatherly message, bade me not to be uneasy, but to get well as fast as I could. In a few days I received an *official release* from Propaganda, and the Bulls, which were in Monsignor Acton's keeping, were formally returned. Here the matter is at an end. No one blames me for what I have done; and I myself feel that I could not conscientiously have done otherwise. In fact, dear Husenbeth, it would have been madness in me to have accepted the mitre. You know *in part* what the state of my health has been for some years. But no one but myself could know how fearfully all the symptoms had increased of late years, but particularly for the last two years of my residence at Oscott. During those two last years the *wear and tear* of mind has been immense. I have sacrificed time, health, studies, every thing to the successful establishment and management of Oscott. My late illness has shown the dreadful state of derangement in which my whole system has been,—stomach, bowels, all disordered,—spirits broken, nerves shattered, *brains smashed;* and but for this respite I must have been in my grave......

still professed hopes of subduing his opposition. Determined to put a stop to this state of things, I last Thursday, September 10th, (having previously obtained permission from the Pope to visit him any day most convenient to myself,) drove over to Castel Gandolfo, and was most graciously received by his Holiness. I pressed upon him to allow me to tell DR. WEEDALL positively that he was free, and to order Progaganda to send the usual notification. He granted both requests, and on Saturday evening the official notification arrived, exempting DR. WEEDALL from his charge; and directing him to return the briefs of his appointment. He was ill in bed when the letter came; and I frightened him by reading it as an order for him to accept the office. He was overjoyed when he learned the real fact, and is now nearly well again."

"Adieu! for once a long letter. His lordship, Dr. Baines, desires his kindest regards. Write soon, and address,—English College, Rome.

"Yours affectionately,
"HENRY WEEDALL."

This letter speaks out for itself, and so fully explains every thing, that further remarks would only confuse the narrative, and weaken its effect. The reader, however, cannot fail to peruse with astonishment and deep sympathy the actual memorial which Dr. WEEDALL drew up and presented to his Holiness and Propaganda. A portion of it has been already given in these pages, but it may be well here to repeat it, and thus present this very affecting document entire.

"DR. WEEDALL'S MEMORIAL TO PROPAGANDA.

"The disorder under which I have laboured for so many years is one of no ordinary character: not a head ache, but a mischievous affection of the nerves of the head. Indeed I never found a person similarly affected. It began when I was about ten years old, and went on increasing with intensity and active mischief throughout the whole of my course. I found a difficulty in going through my humanity studies, and when I came to Philosophy and Divinity, it had increased to an alarming height. I could not read even for five minutes in the day, I could not even at times bear the light. I was obliged to give up entirely my course of Philosophy; and the whole of my Theological studies, such as they were, were learned by listening to a fellow divine, who would read me the lesson. I made up the whole as well as I could by chance snatches, just as I was able, but I had serious difficulties in taking Orders. I was obliged to have a dispensation from my office, by commutation for the Rosary, for three or four years after I was ordained priest. I then began with Vespers and

Complin, afterwards the Little Hours, and lastly with Matins and Lauds; which latter I was only able to manage at first by the help of others, until the psalms grew familiar to me. Afterwards, however, by carefully attending to my general health, having the advantage at college of horse exercise, and by the healthy occupation of looking after the farm, and the external management of the college concern, my head and eyes grew rather better, the eyes more serviceable; but I never have been able to make use of them without great inconvenience for a whole day together, and never much by candle light. My studies, therefore, have been very superficially pursued, and as I have been chiefly confined to the teaching of the classics, my theological studies have necessarily been very meagre. Latterly, however, my head and eyes have been getting worse. Owing to the fatigues and anxieties of a large establishment, and all the wear and tear of mind arising from a large building superadded, I have been reduced to such a state of weakness of head and constitution that I thought I should have been obliged to give up every thing. The nerves of the head are so bad, that I fall at times into a helpless lethargy. The utmost often that I can hope to do in a day, is to get through my Office; and if by chance I am obliged to defer it until late in the evening, I tumble and toss about over it. I often know not what I say, am in danger when walking about my room of falling down in a lethargic stupor, and even with the help of an assistant I am obliged frequently to give up the Office, and say it next morning. This happens not once, but frequently. My friends do not know half of what I suffer. And even now, though from a cessation of six weeks, and the natural effects of travelling, I both look and am better, yet even now I cannot kneel down at night to say my last devotions, but am obliged to walk up and down my room, and even so I generally find it necessary after the most painful repetitions to break short in the middle and leave them unfinished. I think this has been the case for the last two years almost every night. A Catholic physician, who knew me well, but is now dead,* told me that it was all the effect of mental anxiety and application, and that unless I remitted in time, I should fall into premature dotage. This I feel to be true. At the college, or with a small congregation, I might possibly be useful; but in the contemplated situation, and with increasing duties, I fear I shall not only sink myself, but endanger the cause of religion. These are the grounds which I conscientiously submit to the Sacred Congregation, and I beg that they will condescend to take the same view of my case, which his Holiness has most graciously condescended to take. I humbly, &c."

On the 17th of September, DR. WEEDALL returned his formal note of thanks to the Secretary of Propaganda for the communication he had received of the acceptance of his resignation of the episcopacy and Apostolic Vicariate. His mind was now completely set at ease; he was relieved of a most oppressive burthen, and intense anxiety; and he had reason to rejoice that in the face of the gravest efforts to deter him, he had taken the wise resolve to ascertain the truth at the fountain head, and throw himself confidingly at the feet of the Vicar of Christ, who he knew would be kind, considerate, and paternal.

* Dr. De Lys, who died at Birmingham, August 25th, 1831. *(Note by the Author)*

CHAPTER XV.

Dr. Weedall Presented to the Pope—Uncertainty of His Future Position—Offers Made to Him—Remains in Rome till the End of Spring—Returns to England—Visits Cossey and Oxburgh—Goes to Reside at Old Oscott—Is Invited to Remove to the Eastern District—Relieves and Succeeds Mr. Foley at Hampton-on-the-Hill—Undertakes the Mission at Leamington.

It was natural to consider that Dr. Weedall, now released from his unsought for, and unexpected appointment to the episcopacy, reverted to his previous state, and might justly claim to resume his position at St. Mary's College, which he had filled so long, and with so much dignity and efficiency. It has been seen that Bishop Walsh declared that the appointment had quite astounded him, and that he had not the least expectation of it. He added, moreover, that he had not "the most distant idea of thus displacing Dr. Weedall," to make room for another, and that Oscott "would suffer materially from the loss of its worthy President." After all this, the obvious conclusion was to invite him at once to resume his former honourable position. This, however, to the surprise and disappointment of his many friends and admirers, was not done; not even was there the least sign of such intention exhibited. The Bishop wrote to him, indeed, in very kind terms, professing the greatest regard for him, but ended by very coolly asking him what situation he should like. Of course to such a question poor DR. WEEDALL could return but one answer. It was not for him to say that he should prefer to be as he was before, when he saw that Oscott was plainly closed against him; he, therefore, returned the only answer he could give, that he would not begin to embarrass his peace of mind by choosing for himself. But he was not yet fit to do anything; and it seemed expedient for him to remain some time in Italy to re-establish his health.

The Princess Borghese, the younger daughter of the good Earl of Shrewsbury, died at Rome, on the 27th of October, to the great affliction of the whole city, where her piety and charity were so well known. Even the Pope, when he heard of her death, exclaimed: "*Ecco un' altra calamita per Roma!*" Bishop Baines sent a beautiful account of her death and funeral to the *Tablet* paper, in which it appeared on the 28th of November. In the same paper, December 5th, was inserted another letter with additional particulars, very long, and written with so much elegance and pathos, that though it has no signature, it bears intrinsic evidence of coming from the pen of DR. WEEDALL.

On the 9th of November he wrote: "I am, thank God, quite recovered, at least up to the point at which my barometer usually stands."

On Wednesday, December the 2nd, 1840, Dr. Weedall was presented to the Pope by Dr. Baggs, the rector of the English College, and he offered the tribute of his humble and fervent thanks to his Holiness for having granted his earnest prayer to be released from the contemplated bishopric. The Pope received him most kindly, and expressed his regret at his unwillingness to accept the dignity intended for him, and the reluctance with which he had consented to relieve him from it. His Holiness added that the whole Catholic body in England had desired his elevation. Dr. Weedall replied: "Your Holiness does not speak *ex cathedra*." The Pope was standing, but he immediately sat down, and playfully answered: "Well, now I do speak *ex cathedra*."

Meantime his many friends in England were looking for his return with most uneasy feelings on his account. "What is to be done about him, with him, of him?" wrote one of his intimate friends,— "I am much afraid of the poor Doctor's feelings when he returns, and finds all things going on, and done, and planned without the least reference to him." A Catholic nobleman in England, whose sons had all been educated at Oscott under Dr. Weedall, made him a proposal to become his domestic chaplain. To this he replied, that with a very grateful sense of his lordship's kindness, as he had received no such proposal from his Bishop, Dr. Walsh, he was unwilling to assume, without official notification, *that he was to be removed from a place where he thought he had formed a home*. In a subsequent letter of December 10th, he signified again his deep sense of the kind feeling which prompted the offer, but that considering that he should have no missionary charge, and no further duty than attending to the family and domestics of the noble Lord, he should fear being *prematurely laid upon the shelf*, and not find any field for that quiet exertion which he hoped yet to be able to make. How fully he was justified in looking forward to future exertion, the twenty years more, save one, of toil and indomitable labours which crowned his meritorious course, afford overwhelming evidence.

Early in the following year, 1841, Dr. Weedall wrote from Rome that he had had an active situation offered him, and was in constant communication with Bishop Baines, who was still there; from which it was conjectured that he might go to Prior Park. Nothing further, however, came of this: but it was evident that Dr. Weedall's affections were strongly fixed on Oscott, as well they might, and that he severely felt the humiliation of having it closed against him. He remained at Rome some months longer, and received a palm from the Pope, in St. Peter's, on Palm Sunday. Bishop Baines had quitted Rome on the 27th of March, and was received with the greatest joy at Prior Park on the 21st of the month following. Dr. Weedall had an audience of the Pope to beg his blessing before he left Rome. His Holiness expressed his satisfaction at seeing him so well, and said that now that he knew so much of him, he should not let him off so easily another time. Dr. Weedall had in his hand some rosaries which he meant to ask the Pope to bless with Indulgences, but a gentleman who accompanied him was asking for so many favours of that kind, that his Holiness considered his requests too exorbitant, and said to him: "*No, mio figlio, é troppo: e pur un laico!*"* This paternal rebuke made the humble Doctor keep back most of his rosaries; but he ventured to ask, and of course obtained, the Pope's blessing upon a few, one of them being expressly for his friend the present writer, to which is attached a Plenary Indulgence at the hour of death. It may well be conceived that he has ever treasured that precious rosary, and that now the death of its beloved donor has invested it with a mournful interest and additional value. Dr. Weedall left Rome in May, 1841, and soon arrived in England. It was time for him to re-appear, for it really seemed as if he was well nigh forgotten: *oblivioni datus, tanquam mortuus a corde......ut vas perditum.*† The man who had done so much for religion, who, to use his own expressive words, "had sacrificed time, health, studies, every thing to the successful establishment and management of Oscott," returned with no home to repair to, and no situation provided for him!

On the 23rd of June, the new cathedral of St. Chad's, in Birmingham, was solemnly dedicated, and Dr. Weedall was present as assistant priest

---

* No, my son, it is too much, and for a layman too!
† Psalm xxx., 13.

to Bishop Walsh, who officiated. At the dinner in the afternoon, he proposed in a short but well turned' speech the health of his old friend and schoolfellow in the early days of Oscott, Sir Arnold Knight. He hastened to pay a visit to another old and trusty friend, his present biographer, and found so much consolation in the cordial welcome he received, that he remained with him some weeks, and seemed greatly to enjoy himself with him, and another old friend in the neighbourhood, the Rev. John Abbot. During this visit the writer accompanied him to Oxburgh, where he had the pleasure of meeting another friend who had long been with him at Oscott, the Rev. John Gascoyne. He did not omit, during his stay at Cossey, to visit the holy well of St. Walstan, at Babur, where he washed his eyes with great devotion with the water of the well, invoking the intercession of the Saint.

Mr. Foley, who, it has been mentioned, was at the same time serving the mission at Old Oscott, and conducting a small preparatory school there, felt deeply for DR. WEEDALL, who seemed so lost and neglected; and generously offered to give up his place to him. He knew his attachment to Oscott, and he considered that at the old college he would at least be on a spot where he had resided so many years, and would, moreover, be close to the new college, and in close connexion with it. This offer DR. WEEDALL accepted, as it would bring him to the neighbourhood to which all his affections were rivetted. He arrived at Old Oscott towards the middle of September, 1841. Mr. Foley at once resigned to him the presidentship of his preparatory school, and soon after was appointed to the mission at Hampton-on-the-Hill, near Warwick, at the invitation of Lord Dormer, and arrived there on the 11th of November.

Dr. WEEDALL sat down thus in a very low place, compared with his former dignity and elevation. He was the pastor of a small flock of poor country people, and the president of a small school of young boys. Yet he was never heard to utter a word of complaint; but pursued his humble course patiently and resignedly. "*Crede mihi,*" says even a Pagan, "*bene qui latuit, bene vixit;*"* and this incomparable man, though so close to the scene of his former exaltation, strove to make himself contented in his present lowliness and obscurity. But if he made no complaint for himself, his numerous friends felt and complained for him. They felt that this was not the position where such a man ought to be allowed to remain. A distinguished bishop among the Vicars Apostolic wrote of him: "I am sorry for Dr. WEEDALL. I have heard nothing of him since he became president of Old Oscott. *Of course the thing will not do.*" The worthy prelate was right; it was not likely to do, it *ought* not to do, and it *did* not do long. Dr. WEEDALL wanted instinctively a greater field for the exertion of his very superior talents; and as the new college was closed against him, he naturally sighed to go farther off, and take some active mission.

* Believe me, he that loves obscurity, lives well.—OVID, *Tristium* III., 4.

Indeed, when Mr. Foley repaired to Hampton-on-the-Hill, Dr. WEEDALL almost asked him to keep that mission for him in case he should not find himself at home at Old Oscott. He probably thought that Mr. Foley, having given up that place to him, would be equally willing to resign Hampton to him; and he was right if he did think so, for Mr. Foley was ready to do any thing to promote his peace, and testify his personal affection for him, and his esteem for his great merits and abilities. But he was not the only one who loved and valued a man so worthy. Bishop Wareing, one of his earliest and most attached friends, proposed to him to come and preside over an ecclesiastical seminary, which he was about to commence at Gifford's Hall, in Suffolk, for the Eastern District. He did not at once decline the offer; there were many reasons which might have led him to accept it. But after taking some time to consider it, and after three long conversations with Bishop Wareing, he respectfully declined it, with a deep sense of his lordship's kindness in making the proposal, because he was unwilling to transfer himself to another district, and to remove so far from the neighbourhood of his beloved Oscott; but principally because he could not at his time of life begin again to teach classics, and instruct young students in a seminary. Mr. Foley met him in the month of June in Leamington, and Mr. Foley at once offered to resign to him the mission of Hampton-on-the-Hill, as far as he might make the offer, subject of course to the approval of the Bishop, Dr. Walsh. Mr. Foley declared that he offered him the place because he himself found it agreeable, and he fancied that the little farming attached to it might suit him. It was feared, however, that the long winter nights in a country place, without any society, would be too lonely and wearisome to a man, the weakness of whose eyes prevented him from writing, or even reading by candle light.

Dr. Weedall had no great fancy for the situation at Hampton, though he fully appreciated Mr. Foley's generous offer to resign it to him. He was far from being happy: he felt that he could not remain in his anomalous position at Old Oscott; but he had some wish to go to Nottingham, and assist in carrying out the new cathedral there of St. Barnabas. In this, however, he did not succeed; and he then reverted to Bishop Wareing's invitation, who was very desirous to possess him, knowing well that he would bring to his projected new seminary, those very valuable qualifications, great talent, long experience, and high reputation. At Midsummer, Dr. Weedall requested somewhat urgently to come into the Eastern District; for he was by this time thoroughly and feelingly convinced that he was not wanted at all in the Central District. His friends, who had watched events and movements there, were only surprised that it took so much to convince him. Bishop Wareing gladly consented to receive him; but, on the 27th, Dr. Weedall wrote to his lordship a letter, which showed how difficult he felt it to take any decisive step, and at the same time afforded painful evidence that his uncertain and uncomfortable position was beginning to throw him back to his former wretched state of health. He said in that letter that he could hardly ever see or hear of Bishop Walsh, and when he did, he knew not how to procure an interview. What a position! How humiliating to such a man as Dr. Weedall! He went on to say that he prayed for patience and resignation, and that he might not precipitate any thing. "But at present," he said, "I continue to suffer, and I feel that I am reverting to a state of *head* and health, into which it is easier to sink than to emerge again out of. A constrained suppression of feeling is one of the most painful states of the human mind."

How deplorable that a man with all his merits and claims should have been ever driven by neglect and ingratitude into a state of mind so painful and perilous! About the middle of August, he paid a visit to Bishop Wareing at Northampton, and when he returned he was quite resolved to leave Oscott, where he now saw plainly that his absence was even desired. He was now disposed to supply for a time for Mr. Foley at Hampton-on-the-Hill. He had paid him a visit there at the beginning of August, and perceiving that poor Foley was by no means well, he proposed to come and take charge of the mission for him, thereby affording him opportunity for rest, change of air, and recreation. After seeing the place, he seemed to have some inclination for it. Besides a fair amount of missionary duty, he would have there a little farming, in which he had always taken delight, for there were two cows, half a dozen pigs, thirty sheep, and a stock of poultry. He could keep his horse, and be near Leamington, where he had several friends, and within an easy distance of Oscott. On the 8th of October, 1842, he went to Hampton-on-the-Hill, to relieve his friend Foley, but only as making an experiment; and it was expected that he would soon find, what all his friends saw and knew, that the mission was not likely to be his resting place. Poor Mr. Foley's health rapidly declined; he went in October to Sedgley Park, where his old friend the president, Mr. Bowdon, showed him the greatest kindness and attention. But he removed at the end of November to the New College at Oscott, where he died on the 11th of February, in the following year, 1843. Dr. Weedall was with him the day before his death, and returned on the following Tuesday, to be present at his funeral, which was conducted with much solemnity. His remains were deposited in the first and centre recess in the crypt at the altar end of the chapel.

Dr. Weedall, it has been mentioned, was only making an experiment at Hampton-on-the-Hill. He was still uneasy, unsettled, hesitating, and unhappy, and had soon found that the experiment would not succeed. For one thing, housekeeping on limited means was a thing to which he had not been accustomed, and which he did not understand. In June, 1843, he removed to Leamington, four miles from Hampton, succeeding the Rev. William Cunningham in the charge of that mission. At first he suffered severely in his head, and was very low, timorous, indecisive, and scrupulous. This was the account given of him by respectable Catholics at Leamington. He continued for some time very unhappy there, but grew better after a few weeks, and though he complained of his head at times, as he did indeed all through life, he seemed on the whole more comfortable. These feelings and fluctuations need not cause surprise, when the severe trials to which he had been subjected are borne in mind. A college life was clearly his vocation: and cast down suddenly from the dignified position which he held at Oscott, and thrown unexpectedly into a sphere for which he was never trained, it was no wonder that he could not at once bring his mind and habits to his new line of duty and occupation.

CHAPTER XVI.

Dr. Weedall on the Mission at Leamington—His Difficulties, Duties, and Habits there—Sermon on Fasting—Decoration of His Chapel—His Converts—Sermon at Northampton—Sermon at Leamington on Confession—Newspaper Correspondence Entailed by it—His Address to the Choir—His General Character as a Missioner.

However trying was Dr. Weedall's novel situation on the mission, his deep sense of duty soon prevailed over the feelings of nature, and he resolutely set to work in the discharge of his pastoral functions with a zeal and energy which filled his numerous friends with edification and consolation. If, indeed, he was to be on the mission at all, a place more suitable in several respects for him than Leamington could hardly have been found. The congregation was not too large for his strength, and a good part of it was composed of highly respectable residents, with occasional visitors, being generally persons of superior education, capable of appreciating his talents, and relishing his eloquent and learned discourses. The town was genteel and pleasant, and the neighbourhood on all sides interesting. What he most felt and complained of was the want of provision for the various necessities and contingencies of the mission; and the consequent necessity of constant collections in the chapel, and appeals to the congregation. He was not accustomed to such a state of things, too common, however, in our poor missions; and how much it cost him to make these collections, may be in part inferred from a short extract from an address with which he prefaced one of his appeals:—

"Amongst the unpleasant duties of a pastor's life, one of the most unpleasant is to recur to the subject of money and finance. However, you who know the circumstances of this mission, know that it is entirely unprovided with funds for any single purpose, and that all expenses, whether of chapel, school, organ, or poor, must be provided by the priest from the contingent sources of the voluntary offerings of the faithful. Six collections in the year for these purposes is all that the pastor can bring himself, and that reluctantly, to propose. And were it not for the private liberality of some individuals, the above objects could not in any manner be carried out. But great as has been the liberality of private individuals in giving beauty and honour to this house of God, and in providing efficiently for its service and comfort for all, there must necessarily be a vast variety of minor but expensive details which can only be supplied by the voluntary contributions of all who benefit by them.......Perhaps from an unwillingness to say much, I have not made myself intelligible. But you will probably infer that you are invited to support the organ and choir, as they deserve to be supported, and that the collection may be made, as usual, on Sunday next."

He was assisted, however, in Leamington by kind and generous friends, who knew his great merits, and valued him as he deserved. To their houses he was always welcome. Indeed, he seldom dined at home; for when his ordinary duties of the day had been discharged,—and they were never neglected,—when he had visited the sick, consoled the afflicted, relieved the poor, and instructed the ignorant and the enquirer after truth, he found solace and relaxation in the elegant and cheerful society of several Catholics residing in that fashionable town; which was very important for the preservation of his valuable health. Besides this resource, he had good friends in the neighbourhood, whom he frequently visited, as at Kenilworth, Princethorpe, and Coventry, at the latter of which resided as missioner the present respected Bishop of Birmingham, Dr. Ullathorne, who was also consecrated in the noble church which he had built at Coventry, Bishop of Hetalona, on his being appointed Vicar Apostolic of the Western District. He was consecrated by the venerable Vicar Apostolic of the Yorkshire District, Dr. Briggs, June 21st, 1846.

On the First Sunday of his first Lent at Leamington, in 1844, DR. WEEDALL preached a sermon, which he was induced to publish, with the title of *Vindication of the Catholic discipline of Fasting both in principle and practice.* He said in a note prefixed to it: "The following sermon was not delivered with any view to publication, but simply to discharge an ordinary duty of the sacred ministry. But in consequence of certain misrepresentations afloat, to which the writer's attention has been recently drawn, he yields to a request to publish the sermon, in the hope that it may vindicate the principle of fasting, and justify the practice of the Catholic Church, in this holy and Apostolical Institution." It was in reality a sermon which he had preached at Oscott in 1821. It is a well argued, spirited, and persuasive discourse; and the following extract will give an idea of its style and composition:—

"My brethren, with such evidence of its utility and necessity, with such weight of authority in its favour, comprising all the great, and good, and illustrious, whether of the Jewish or the Christian Church; with the positive injunction of Jesus Christ, backed by his own divine example, is it well done by our separated brethren, to renounce the wholesome ordinance? Is it wise, is it safe, to strike out from their practice so intrepidly, this efficient medium of sanctification? And having thus decided for themselves against both reason and Scripture, is it decent to stigmatize our Church with Judaism and superstition, because we still cling to the holy custom, every where commended in the sacred writings, and consecrated by prophets and apostles, by the head and master of the Christian Church? Above all, is it rational, is it consistent in terms, or with the common usage of language, that a Church, or a body of men, should strip the religion of Jesus Christ, which is essentially the *religion of the cross*, of all that is penal in it, and mortifying to nature, of confession, of obedience, of poverty, of celibacy, of fasting, and of its other corporal austerities; in a word, of every character which could stamp it as the religion of the first Christians, and then publish it forth to the world as the *reformed* religion: whilst that which has guarded, with a superhuman fidelity, the counsels, as well as *precepts*, of her beloved Founder, the Church which is Catholic in its faith, and Catholic in its practice, and Catholic and Apostolical in its essential discipline; that Church which assumes no license to recede from the letter of her instructions, nor to explain away, or to quibble with the words of the Testament, the Church which, in her simplicity understands the commandment to fast, to abstain, to mortify the appetites, as implying a real obligation to fast, to abstain, and to mortify the appetites, and practises these austerities accordingly with an honest and cheerful submission; that this Church should be branded as the corrupt, the degenerate, the superstitious Church, which needed to be *reformed* therefore, and brought back to the spirit of its Founder! Is this rational? Is it intelligible? Is it conformable to the simplest elements of justice, thus to make her very merits the heads of her impeachment, and to condemn her, not by the evidence of the Gospel, but by the convenient decisions of irreligion and licentiousness?"

St. Peter's Chapel, at Leamington, was built by the meritorious exertions of the Rev. B. Crosbie, and opened in October, 1829. It is a handsome building, in the Grecian style; but DR. WEEDALL, soon after he came to Leamington, being quite enamoured of every thing Gothic, had a great wish to *gothicise* the interior, so far as this could be done consistently in a building of a widely different character. He did this, however, successfully, by adopting that style of transition, or Oriental Gothic, usually termed Byzantine; and the chapel was superbly decorated in that style. His eloquent and impressive sermons attracted many to the chapel, and he had the happiness to witness many conversions. His own amiable manners, and his humble and unostentatious life, had their share in winning for him the respect and confidence of the inhabitants of Leamington in an extraordinary degree. He was frequently consulted by correspondents, who concealed their names, while they candidly opened their minds, and laid before him their difficulties. This imposed upon him a labour particularly trying; for he had occasionally to write long letters to resolve the religious doubts of enquirers, who little knew how painful it was 'to him to write at all, from the peculiar affection of his head and eyes. Yet he patiently endured the distressing labour, becoming all to all, that he might gain all, and spending himself, and being spent, for the conversion of erring souls. He kept their correspondence inviolably secret, when desired, and received into the Catholic Church one lady of great respectability, without even enquiring her name. If some of his letters of this kind could with propriety be made public, they would excite great admiration at the force and ingenuity of the arguments, and the holy and attractive charity which distinguishes them.

In the summer of 1844, his old friend and schoolfellow, Bishop Wareing, had completed his new church of St. Felix, adjoining the episcopal residence at Northampton. The opening was to take place on the 25th of June, and the Hon. and Rev. G. Spencer had engaged to preach on the occasion. He was unfortunately prevented by illness; but DR. WEEDALL willingly undertook, at the request of Bishop Wareing, to supply his place. The notice was too short to allow time for him to prepare a new sermon, so he delivered again the same beautiful discourse on Prayer, which he had given when the former chapel was opened which had been built by Mr. Foley, in 1825. He considered that the sermon would be as acceptable as if new, after the lapse of nineteen years; and, in fact, there were but two or three persons present who remembered it on the former occasion. He came again in the week following to Northampton, by invitation of the Bishop, to attend, as a visitor, the annual meeting of the clergy of the Eastern District. The writer had the pleasure of meeting him there, and spending some days with him. He was in excellent spirits, and seemed in as good health as at any period of his life.

On the 18th Sunday after Pentecost, in 1846, DR. WEEDALL preached at Leamington a very able sermon on Confession. He had composed it at Oscott, and preached it there, on the same Sunday, in the year 1829, during the Jubilee granted on occasion of the election of Pope Pius VIII. He was earnestly solicited by his congregation to print this sermon, and it appeared under the title of *A Vindication of the Catholic Doctrine and Discipline of Confession.* He wrote the following introductory note for it, from Ramsgate, where he was on a visit, though the first sentence only was prefixed to the sermon when published. It is, however, so excellent and so characteristic of the author, that no apology can be needed for giving it here entire:—

"The present homily is printed at the request of certain persons, to whose judgment the writer deems it reasonable to defer. Though recently preached, it has not been recently written. It was composed several years ago, with no view to publication; so that at this distance of time, and at a distance also from his books and papers, the author cannot now remember how far and what acknowledgements should be made to any extraneous sources of information. He has, however, a grateful recollection of the admirable work, which had just then appeared, of the late Bishop of Strasbourg, and he would be well pleased to find that he had successfully adapted any of the lucid views and masterly reasonings of that illustrious and highly gifted prelate. However this may be, he hopes he does not depart from the spirit of the 'Discussion Amicale,' that no bitterness of controversy pervades his sermon, that in vindicating Catholic doctrine, he assumes the defensive position, rather than the aggressive, and that if he aims to refute error, he refutes it only by establishing truth.

"In controversy, indeed, originality of matter is as little to be wished for as expected. Old doctrines will best be sustained by old arguments. It is only they who invent new theories to overturn old truths, that can afford to be original and ridiculous. The quiet province of the Catholic controvertist, is to collect and adapt, rather than to invent, to resemble the householder in the Gospel, to re-produce old matter under new forms only, and thus to become the Scribe learned in the kingdom of Heaven, who brings forth from his treasures new things and old: *Ideo omnis scriba doctus in regno cælorum similis est homini patrifamilias.*

"Ramsgate, Feast of St. Wilfrid, 1846."

This sermon led to an animated correspondence in the *Leamington Spa Courier*, between DR. WEEDALL and the Rev. Frederick Chalmers, who began it by a long letter of remarks upon the sermon. It would only encumber these pages with very uninviting matter to detail the common place arguments and unfounded accusations of Mr. Chalmers, in his long, wearisome letters. He was little aware what a man he attacked when he encountered DR. WEEDALL. With the cool self-possession of a veteran who feels his power, but has no need to put it forth against an adversary by no means formidable, he playfully defended his sermon, and made his opponent appear rather ridiculous. A few extracts from his letters will illustrate his happy mode of rebutting the worst charges brought against his admirable sermon. Mr. Chalmers had ignorantly asserted that the Greek church owns neither the doctrine nor the practice of confession. DR. WEEDALL having directed his attention to quotations in the sermon from various Greek Fathers, thus amusingly proceeds:—

"I might also, if space could be found, narrate to Mr. Chalmers a very pleasant story on this subject, about certain theologians of the celebrated Protestant University of Wittemberg sending up a deputation to a certain Jeremias, Patriarch of Constantinople, the then acknowledged Head of the Greek Church, with a copy of the Augsburg Confession of Faith, for his examination and approval; and how the said Jeremias severely rapped the knuckles of the said deputies for presuming to suppose that the faith of the Greek Church, on the leading points of Transubstantiation, *Confession*, Invocation of Saints, &c., &c., was not precisely the same as of the Church of Rome, *coming down to both by uninterrupted tradition.* And how he thereupon bundled out the deputies, together with their bundle of Articles, as is more particularly narrated in the 'Perpetuité de la Foi.'"

Mr. Chalmers had closed his first letter very disgracefully, with denouncing what he chose to call the immoral tendency of the Confessional. This drew the following merited castigation from DR. WEEDALL:—

"But his last paragraph I severely blame, not merely as injudicious, but as eminently unjust. What right has

Mr. Chalmers to cast infamy on the Catholic Church, and wantonly to dishonour his own mother? Does he not know that in doing so he defames millions of the fairest and brightest characters of the Christian Church, and the majority, even now, of the Christian World? But to speak only of our own times. Let him look to the large portion of his own Church, who have a yearning for the practice of Confession. Let him inspect the bright and brave array of converts who have recently joined our Church. Are their names less honourable,—are their minds less cultivated,—their judgment less sound,—their morals less unimpeachable than his own? Have they been educated in a school less pure than his,—and have they imbibed sentiments of religion less perfect and less exalted? Are they his inferiors in literature, morality, and theology? And if on trial they had found our Church to be what Mr. Chalmers describes it, would they not have immediately abandoned or denounced it?

"I do not say that I fling back the charge with indignation; it would imply more excitement of temper than I really feel; but I tell Mr. Chalmers, and I tell him firmly, that his charges are unmanly and unmannerly; as worthless in argument, as ungenerous in sentiment."

After Mr. Chalmers, the Vicar of Leamington came forth; and Dr. WEEDALL wrote in answer to him two long and admirable letters, full of theological lore, and enlivened by clever sarcasm, cutting, though courteous. The concluding paragraph will suffice to give the reader a specimen of his felicitous handling of this opponent:—

"There is an instinct, too, of human nature to connect truth with good humour. If, in the case of two opponents, there are manifested the opposite extremes of good and bad temper; if one laughs, and the other frets; if one flings a joke, the other a firebrand; prepossession will be in favour of the first. I do not hereby insinuate that either the Vicar or myself illustrate these opposite extremes. It is an abstract comparison only, which I plead in abatement. But, at the risk of being thought somewhat officious, I will venture to suggest to the Vicar, that if his heavy columns had been relieved by a little cheerful sprightliness, if he had worked into the pasty matter a little less of the leaven of *iniquity*, and a little more of the leaven of *sincerity and truth*, it would have been quite as light and agreeable, and much more readable than fame reports it to have been."

Thus, then, Dr. WEEDALL, during his career at Leamington, experienced the various phases of missionary life. While he fulfilled the several obligations of his charge, and fed his flock with the assiduous care of a good shepherd, he had in his turn to defend them against the wolf, and prevent their straying from the fold, and feeding in noxious pastures. In all, he proceeded with that serene temper of holy charity, which is laid down by the great St. Augustin as the sum and perfection of a Christian life : " Semel ergo breve præceptum tibi præcipitur, dilige et quod vis fac : sive taceas, dilectione taceas ; sive clames, dilectione clames ; sive emendes, dilectione emendes ; sive parcas, dilectione parcas : radix sit intus dilectionis : non potest de ista radice nisi bonum existere." (Tract 7 in 1 Joan.)* His behaviour to all was kind, benevolent, and attractive, which made him always

---

* Once for all, therefore, a short precept is commanded thee,—love and do what thou wilt : if thou art silent, be silent with love ; if thou speakest loudly, speak loudly with love ; if thou amendest, amend with love ; if thou sparest, spare with love : let there be within a root of love : nothing but good can exist from this root.

W

loved, while his very superior abilities and gentlemanly manners always procured him real respect.

As a good example of Dr. Weedall's cheerful and happy style of address on familiar occasions, the following portions may be taken of a speech at a supper, which he gave at his own house to the members of the choir.

"My good Friends,

"It is usual on occasions like the present to address the company as 'Ladies and Gentlemen:' but I think it more suitable to the simplicity of my feelings, as well as to the ordinary style of my addresses, to say, my dear friends, my good friends.

"Good friends then let it be. And now let me tell my good friends that I am not going to make this a speechifying night, to turn our meeting into a debating club,—to turn *concord* into *discord*. If I express to you the pleasure I feel in meeting you, and my gratitude for the great exertions you make for promoting objects so dear to me, I shall not ask any one to make a speech in return. If only my sincere thanks shall be thought not unworthy of your acceptance, I shall wish you to keep them, and not to return them. So much for the character of our meeting.

"I feel quite delighted that circumstances this year have enabled me to receive you in my humble habitation, and at my humble board. Perhaps you may think that I am here affecting a false modesty, and that I deal unjustly with the *board*, when I style it *humble*. But I assure you, I mean what I say. For excepting only the sincere good will, and the hearty welcome which I proffer you on this occasion, I can claim very little of this entertainment but the *simple board below*. The viands above are all the contributions of good friends to you and me; some of whom I will not name, because they may happen to be here present, and others I need not name, because they are absent. All of them by this act wish to acknowledge the utility of your services, and to make substantial demonstration of the warm interest they take in the little party assembled."

It was the year 1847, when the famine prevailed in Ireland, and subscriptions were every where making to relieve the dreadful distress in the sister isle. This will explain the following beautiful and feeling continuation:—

"For another reason I rejoice that they have evinced an interest on this particular occasion. For had it been otherwise, I should scarcely have had the heart at this crisis of want and woe to appear to luxuriate in the table, or have deemed it consistent with my particular character as steward of the poor,—much as I wish to show honour and attention to my present company,—I should scarcely have had the courage to divert any available resources towards furnishing what is familiarly termed a supper party, whilst famine is raging in the land, with a fury and fatality unparalleled, perhaps, in the history of the world. But we may take comfort that in partaking of what friends have provided, we do not exhaust their benevolence, nor do we diminish our own means and will to sympathise practically with others. So that the result may prove to be that charity may be augmented, that the fragments may exceed the original provision, and that we shall only think with a more *determined* charity on the hearts which are bursting, and the frames that are breaking, and the souls that are passing, from sheer want, to a farther and a better land. And we shall fervently pray that abundance may tax its means, and mediocrity husband its resources; that small hearts may be enlarged, and large hearts may be widened still, to meet the pressing, the appalling exigencies of so many millions of our fellow-creatures perishing with hunger.

"Forgive me for dwelling on this point; for on these occasions it is uppermost in my mind, as I doubt not it is in yours. Let me now acknowledge, and thank you all, collectively and individually, for your useful services to our little church."

He proceeds to show how the Catholic Church herself acknowledges and regulates such services, and concludes by pointing out beautifully and practically what should be the guiding spirit of those who sing in our holy services:—

"They should aim to give majesty to Religion, and to nourish devotion and humility in their hearts. Singing in *grace*, as the Apostle says, *singing in grace, in your hearts to God*; so that those who listen may be worked upon, as was the great St. Augustin, who thus leaves it recorded in one of his celebrated works: 'O how much did I weep in hearing thy hymns and canticles, being exceedingly moved by the voices of thy harmonious Church. Those voices flowed in at my ears, and thy truth distilled into my heart, and from thence the affection of devotion boiled over, and tears flowed from me, and I found much comfort in them.' Conf. ix., 6.

"These are my simple wishes to God for you all, and this is my best expression of thanks, that the harmony of your voices should bespeak the harmony of your faith and your virtues: that through those voices truth should distil into ears, and devotion be transfused into hearts: that tears should be made to flow rather than admiration be excited, and that from an earthly choir you may be raised to an immortal one, whose merits are more justly recognised and better rewarded. We will now sing: *Non nobis Domine, non nobis*, &c."

Thus did this incomparable man possess the secret of treating the most ordinary affairs in a way peculiarly fascinating, and at the same time instructive. The reader cannot fail to admire the vein of humour, and playful pleasantry in which he manages the simple matter of thanking his choir, and welcoming them to his entertainment, and much more the ingenuity with which he almost imperceptibly elevates the occasion to a higher purpose, and contrives to make it serve the great ends of charity and devotion. But he had an original way of treating the commonest subjects: he invested the most unattractive themes with some elegant adornment, and worked out every topic with grace and felicity peculiarly his own. Indeed his compositions were often overlaboured; for he was never contented with ordinary precision and elegance. Great care and scrupulous attention pervaded all his performances, and as a necessary consequence were conspicuous in all his missionary duties.

It will at the same time be easily understood how a missioner, zealous as he was even to anxiety: and particular even to scrupulosity, must occasionally prove a trial to his flock; and it must be owned that this was too frequently the case with Dr. WEEDALL. His sermons were often tediously long, and so severely tried the patience of the congregation, that they had recourse to the expedient of putting up a clock in the chapel, where it could be seen by the preacher, and might warn him not to exceed a reasonable time in his discourses. But this produced no effect: he was too much absorbed in his subject, to attend to the progress of time; and so it was with him to the end of his career. In every function he was apt to be very long and often tiresome: he did not make allowance for the feelings of others, but measured their capacity by the exalted standard of his own zeal and devotion. Accustomed for so many years to college discipline and command, he would often keep persons waiting for him; and was hardly ever punctual. He has been known to interrupt hearing Confessions, and keep a number of penitents waiting a long time, because he had his Office to say. In many things of this kind he was certainly more attentive to his own convenience, than to that of his people. Nevertheless they always loved him and respected him; for they knew how much his great virtues and talents outweighed these defects. But the truth was that the mission was not his precise vocation. When placed upon it indeed, he gave his heart and soul to its duties, and discharged them faithfully to the best of his judgment and ability; but as a missioner he was not exactly in his element.

CHAPTER XVII.

Dr. Weedall's Address at the Instalment of Bishop Ullathorne—He is Called to St. Chad's, Birmingham, and Made Vicar General and Dean of the Cathedral—His Funeral Sermon on Bishop Walsh—He Retires to Handsworth—His Sermon at the Funeral of Lady Throckmorton—Funeral of Dr. Kirk—Dr. Weedall's Memoir of Him—Dr. Weedall Appointed Provost of Birmingham—Assists at the First Council of Westminster—Accompanies Bishop Errington on his Visitation—Meets with an Accident—Death of John Earl of Shrewsbury—Dr. Weedall's Funeral Oration over Him—Death of Earl Bertram, his Successor.

In the month of August, 1848, the Right Rev. Dr. Ullathorne was appointed Vicar Apostolic of the Central District, vacant by the translation of Dr. Walsh to the London District, preparatory to his being nominated, as was intended, the first Archbishop of Westminster, when the new hierarchy should be constituted. Bishop Ullathorne was translated therefore from the Western to the Central District. He was installed in St. Chad's Cathedral, at Birmingham, on the 30th of August, and Dr. Weedall, having been appointed his Vicar General, received him at the door of the

Cathedral, and read up in the church the Brief of Institution. After the ceremony of installation, the attendant clergy, numbering almost one hundred, were entertained in the Bishop's house; and before they separated, DR. WEEDALL delivered an address of congratulation, in the name of the clergy to their new bishop. After alluding in feeling terms to the loss of Dr. Walsh, who had for almost half a century been "the zealous supporter and propagator, as well as the meek ornament of religion in this district, heading and cheering forward its onward march," he expressed nevertheless "sweet confidence in the zealous, and pious, and energetic, and talented successor;" and thus continued:—

"He is no stranger amongst us; he has laboured successfully and enduringly at our side; and I venture to tell his lordship that he will find an obedient and confiding clergy, willing and ready to sustain his energies, and to concur in all his plans for the promotion of one endeared and common object. We tender him this day our hands and our hearts *de jure* and *de facto*:.........

"May clergy and people find in him a father, and may they prove to him, in return, *his joy and his crown*.

"Health be his, and strength, and lengthened days of successful and meritorious labour."

Bishop Ullathorne well knew, and properly appreciated the talents and merits of his intimate friend DR. WEEDALL, and he lost no time in availing himself of his valuable counsels. In a Pastoral Letter of November 16th, 1848, his lordship made the following announcement respecting him:—

"Having considered that a Bishop must extend his personal vigilance, and a watchful solicitude to every portion of his district; that he must of necessity be much and frequently absent from his residence; that, nevertheless, there should always be found some one there possessed of authority to meet such exigencies as may arise, and require immediate attention, and to represent the Bishop during his absence even in his district; and well aware that this is the usual practice of the Church; desirous also to have near us a prudent ecclesiastic to share our counsels; we have, therefore, appointed the Very Rev. Dr. Weedall to reside with us as our Vicar General both in temporals and spirituals; whom we have also appointed Dean of our Episcopal Church, and to whom we beg to refer all persons who call upon us on matters of business in our absence, unless they should particularly wish to consult ourselves."

As further proofs of the Bishop's esteem and confidence, he signified in the same Pastoral his appointment of DR. WEEDALL to preside over three important councils,—those of the temporalities of the district,—of the temporalities of Oscott College, and of the temporalities of the school at Sedgley Park. In consequence of these important appointments, DR. WEEDALL, in the month of December, removed from Leamington, and came to reside with his Bishop at St. Chad's, Birmingham. On the ensuing Feast of the Purification of our Blessed Lady, he assisted at the head of the clergy of the town at the opening of the new chapel of the Oratory recently established in Birmingham, under the venerable superior, Rev. J. H. Newman, who preached an affecting sermon on the occasion.

He was soon after called upon to discharge a more important and trying duty, to preach the funeral Oration over his late Bishop and lamented friend, Dr. Walsh, who died in London, on the 18th of February, 1849, aged 72. His funeral obsequies took place first at St. Mary's Church, Moorfields, London, on the 28th of February. His honoured remains were, however, removed on the following day to St. Chad's Cathedral, Birmingham, where another solemn service was performed for him on the 2nd of March; and his body was finally deposited in the crypt of the cathedral. On both occasions DR. WEEDALL delivered the same funeral oration, with the slight exception of the introduction, which was substituted at St. Chad's, for the exordium at Moorfields, that having been "merely apologetic of the preacher's peculiar position," as explained in a note to the Oration, afterwards published. The circumstances of its having been delivered but a few years ago, and subsequently published, render it unnecessary to dwell much upon its contents. It is eloquent, earnest, and pathetic; but, perhaps, hardly equal to DR. WEEDALL's previous productions. It is a laboured and studied composition, in which, however, he undertook to establish more than he could have justly hoped to accomplish. He selected for his text: *Behold a great priest, who in his days pleased God, and was found just.* (Ecclus. xlvi.; 17.) He felt that it would be thought "not exactly to delineate the peculiar characteristics" of the deceased prelate, "yet," he said, "the more I consider the prominent features of his life, and the structural machinery of his character, the more I am persuaded that there were the elements of *greatness* within him, as there were confessedly the elements of *goodness*." The latter will be universally and gladly admitted; but the preacher, able as he was, could hardly establish satisfactorily any other *greatness* in the character of Bishop Walsh than that of virtue. Good, pious, humble, amiable, zealous, meek, patient, and persevering he certainly was; and so far he was *great*, but no farther. DR. WEEDALL first undertakes to prove him *great* in his personal character, that is a man of great virtues; and here no one will dispute his success. But he also professes to show that he was *great* in his "enlarged views of prospective utility," and in his means and measures to realise it; and lastly, that he was *great* in the results which he achieved. These two latter points he treats together, as naturally resolvable into one: but those who knew the holy prelate well, and are well acquainted with the course of his episcopacy, will hardly consider that the preacher has established his propositions. He enumerates indeed a number of good and great works planned and begun, and in some instances perfected: but though they all happened under his episcopacy, it does not follow that they were all owing to him. It would be safer, and nearer to the truth, to say that he was carried along by these events, rather than that he devised or directed them, or at least many of them. They certainly rendered his episcopacy memorable: but it is too well known that they are not unclouded in some instances with very painful associations; and even the preacher felt obliged to hint that he "adventured" occasionally "a noble daring, a little beyond the technical caution of human policy." But Dr. WEEDALL did himself injustice, when he modestly ascribed to Bishop Walsh the merit of erecting "a College and Seminary, perhaps the largest and most complete that has been erected, *de novo*, since the days of the Reformation." That work would never have been accomplished, or even attempted, without a WEEDALL: he had indeed the willing sanction and cordial co-operation of Dr. Walsh; but to WEEDALL are due the erection and organisation of that noble College.

Though compared with DR. WEEDALL'S previous discourses, this Sermon is so far defective as it undertakes to prove him generally *great*, who could be called so only in the sense that he was *good*; it is nevertheless a very fine composition. It bears the marks of labour and rhetorical artifice; but it is still a production of very great merit. One extract, describing in 'language of unequalled power, the horrors of the first French Revolution, will suffice in illustration.

"Like a wild tornado, it swept away our foreign colleges and educational establishments, commingling all things, sacred and profane; and in the face of God and man, heaping up a monstrous accumulation of murder, rapine, sacrilege, perjury, cruelty, and impiety, so that no tongue could repeat, no pen could record, save the pen of the recording Angel, the indescribable horrors of those frightful times. Suffice it to say, that all our foreign establishments were dismantled,—St. Omers, Douay College, that mother of martyrs, and bulwark of the faith,—the houses of the Benedictines and Franciscans were all cleared out and plundered, and their holy inmates, seniors and juniors, were forced away by ruffian soldiers, and crowded into the gloomy prisons of Arras and the Citadel of Douriens."

DR. WEEDALL'S residence at the Bishop's House, and position as the head priest and Dean of St. Chad's, Birmingham, were of great benefit to religion, and great comfort and support to the Bishop, Dr. Ullathorne. In placing him there, his lordship had two objects in view,—the service of the District, and the putting him in his proper position as the first priest of the District. Many difficulties were overcome by his counsels and co-operation; and his presence was of material service in aiding to bring things to a bearing, and in inspiring confidence. But the charge was of a nature too oppressive for his health and strength, and towards the autumn of this year, 1849, he was in a state of great suffering, and his eyes much worse. He went to London for a little change and recreation in October; and in his absence his old friend and schoolfellow, Bishop Briggs, V. A. of the Yorkshire District, conveyed through Dr. Kirk, of Lichfield, his apprehensions to Bishop Ullathorne, that DR. WEEDALL could not continue in his position at St. Chad's without serious danger to his life. His kind and good Bishop immediately signified to him his sincere wish to relieve his mind from all anxiety arising from his position at St. Chad's, and that he had no other object than to consult his feelings. The Bishop thought he might like to return to Leamington, and offered in that case to place a second priest there to assist him. But he begged Dr. WEEDALL, whom he addressed as his "dear and venerable friend," that he would not consider *him* (the Bishop), but only himself and his own health and happiness, in any conclusion to which he might come in the important matter, adding that had he anticipated so much trial to Dr. WEEDALL, he certainly never should have proposed his coming to St. Chad's. Dr. WEEDALL preferred retiring to the Convent of our Lady of Mercy, at Handsworth, close to Birmingham, where he would have only a small congregation to attend to, besides the community, and the children of the orphanage. He accordingly quitted St. Chad's, and removed to Handsworth on December 18th, 1849.

He was called a few months later to preach another funeral Sermon. Elizabeth, Lady Throckmorton, the wife of Sir Robert Throckmorton, Bart., and sister of Cardinal Acton, had taken a voyage to Madeira, in the hope of benefit to her health; but unhappily in vain. She died there in April, and was brought home for interment in the family vault at Coughton, Warwickshire. The funeral took place on the 1st of June, 1850, and Sir Robert, an intimate friend and former pupil of Dr. WEEDALL's, requested him to preach on the occasion. His discourse was so original and touchingly beautiful, that the reader cannot fail to be gratified with some extracts from it. Those who have had experience in preaching funeral discourses, know how difficult it is in such compositions to produce any thing new: but DR. WEEDALL was never at a loss, his fertility was never exhausted. Accordingly, in this Sermon he takes a new and striking text, and draws it out with the happiest ingenuity:—

"*And the Angel of the Lord...said to her: Agar, handmaid of Sarai, whence comest thou? and whither goest thou?* Genesis xvi.

"How different the reception to-day from that which our hopes had formed! How different is she who comes in, from her who went out in gladness! From her who went out, the crown of her family, the ornament of her house, "a joyful mother of children." Ask the question again: *Whence comest thou? and whither goest thou?* There is no ear to catch the greeting, no tongue to answer. And I am commissioned to answer for what portion of mortality that coffin contains. She is come from a pilgrim land, from a voyage of experiment, where she fulfilled a duty of prudent piety. She is come from a land of salubrity, where she was enjoined to seek for restoration. And she comes back the mute evidence of unintermitted patience under protracted sufferings, and of meek resignation to the adorable will of God, to which she had learned completely to subject her own: *Not my will, but thine be done!*

"And now she is come to her last home on earth, to bespeak the prayers of relatives and friends who honoured her, to receive the benedictions of her holy Mother the Church, and to be signed and sealed within her final mansion, until she be transferred to the valley of Josaphat. And her soul, whither is it gone? It is gone *to the house of her eternity* (Eccles. xii., 5): and if it have met with a just Judge, it has also met with a merciful one.

"My brethren, we do not augur rashly when we augur favourably of the general issue of that last trial to which she has been subjected. Her life and conversation among you was familiar to all; and by all was her character justly appreciated. Singularly endowed both by nature and by grace, a sound mind and a solid judgment moderated and regulated a religious heart. Piety was engrafted in her infant soul. She seemed to have shared it as an inheritance with her saintly brother, who though exposed in his youth by a Protestant guardian to the discouraging atmosphere of an English University, yet, as soon as he became emancipated from his tutelage, renounced, like St. Aloysius and St. Stanislaus, the brilliant prospects of life, and postponing earthly to heavenly enjoyments, he threw himself generously into the ranks of the Church. Under her tuition he became successively priest and prelate, counsellor and judge in her ecclesiastical courts, and prince and cardinal in the Church of God.

"As it was an honourable privilege to have been the sister of such a brother, so was it presumptive evidence of a kindred piety. And were it not that while the many would be gratified to hear the detail of her virtues, the recital might disturb a sacred grief, which it were not seemly to disturb, I might tell of her unaffected and deep sunk piety, of her love of the Church, and all its holy institutions, of her ardent love of Jesus Christ in the holy Sacrament of the altar, of her wise and enlightened care of her children and household, of her tender solicitude for dependants and the poor, of her bountiful provision for the religious education of the poor children of the neighbourhood, and of her many secret charities that flowed from her resources to relieve the widows and the orphans, the sick and the destitute, and to clothe the aged and the naked, as their wants might respectively plead. I can even figure to myself the interesting description in the Acts of the Apostles (ix., 36), of the holy widow *named Tabitha, which by interpretation is called Dorcas. This woman was full of good works and alms deeds which she did. And it came to pass in those days that she was sick and died. Whom when they had washed, they laid her in an upper chamber. And forasmuch as Lydda was nigh to Joppe, the disciples hearing that*

Peter was there, sent unto him two men, desiring that he would not be slack to come unto them. And Peter rising up went with them. And when he was come, they brought him into the upper chamber. And all the widows stood about him weeping, and showing him the coats and the garments which Dorcas had made them.

"And here the parallel must end. We cannot realize the conclusion of the scene: *And they all being put forth, Peter kneeling down, prayed, and turning to the body he said: Tabitha, arise. And she opened her eyes: and seeing Peter, she sat up. And giving her his hand, he lifted her up. And when he had called the saints and the widows he presented her alive.* This we cannot realize. We cannot pray with the authority of St. Peter: *Tabitha, arise.* But we can meekly commend her to St. Peter and to all the saints of God, and fervently pray that her soul *may rest in everlasting peace.*"

Further on he thus strikingly personifies Death:

"*Remember that Death is not slow.* (Ecclus xiv., 12.) It is not enough to admit that Death will come; we must be convinced that it will *come quickly, as the torrent that passeth swiftly in the valleys.* (Job vi., 15.) For indeed it sets us in our cradle, and crouches at our heels in our earliest paths. It follows us foot by foot, and step by step; and though we plunge into the thickest of the throng, and think to hide ourselves as individuals among the multitude, yet Death never loses either sight or ground. And there he stands and watches each. You see him described in the old tapestry before you, standing on the earth, as if to claim it. His hour glass at hand, nicely adjusted, for one an hour, for one half an hour, for another ten minutes, for another three. And whether high, or low, or rich, or poor, whether young, or aged, healthy, or infirm, when once a man has reached the term which God has prescribed, those *appointed bounds which cannot be passed*, (Job xiv., 5,) he crouches towards him without regarding face or person, and when the last grain of sand has dropped below, he smites him down without remorse, and in royal guise he sets his foot upon his neck." Job xviii., 14.

At the close of the year 1851, the venerable Dr. Kirk died at Lichfield, at the very advanced age of 91. DR. WEEDALL, his old friend and early pupil at Sedgley Park, sung the solemn Mass of Requiem at his funeral, in his little church of St. Cross, at Lichfield; and he afterwards wrote a very interesting memoir of him, which appeared in the Catholic papers, *The Tablet* and *Catholic Standard*, Jan. 24th, 1852, as also in the *Ordo recitandi* for the year 1853. The introduction deserves to be transferred to this page:—

"A pillar has just fallen in our little church, a master mind has fled, carrying with it the records of three generations, a great man has departed, or what is better, a good man and a holy priest, *whose praise was in all the churches*, has gone to his eternal home......Of patriarchal age, and patriarchal simplicity of manners, ranging through near a century of Catholic affairs, with many of which he was actively and intimately identified, *quorum pars magna fuit*, he moved a living chronicle of persons, places, and facts, which our little English church will long desiderate, perhaps never replace. Affection would fain dwell on his memory, and if possible, adorn it; but time and occupation can afford only a brief memoir, which the future annalist may extend. *His saltem accumulem donis.*"

In June, 1852, the new Chapters were erected in the Dioceses of England; and again the Bishop of Birmingham paid a just tribute to the merits of DR. WEEDALL by appointing him the first Provost of his Cathedral Chapter. He assisted, as the proxy of the Chapter, at the First Provincial

Council of Westminster, held at St. Mary's College, Oscott, in the beginning of July, was assistant priest at the Pontifical High Mass, and read out each day at the conclusion of each of the three Sessions, the three points of Meditation. Soon after the Synod, he accompanied the Bishop of Plymouth, Dr. Errington, on his first episcopal visitation of his diocese; but unfortunatey met with an accident, by scraping the shin bone of his leg against a step, which obliged him to lie by for several days; so that the Bishop was reluctantly obliged to leave him behind in Cornwall, in September, and forego the further benefit and pleasure of his accompanying him for the rest of his visitation. For several days he could neither go up nor down stairs; but the wound healed soundly, though the process was slow and painful.

An event occurred at the close of this year, which cast a heavy gloom over the whole Catholic body in England, which has only gone on deepening since, by the inscrutable dispensation of Divine Providence. This was the unexpected death of John, Earl of Shrewsbury, which took place at Naples, on the 9th of November. It was felt in England as a perfect calamity; and time has only too fatally justified the estimate of that very desolating event. On the 14th of December, the precious remains of the great and good Earl having been conveyed to his princely mansion at Alton Towers, a solemn Mass of Requiem was sung in the beautiful family chapel, and DR. WEEDALL delivered a sermon, justly characterised as "a magnificent funeral discourse, which did honour to his head and heart."* It was indeed "magnificent," a model of pulpit eloquence, worthy of the exalted subject, worthy of the gifted orator. It is equal, if not superior, to any of his previous productions; and no feebleness, no commonplace, no falling off in any way can be detected in any part of it. A more strictly appropriate text might have been suggested; but a nobler use, or a grander application of the text chosen could not have been imagined. The sermon, of course, was immediately published; and it is too fresh in every one's remembrance to require much to be quoted from it here. A few of its most interesting passages may, however, be selected:—

"Born to the highest earthly pretensions, possessed of fortune in princely amount, and of domains corresponding to his fortune, descending from a line of ancestry, whose martial prowess had shed a lustre over the palmy days of England's glory, the good Earl of Shrewsbury might have trod the most select paths of fashionable life, might have rioted in all the luxuries of refinement, and have affected a notoriety which many would have deemed most fitting, and more would have considered, at least, not unhonourable. But his judgment was formed on a safer rule. His wisdom was of a higher order. Built upon the maxims of the Gospel, and the assumed insecurity of worldly policy, he was poor in the midst of plenty. He made *friends of the mammon of iniquity*,† and regarding his wealth as a *deposit*, rather than an *absolute property*, he expended, without limitation, in charity, and laid up his

* Memoir of the Earl of Shrewsbury, in the *Ordo* for 1854, by Rev. Edward Price.

† St. Luke xvi., 9.

goods in the bosom of the poor. He transmitted rich treasures, in secret, to Heaven; and whilst his memory will *be in benediction before God and man, his good works*, we need not doubt, *will commend him to mercy in the gate*. *Et laudent eum in portis opera ejus.**

"And this is the true point on which to fix his character. It would be a waste of time to trace out his early history, and chronicle his years from the boy to the man. He ran through the usual course of Catholic studies, partly at college, partly under private tuition, with credit and success; and his sound acquirements and solid judgment evinced the ability of his instructors; as did the gentleness of his demeanour, and the purity of his principles speak well for the excellence of his moral training. His abilities, in fact, were of a very high order, and, improved by habits of studious application, made him equal to his station on every emergency. He rarely indeed appeared in his place in the House of Lords, because his habits were estranged from political contention; but when he did speak, he was received by his peers with great courtesy; and the marked attention which was paid to him, showed the weight which was acknowledged to attach to his arguments. *Nobilis in portis, quando sederit cum senatoribus terræ*†.........

"It is from the heart that spring the hero and the sage. It is the heart, sublimed and ennobled by true wisdom and virtue, that constitutes the excellence of personal character, and decides the moral worth, and the solid greatness of a Christian nobleman. This was the heroism, the gentle blood, the noble chivalry of the good Earl of Shrewsbury, whose patent of nobility is registered in heaven, which tests so severely the proud pretensions of earth. His was the true estimate of greatness, that without religion, greatness was a *great vanity;* and his also was the just estimate of riches, on the principles propounded in the Holy Scriptures, that whilst *they are* indeed a *crown*

* Prov. xxxi., 31. † Prov. xxxi., 23.

of the wise, they are *the folly of fools*.* And that the immoderate affectation of them only *leads into temptation, and drowns men in destruction and perdition*.† And hence arose the two distinguishing features of his life, his genuine piety, and his unexampled munificence."

At the end of a beautiful exposition of the virtues by which this lamented nobleman had rather adorned his riches, than was adorned by them, the preacher exclaims :—

"Herein consists the felicity of wealth, and none enjoyed this luxury more than the 'Good Earl,' the emphatically 'Good Earl of Shrewsbury.'"

But the conclusion of this noble Oration is touching indeed, and doubly so now, after all that has since befallen to cast us deeply down in humiliation and bewilderment.

"And here I think that your keen sensibilities forestall me, and revert to the critical contingencies that hang around that House. Would that I had upon me a *burthen* of prophecy, and that I were commissioned to predict, as Nathan of old—*The Lord foretelleth to thee, that He will make thee a house. And when thy days shall be fulfilled, and thou shalt sleep with thy fathers, I will raise up one after thee... ...And I will establish him, I will be to him a Father, and he shall be to me a son. And thy house shall be firm and faithful.*‡

"May these words be prophetic, as in the mouth of Nathan! Our English Church implores it. Thousands of prayers, from pure lips and fervent hearts, will be incessantly poured forth for the heir and successor to the noble House of Talbot. BERTRAM and JOHN will share in our holy sacrifices, and we shall instinctively commemorate the one in the 'Memento for the living,' when we commemorate the

* PROV. XIV., 24.   † 1 TIM. VI., 9.
‡ 2 KINGS VII., 11; 12, et seq.

other in the 'Memento for the dead.' May God show him the path in which to walk, and perfect his steps therein. For there is a *path and a way* before him. A glorious destiny to accomplish, and a noble example to pursue. May the Lord preserve him, and give him life, and make him happy on the earth. '*Dominus conservet eum, et vivificet eum, et beatum faciat eum in terra.*'"*

Alas! Alas! how bitterly have these holy aspirations been disappointed! Young Earl BERTRAM, his pious and amiable successor, survived not quite four years, and was carried off on the 10th of August, 1856, in his 24th year. But how deep was his love and veneration for his saintly predecessor, whom he always called his uncle, though he was in reality his cousin, the following extract will show from one of his beautiful letters to the present writer:—

"But, my dear Dr. Husenbeth, can words express the extent of our grief at having lost our greatest benefactor, Catholic England's brightest star? Can we cease wondering why he was taken; and is it not natural we should say, 'Why, O Lord, didst thou not leave thy servant yet a little longer?' Truly God's ways are inscrutable, and never shall I be able to conceive why the excellent and virtuous Lord Shrewsbury was taken so soon, in the midst of his good works, unless the reason be that he was ripe for heaven, and God wished to crown him with the bright diadem he had gained by his pure, holy, and angelic life. At present my daily prayer is that I may be like unto him, and that I may live the good and holy life he ever lived. I beg also your good prayers, my dear Dr. Husenbeth, for this end.

In another letter to the author, the amiable young Earl thus expressed his vivid recollection

* Litany of the Church.

and appreciation of Dr. Weedall's beautiful allusion to himself in the funeral oration :—

"Your letter is full of that holy advice I love so much to hear, and which I truly hope to follow. Those words of Dr. Weedall, preached, too, on so solemn and mournful an occasion as that which took place exactly this day twelve-month, are constantly before me. 'For there is a *path and a way* before him. A glorious destiny to accomplish, and a noble example to pursue.' So there is, and God only grant I may walk steadfastly in that path, and make God and my holy religion the first, yea, the sole great object of my thoughts. But we must have God's grace, and that I shall receive through the pious and earnest prayers of the faithful."

How unsearchable are the ways of Divine Providence! *For who among men is he that can know the counsel of God? or who can think what the will of God is?* * He, whose praise was in all the churches, whose varied and multitudinous charities were familiarly known, but too numerous to recount, who relieved so many destitute, fed so many hungry, protected so many widows and orphans, sheltered so many houseless, liberated so many imprisoned, relieved by his angel-hand from debt and anxiety so many heart-broken priests, whose zeal rather than imprudence had involved them in difficulties, and restored them in joy and peace to their holy ministry and sorrowing flocks; he whose munificence to the Church was unbounded—almost startling to record—outstripping the deeds of the early patrician senators, and emulating in piety the

* Wisdom ix., 13.

merchant princes of Venice and Genoa, with whom a glorious church was their policy of insurance, and a costly altar the price of a vow;* he the great benefactor, support, and glory of Religion in our land, was suddenly taken from us; and his virtuous successor, fully prepared to walk in his holy footsteps, was scarcely permitted to set foot in them, when he too was snatched away; the last spark of the noble race of Talbot was extinguished, and the whole Catholic body in England made very sad, and very desolate. *He hath destroyed and hath not spared, and he hath caused the enemy to rejoice over thee, and hath set up the horn of thy adversaries.*†

* All this is taken almost word for word from DR. WEEDALL'S eloquent enumeration.

† LAMENTATIONS II., 17.

CHAPTER XVIII.

DR. WEEDALL IS REINSTATED AS PRESIDENT OF OSCOTT COLLEGE—SERIOUS ATTACK OF ILLNESS—IS MADE A DOMESTIC PRELATE OF HIS HOLINESS—HIS LETTER OF THANKS TO THE POPE—CELEBRATION OF THIS EVENT, TOGETHER WITH HIS JUBILEE.

*Believe God, and he will recover thee: and direct thy way, and trust in him.** DR. WEEDALL had now been separated from his beloved Oscott, his own creation, and the polar star of his whole life, for the dreary term of thirteen years: but he had been proved in the furnace, and found faithful; he had rightly *directed his way*, and *believed* and *trusted in God*, and the time was now come when he would *recover him*, and order for his restoration to his proper position, as the President of St. Mary's College. *And I said: I shall die in my nest, and as a palm-tree shall multiply my days....My glory shall always be renewed, and my bow in my hand shall be repaired.*† In all the places where he had been located on the Mission, he had been zealous, exemplary, and indefatigable; but he was not in his true position, and he was not happy. Every one

* ECCLUS. II., 6.   † JOB XXIX, 18, 20.

saw that the Mission was not his peculiar line of action and duty, and that he was not in his proper element, or sphere of exertion. His kind Bishop, Dr. Ullathorne, seized the earliest opportunity to honour him as he so well merited, and to restore him to his deserved and dignified position at St. Mary's College. He returned thither, and resumed the presidentship on the 2nd of July, 1853. He was now in his 65th year; but, always allowing for his constitutional nervous affection of the head, and weakness of eyes, he had no appearance of age, or decay.

> " His thoughts,
> His feelings, passions, good or evil, all
> Have nothing of old age ; and his bold brow
> *Bears but the scars of mind, the thoughts of years,*
> *Not their decrepitude.*"
>
> MARINO FALIERO. *Act II.*

It was indeed high time that DR. WEEDALL should come back to save Oscott from utter decline and decay. " In his vigour of life," said Bishop Ullathorne of him, in his circular to the clergy upon his death, " he raised that college up in its splendour, and left it prospering: he returned to it *in its hour of difficulty*, and expended on its service all the energies of life that yet remained to him. God blessed his work." It was indeed for St. Mary's College the *hour of difficulty*, and very different did he find it, from what he left it. A work of arduous labour was before him, but he did not shrink from it; a discouraging prospect, but it did not dishearten him. He was supported by three other Superiors, who gathered about him all old and tried Oscotians; and with their valuable aid, counsel, and experience, he set himself to the work again with all the courage and cheerfulness with which he had laboured in its first organisation, so many years before. The Bishop truly said that "God blessed his work:" his very name had a magic influence: it was almost an essential adjunct to Oscott; and as soon as it was again associated with the college, patronage returned, and confidence revived. By that wise government and prudent administration which were so familiar to Dr. Weedall, he gradually, unostentatiously, and safely performed his arduous work; and soon had the satisfaction to see the prospects of St. Mary's begin to brighten. It was not the labour of a day, but a work of steady confidence and unwearied perseverance. But these Dr. Weedall eminently possessed; and by these, under the Divine blessing, his efforts were crowned with success. In the month of November following he went to London, and attended, for the first time since his election, a meeting of the members of the old, and now defunct, Chapter of England. The writer was present, and witnessed with delight how cordially he was welcomed by all assembled, when quite unexpectedly he made his appearance. He dined with his brethren, was very cheerful, and evidently enjoyed himself highly. But alas! this first visit was to be also his last, and the prelude to a state of great suffering. After a very pleasant evening, he went back by the mail train to Birmingham. But he was seized with distressing pain on the journey, and on arriving at Birmingham was obliged to go to bed, and call in surgical aid immediately. He kept his bed, and was obliged to remain in Birmingham a fortnight. From that time, he was always more or less in a state of suffering; and, as Dr. Newman so truly described it in his funeral sermon, "it pleased Almighty God to send upon him a disorder which, during the last six years, fought with him, mastered him, and at length destroyed him." It was known, however, to his intimate friends, and to the writer among them, that he had all through life had symptoms which prepared the way for this final affliction.

Dr. WEEDALL was, however, cheered and encouraged in the following year by a special mark of favour from the Holy See. He received, quite unexpectedly, the high honour of being named a Monsignor of the second rank, as Domestic Prelate of his Holiness, and entitled to the style of Right Reverend. The Brief of appointment was dated May 9th, 1854. The humble man was again confounded, almost as much as when by the former Pope he had been appointed a Bishop. But his present Holiness had now conferred upon him all the honours of the prelacy, which could be given without the actual episcopal character, and consequent responsibility. He hastened to offer his thanks at the feet of the holy Father, in the following beautiful letter:—

"BEATISSIME PATER,

"Acceptissimum nuper, et quidem inopinatum pervenit ad me gratissimum illud Breve Apostolicum quo Beatitudo vestra immeritis honoribus me decorare benignissime velit. *Et quis sum ego servus tuus quoniam respexisti super me, abjectum in domo Dei!* Quam parum merui ut oculus ille, qui circumspicit totam Ecclesiam, in me humillimum, ictum præcipue injiciat! Ut in auribus meis illa vox sonet quæ fidem errantibus, monita periclitantibus, solatium afflictis usquequaque in Ecclesia præstare soleat! Ut venerabilis Petri successor tot præsulibus illustrissimis merito circumfusus, me indignissimum cooptari dignetur in numerum domesticorum Antistitum! Sane in illo munere latet aliquid subtilius excogitatum; innuendo scilicet dotes, monet interea Sanctitas vestra, quibus me virtutibus et quantis vestiri deceat, et quomodo me oporteat in *domo Dei conversari, quæ est Ecclesia Dei vivi, columna et firmamentum veritatis*. Sed quo ego indignior, eo magis elucet cura boni Pastoris, qui 'novit in area sua triticum, novit et paleam, novit segetem, novit et zizania.' Novit et fovet benigne, ut bonum semen tandem evadat.

"Mihi autem justa reputanti, minus propter me ipsum, quam propter alios hic honos conferri videatur, nempe ut Seminario cui parum idoneus præsideo, decus aliquod effulgeat, et ut laureola quædam nova innectatur Collegio Sanctæ Mariæ. Melius ergo relinquatur alumnis ut grates dignas persolvant. Placeat ergo Sanctitati tuæ devotissimorum accipere obsequium filiorum.

"Omnes nos denique Sanctæ Sedi et Beati Petri successori addictissimi, et magis ego, quo proximior nunc Capiti addictus et obstrictus, omnes nos, ad pedes Sanctitatis vestræ provoluti, iteratis precibus Deum invocamus ut omnia Sanctitati vestræ feliciter succedant, et ut cuncta

prosperè eveniant, et ut Deus et Dominus noster salvum-
atque incolumen custodiat Ecclesiæ suæ Sanctæ, ad regen-
dum populum sanctum Dei.

"Hæc exigua sinceræ pietatis testimonia accepta
habere dignetur Beatitudo vestra, nobisque Apostolicam
denuo elargiri benedictionem, quam similiter enixè pro
omnibus postulat.

"Beatissime Pater,
"Sanctitatis vestræ
"Humillimus, obsequentissimus, et addictissimus
Filius et Servus,
"HENRICUS WEEDALL."*

* [Translation.]

"MOST HOLY FATHER,

"That most welcome, and indeed unexpected and most gratifying Apostolic Brief has lately reached me, by which your Holiness has been pleased most graciously to honour me with unmerited favour. *And who am I thy servant, that thou hast looked upon me, an abject in the house of God?* How little have I deserved that that eye, which looks around the whole Church, should particularly direct its view to me most lowly as I am! That in my ears should sound that voice which is wont on every side to give faith to the erring, warning to those in danger, and solace to the afflicted! That the venerable successor of Peter, deservedly surrounded by so many most illustrious pontiffs, should vouchsafe to adopt me most unworthy among the number of his domestic prelates! Truly in that favour there lies something more profoundly hidden; namely, that in alluding to qualifications, your Holiness in the meantime admonishes me with what and how great virtues it behoves me to be adorned, and how I ought *to behave in the house of God, which is the Church of the living God, the pillar and ground of truth*. But the more unworthy I am, the more conspicuous is the care of the good Pastor, 'who knows in his threshing floor the wheat, and knows also the straw, knows the corn, and knows also the tares:' knows them and kindly cherishes them that they may in the end become good seed.

"To me, however, if I estimate rightly, this honour appears conferred much less on my account than on that of others; namely, that a certain degree of distinction may adorn the Seminary over which I unworthily preside, and a fresh wreath of laurel encircle St. Mary's College. It may

The reader cannot fail to notice with admiration the ingenious humility of this Letter, by which the whole merit of the honour received is referred to the College, and not to him who so justly deserved it in the estimation of every one but himself. It was indeed matter of universal joy and congratulation that the merits of this great and good man should have been so signally recognised by this high mark of favour from the Holy See. It was an event not to be passed over with any ordinary festivity; and as it happened just at the time when Dr. Weedall* had completed the fiftieth year from his first coming to Oscott from Sedgley Park on the 11th of June, 1804, it was determined to celebrate both his new dignity, and his Jubilee, in one grand

then be best left to the students to return befitting thanks. May it therefore please your Holiness to accept the homage of most devoted children.

"We all, finally, being most attached to the Holy See and the Successor of Blessed Peter, and I more especially as being now nearer and more closely devoted and bound to the Head, we all casting ourselves at the feet of your Holiness, call upon God with repeated prayers, that all prosperity may attend your Holiness, and all things may have a successful issue, and that our God and Lord may keep you safe and secure to his holy Church, to rule the holy people of God.

"May your Holiness deign to accept this imperfect testimony of sincere devotedness, and again grant us your Apostolical benediction, which is entreated alike for all by

"Most holy Father,
"Your Holiness'
"Most humble, most obedient, and most devoted Son and Servant,
"HENRY WEEDALL."

* It was agreed upon at the College, as most convenient, and most acceptable to his own feelings, that he should still be addressed by his old familiar name of Doctor: and so it is retained in these pages.

College Festival, which accordingly took place on the 12th of June, as the 11th fell on a Sunday.

The celebration of that day was devoutly commenced by High Mass. At three o'clock in the afternoon a large company assembled in the Library, honoured by the attendance of the Bishop of the Diocese, Dr. Ullathorne, the Bishop of Shrewsbury, Dr. James Browne, and many of the clergy and laity who had been educated at Oscott. Addresses were presented to the new MONSIGNOR by the superiors and students, followed by a cordial address of congratulation from the Bishop of Birmingham, and a feeling speech of grateful reminiscence from the Bishop of Shrewsbury. The whole proceedings were reported in the Catholic journals, but some extracts cannot but be acceptable in this biography.

The first address, which was from the Superiors and Professors, after alluding to Bishops Milner and Walsh in connexion with Oscott, paid this well-merited compliment to DR. WEEDALL:—

"Thus whilst we see in this college the work of three great names, our eyes on this day naturally rest upon one; and yet the name of that one relieved and adorned by its surrounding associations. Truly then may we say—

Finis coronat opus.

"This consummation of long toils can, however, be appreciated only by estimating aright its scanty commencement. When Sedgley Park first resigned you to the care of Oscott, the latter was a weak sapling just transplanted to an apparently unpropitious soil. How this sapling had taken root in England; how it survived its parent tree, when that had been struck down by the French revolution;

and under what care it throve, like the other offshoots of the old Douay College, be it for others to tell; enough that all have thriven; enough that the little schools of the half-discouraged men, that fled from old Douay, have increased and dilated into the present English colleges, colleges which undoubtedly have to struggle, more or less, with difficulties, but which, we may reasonably believe, have the innate vigour to overgrow every obstacle, and, alike in sunshine and in storm, to become, before many years have passed, the wide-spread giants of the forest.

"When from such a commencement we already see such results, we may well, at the close of half a century, turn our eyes to one, who is both a witness, and, in his own allotted sphere, in no small degree a cause of such undeniable progress. When this witness, moreover, is one whose personal merits have been so recently recognised and honoured by the Holy Father himself, and whose knowledge and experience, kindliness of disposition, and refined tact, delicacy indeed may forbid us to dwell upon, but gratitude has stored up in the memory of hundreds; then, indeed, does such a day as this become a day, not only of interest, but of unfeigned, affectionate felicitation and joy."

The address of the Students came next, and was the warm and affectionate ebullition of youthful hearts; as the following passage will testify:—

"If ever there was a Superior who has well nigh realised the ideal substitute for a parent; who has felt the joys and griefs of those entrusted to his care, and identified their feelings with his own, it is he with whom we this day congratulate. Whom we honour as Rome honours, whom we love as all must love, who have been blessed with his care. Father! we speak from the abundance of the heart, yet not in language adequate to its fulness. Our hearts are young and overflowing; our expressions barren, and not yet rounded for congratulation. But appreciate our humble demonstration. Listen to the expression of our joy for your new dignity, of thankfulness to God who has so long spared you to us, and of anxious wishes that your years may be prolonged. Hear our vows of devotion to Alma Mater. Yes! Oscott is still dear to her sons; *dearer now that her founder is restored and has drawn upon her the blessing of Rome.* The shadow of Peter that flitted over the infirm, and left health and joy in its train, encompasses us round; the hand of Peter, that lifted the cripple to wholeness and activity, is extended in honour to you, and in blessing to your charge; and when did Peter's blessing fail? Oscott shall yet again arise, and her best years be counted by the years of her beloved Superior and President, DR. WEEDALL."

The address of the Bishop of Birmingham is too beautiful, too eloquent, and too richly applicable, to bear any excision. Here it follows entire:—

"I feel a singular pleasure, Right Reverend Sir, and my dear friend, in uniting my congratulations with those that have been presented to you by the Superiors, Professors, and Students of the college, on this auspicious occasion. *For fifty years your name has been associated with this institution, from which it never can be in future separated. In its present expansion and completeness the College of Saint Mary's, Oscott, recognises you as its founder.* Admirably as experience has shown this large structure to be adapted to its purposes, finished as are its arrangements, suitable and harmonious as are its appointments, even to the least details, it was the emanation of your mind; and the time through which it has flourished, from its foundation on this beautiful site, has but indicated more perfectly the judgment and foresight which you exercised in its projection. And, in your venerable yet vigorous age, you have come to renew that peculiar spirit of ecclesiastical piety and discipline within its walls with which your character imbued it from the first.

"The Supreme Pontiff, in that document which has just been read, has shown how well he understands and how thoroughly he has appreciated your merits, even in their detail; and the distinction which, unsolicited and unlooked for, the Father of the Faithful has, out of his high consideration, and of his own motion, conferred upon you at this interesting moment of your career, reflects honour from you upon me, upon this college, upon this diocese; and I know how thoroughly, how heartily the Clergy join with me in congratulating you upon this well-merited proof of Apostolic favour. One thing only I regret in this festive commemoration. You have been deceiving us. So gentle has the green vigour of your spirit grown over this half century, in companionship with the college, that the term has come upon us suddenly and unawares. It was a sudden discovery. And the discovery came so late, so near on the day, that there was not time left for ample preparations. I myself knew of the arrival of this jubilee only three days ago. Had there been but time for the invitations I am sure that many Clergymen from the adjoining dioceses, that distinguished Prelates, that many of those once your pupils, of more than one generation or even two, who occupy dignified positions in the world, would have gladly come here this day to give you cordial proof that their esteem and veneration for you has undergone no change.

"After the discriminating appreciation of the Sovereign Pontiff my commendations were vain. But if only for my own satisfaction I will dwell a moment on that modesty and gentleness which, instead of impairing, adds force to firmness when fit occasions call it forth. That keen spirit, always of the Ecclesiastic; that kind and loving heart. Witness it, Rev. Brethren; Dr. WEEDALL has passed those fifty years, and has never made an enemy. With whom did he ever come in contact whom he did not make a friend, and a constant friend? Then that eye for the beautiful, that perception for the true, that exquisite taste in literature, that learning of which the Sovereign Pontiff speaks.

Justly, my dear friend, are you esteemed the Father of this College; nay more, as the Father of the Clergy; nay more, as the Father of Bishops; and the Right Rev. Prelate at my side is not the only one who is prepared to acknowledge in you that endearing title which you share with Louis of Grenada.

"Pius the Ninth is not the only Pontiff, my brethren, who knew the merits of our venerable friend. When our little Church was expanded from the number of four to that of eight Vicars Apostolic, we remember, if he does not, that Gregory the Sixteenth set his mind upon him for a mitre. But from that modest and humble estimate of himself, and doubtless from a deep and elevated sense of the Episcopal responsibility, he dared to struggle with the Apostolic will, and when he left that Rome where he at last succeeded in winning his liberty, the great Pontiff said to him—'Now that I know you so well, I will not so easily let you escape a second time.'

"Half a century since you began your labours in this college! There is a vein of melancholy in the recollection. Would that the fifty years past were fifty years to come! But may God long sustain your spirit, young and fresh as it still is, and may Time touch your frame in a manner as gentle and kindly as your own; may you find Heaven late, but find it well. In the old monastic rite the Jubilarian receives his staff to support his declining years. Your spirit still sustains your frame with ease; but may the love and veneration of the Clergy of this diocese be your staff and support, and may God within your heart be your consolation."

Dr. Weedall's reply to these addresses was fervent, feeling, elegant, and eloquent. It is too long to be given here entire: yet too beautiful to be much curtailed. It is the last, however, of his glorious effusions which can be presented to the reader; and he will bear with the insertion of at least the greater portion of this masterly production.

"My dear Lord,

"Before I proceed to reply to the addresses just presented to me, let me acknowledge how profoundly I am humbled and confused by your Lordship's unexpected and unmerited eulogies. I dare not admit their applicability, yet know not how to shape a protest. I feel, however, deeply grateful, though I can scarcely describe my emotions. Your Lordship must be indulgent to my feelings and suffer me to proceed in my course.

"My dear Young Friends,

"I accept your kind affectionate address with feelings of reciprocal affection. It is fresh, and warm, and generous; and I assure you that so sympathetically does it reach the heart and stir the current in the veins, that I go back to the years of comparative youth, and fancy I am anticipating my jubilee by an error of calculation. It is only too flattering and too kind. You must, many of you, have taken me on credit, and, even so, have credited me largely. But if youth is generous and confiding, age is trusty and true; and what you so kindly have assumed me to have been and to be, that with God's blessing, I hope you will ever find me. The titles of father and of children bespeak exactly the relationship which I love to contemplate between us.

* * * * *

"But besides receiving an address, which I do with a joyful heart, I must not forget that I have to make one; and particularly now that I have to advert to the most valuable and valued compliment which my dear friends and associates, the Priests and Professors of the College, have just now so unexpectedly offered, and which calls for especial notice, as for special and grateful thanks......

"I will refer, however, to this address to justify a line of reply which I had previously planned, touching as it does so pointedly on a subject which involves, indeed, a common interest......I mean the subject which has created the present commemoration—*my long connection with the college* for the *admitted period of fifty years*.

"I have witnessed during the period in question great undertakings, great personages, great changes, great difficulties, great struggles, and great success. I watched at the cradle of the college, saw its infancy, its growth, its maturity, its vigorous development, and final translation hither. Fifty years have seen its Genesis and its Exodus. Fifty years nearly touch on those patriarchal times when Douay, and Lisbon, and Valladolid, and St. Omer's, poured out their devoted Missionaries to wage the holy battles of our misguided country. *There were giants in those days.* We sprang from the good old race that had studied in the venerable halls which Cardinal Allen and so many martyrs had consecrated, and who brought back with them the sacred fire which they had kept alive during the desolation of captivity. Two or three little brave colonies dotted themselves down here and there over the country, reckless of personal sacrifice, to secure religion and education to Catholic youth, and holy successors in that ministry which they themselves so meekly adorned. Ours was the smallest of these little colonies, the scantiest, the worst provided. It was founded in troublous times, when prudence ventured not beyond the exigencies of the day. It had been first the residence, and then the legacy of a holy martyr, the last victim of that astounding calumny which so long remained the opprobium of the statute book and of the country—the legacy of one who was condemned to death for the technical treason of wearing a surplice and saying Mass!

"In due course of events it became the lot and the portion of the illustrious Milner, under whose ample ægis we rose into confidence and strength. He *planted and watered*, and *God*, benignantly, *gave increase*. Sturdy missionaries went forth from his camp, grave, sedate, and earnest labourers, men of zeal and men of prayer—for Dr. Milner was not an historian only, or only theologian and controversialist, but he was a man of primitive piety, of deep asceticism, humble, benevolent, mortified; a man of the cloister as well as of the camp, who could infuse a spirit into others, and pour over a college a precious ointment which emitted a perfume, and filled the house long after his frail *vessel was broken, and his pitcher crushed at the fountain head.*

" I have said that Oscott was the smallest, the scantiest, the least provided of the Catholic colleges. But under such a guidance it supplied its contingents with a generous fidelity, and worked out the common objects in proportion to its means. But its frame was not equal to its spirit. It soon had fulfilled its limited destiny, and had reached the extreme term which men and materials had originally assigned it. It was confessedly inadequate to the wants of the mission: it had no ecclesiastical character about it, no capacity of usefulness, no elements of durability, And hence circumstances concurred—human, physical, and moral circumstances concurred and combined to warn us that we could no longer dwell there. We followed, therefore, an overruling Providence, and pitched our tents in the wilderness. *And now the beautiful places of the wilderness are springing up. The tree beareth its fruit, the fig tree and the vine have yielded their strength.* Joel ii., 22.

" I bless God for the share which he vouchsafed to me in this great work. It is the brightest vision in my remembrance of the past—the greenest spot in my lengthened career—the sweetest delight to have been an humble instrument in the erection of this house, and of thus *mechanically* assisting—for we can claim no more—*mechanically* assisting the great movement which in the hands of God has already produced such wide-spread benefits, and in His blessed hands, we humbly pray, may be productive of indefinitely more.

He proceeded ingeniously to quote from his own Sermon on the opening of the New College, his prediction and prayer for its success; speaking thus amusingly of the author of the passage:—"And one from whom I have a right to quote, and whose words aptly express my present thoughts on the subject," and after beautifully pointing out the striking fulfilment of his hopes and predictions in various ways, he continued as follows:—

"And now, my young friends, having suspended your hilarity so long, you will be glad to excuse me from saying much about myself. In truth, I have very little to say, except to qualify your kind commendations, which are more generous than just. I was taught by my Superiors to believe that the post in which they placed me was the post which God designed for me. So I threw myself into it with hearty good will. I loved my work, and I stuck to it, and became, *totus in illis*, identified with it.

"My principle in government invariably has been this, to be always firm and always just; to encourage, not to deter; to make study attractive, not repulsive; to *draw*, rather than to *drive*; to reach the head through the heart; not rudely to rub off the soft, peachy down of an ingenious mind, but to shield it, to foster it, to preserve carefully its delicate tints, which blends so softly with the flowers of piety, and bring out into rich relief their varied hues and colours. My object has been to make scholars as far as I was able, but to make happy and virtuous scholars. To those two objects have been directed my feeble efforts and feeble prayers. Let philosophers classify as they will the various branches of learning, my classification has been that of an inspired master—*Bonitatem, et disciplinam, et scientiam, &c. Piety*, good *discipline*, and *knowledge*; not knowledge *first and at any rate*, then discipline, and piety *as you can*. But, first piety, next the discipline of obedience, docility, and self-control, and then, as a rich fruit and natural consequence, *knowledge*—knowledge, sound, useful, suitable—knowledge that hath no pride about it, no arrogance, or self-sufficiency. Such knowledge leads directly to God as its end and aim, and inculcates in due subordination, the various duties of man. It qualifies for every department of life, forming in each the saint, the scholar, and the gentleman.

"But learn the lesson correctly—*Bonitatem, et disciplinam, et scientiam doce me.* Keep that order, and you go right; reverse it and you go wrong. Seek for wisdom in the first place. For *wisdom is better than strength*, says Solomon, *and a wise man is better than a strong man. For if one be perfect among the children of men, yet if wisdom be not with him, he shall be nothing regarded. For wisdom is an infinite treasure to men, which they that use become the friends of God, being commended for the gift of discipline. And the care of discipline is love, and love is the keeping of the laws, and the keeping of the laws is the assurance of incorruption. And incorruption bringeth near to God; and therefore the desire of wisdom bringeth to the everlasting kingdom.* Wisdom vi., *passim.*

"My dear friends, I began with an address; I finish with a sermon. But whether an address or sermon, it is the expression of my best wishes for you all, and of my most continual and most fervent prayers, that you may accomplish an education commensurate with the great end of your being. That, though subject here to many pedagogues, you may chiefly aspire to be *taught of God;* and that, whilst grounded in the elements of human learning, *you may be rooted and founded in charity, which is the bond of perfection.*

"In conclusion, let me first respectfully offer my sincere thanks to our venerated Bishop for his condescension in coming here to give solemnity to this day, to my various friends, both of the Clergy and the laity, for their kind congratulations on the occasion, and to my valued coadjutors in the college, of every rank and degree, without whose hearty and affectionate co-operation I could do nothing efficiently in the house. And then, turning once more to my young friends, and reverting to their kind, too kind address, let me embody my thanks and my feelings in one fervent prayer, that He who is the protector of little ones may have you always in His holy keeping, that, in the beautiful prayer of the Church which we sang this day in the Holy Mass, ' being established in the love of God, you may never by any temptations be separated from Him— *ut in tua charitate firmati, nullis à te tentationibus separemur ;'* but that, journeying together through life in the same blameless path, and having fulfilled our respective duties faithfully and perseveringly here below, we may all meet again—pupils and preceptors—to celebrate, with our guardian angels, an eternal jubilee in Heaven."

"At the close of the reply," says the report in the *Tablet*, "the company, superiors, and students, proceeded to the college refectory, where dinner was served; the Bishops, the president, and the more distinguished visitors being seated at a table a little elevated above the rest. During the dessert, a cantata composed for the occasion was sung by the students, and acknowledged by DR. WEEDALL in his usual happy style. The entertainment proceeded with pieces performed by the brass band recently formed among the students, and with various vocal and instrumental pieces suitable to the occasion. The company subsequently met in the room appropriated to the public exhibitions, where the entertainment was sustained by music and humorous recitations.

"Night prayers and Benediction of the Blessed Sacrament in the college chapel closed the solemnities of the day."

It will be easily imagined how gratifying such a day must have been to the feelings of DR. WEEDALL. It went far towards atoning for the humiliations of the long dreary years that he had spent away from his true home. Oscott was fast becoming herself again; and he was beginning to reap the harvest of his renewed labours for her prosperity: *Eat this year the things that spring of* *themselves, and in the second year eat fruits: but in the third year sow and reap, and plant vineyards, and eat the fruit of them.*[*] All this was verified in these few years of his final presiding over St. Mary's College.

[*] Isaias xxxvii., 30.

CHAPTER XIX.

Dr. Weedall's Active Labours in the College—Exhibition at Midsummer, 1854—Festival on the Feast of St. Cecily—Proposal to Erect an Academic Hall—Dr. Weedall's Visit to the Manchester Exhibition—Dangerous Illness in Lent, 1859—Partial Recovery—Visit to Malvern—Return to Oscott—Last Sickness—Death—Funeral—Proposed Chantry to His Memory.

Though Dr. Weedall's health was but indifferent generally, and though at times he suffered very severely, he was still very active, and laboured on with the same devotedness, energy, and holy cheerfulness. He was always stirring, and never idle. A holy writer has said: "Otiositas inimica est animæ; si non legeris, si non studueris, dormitabit anima tua præ tædio, et hostes tuæ animæ sabbata tua deridebunt."*

The Exhibition at Midsummer of this year, 1854, the first under the restored president, was particularly brilliant; and was honoured by the attendance of the Bishop of Birmingham, who distributed the prizes; of Dr. S. Ives, a distinguished convert, who had been a Protestant bishop in

---

* Idleness is the enemy of the soul; if you do not read, if you do not study, your soul will *slumber through heaviness*, and the enemies of your soul will *mock at your sabbaths*.—Peter of Blois, *Tr. de Inst. Episc.*

America; Lord Henry Ker, who had been an Anglican clergyman; William Acton, Esq., an old Oscotian, and many other highly respectable visitors. Dr. WEEDALL gradually introduced salutary reforms, and made various beneficial changes and improvements. The playday on the feast of St. Cecily, November 22nd, had been enjoyed exclusively by the choir, and those who served at the altar, or were employed in the sacristy. It was generally spent in some excursions away from the college; but it was judged better to make it in future a home festival for the whole of the students. It was accordingly celebrated with great spirit, as a grand day of festivity, in which all partook with the greatest hilarity and enjoyment. Games of "bandy" in the morning, a capital dinner, with music during the dessert, and a dramatic performance in the evening, filled up the day, to the great gratification of the whole establishment.

At the Midsummer Exhibition of the year 1856, the numbers of the College having happily gone on increasing, it was found impracticable by the superiors, "with even an ordinary regard to the comfort of their friends," as Dr. WEEDALL expressed it, to invite them to be present. No remedy could be foreseen for this increasing inconvenience, but the erection of a large, commodious Academic Hall. Dr. WEEDALL issued a short circular, inviting the friends of the College to assist in the work of erecting "a suitable ACADEMIC HALL for Lectures, Examinations, Public Exhibitions, &c." He explained that the want of such a building had arisen from the necessity of appropriating the room originally built for these purposes to the reception of the Marini or Walshian Library. "We are compelled therefore," he said, "to build, however unprepared in the outset. But the spirit which encourages us to begin, gives omen of a successful completion; and if the same sympathy which cheers us forward, continue throughout, we may soon see a suitable building erected, commensurate with the varied wants, and in harmony with the style and character of the College." The same peculiar elegance of diction and comprehensiveness of language will be observed here as in every thing that he spoke or wrote. This circular was dated November 4th, 1857, and deserves to be embalmed as the last paper which he printed.

But he had nearly accomplished his allotted labours on earth. The great object of his life was now happily attained, the resuscitation of St. Mary's College from its deep depression, and its establishment in secure dignity, with every prospect of increasing prosperity. He had borne the burthen of the day and the heats; he had even toiled on to the eleventh hour, and his Lord and Master would shortly call him to his reward. In the Autumn of 1857, he made a little excursion into Lancashire to recruit his strength and benefit his health; for both had begun to give way under his severe labours. The writer of these pages had the happiness to meet him at Manchester on the occasion of the Great Exhibition of Art Treasures there. Dr. Weedall was the guest of Daniel Lee, Esq., at

Springfield, near Manchester. There the writer spent some time with him very agreeably, and met him also at the house of the worthy Bishop of Salford, Dr. Turner, where he himself was receiving most kind hospitality from his lordship. Dr. WEEDALL appeared tolerably well, and paid several visits to the memorable Exhibition, though he was unable to bear the fatigue and excitement of it long together. The writer parted with him at Springfield, but did not think it would be the last time he should meet him on earth, as it unhappily proved. He found him the same amiable, cheerful, delightful friend that he had ever known him through the long period of years from childhood:—

> " The virtuous man,
> Who keeps his tempered mind serene and pure,
> And every passion aptly harmonised
> Amid a jarring world with vice inflamed."
>
> THOMSON.

He shared in a great degree the writer's own love of old days, and old reminiscences, quite agreeing that

> "Hoc est
> Vivere bis, vita posse priori frui."*
>
> MARTIAL.

And so they enjoyed together, neither probably suspecting that it was for the last time, long conversations on olden times, and laughed over anecdotes which each in turn fetched up from the stores of faithful memory.

---

* This is the art to double life's few days,
To live again our former life and ways.

From the time of DR. WEEDALL's severe attack, on his return from London, in 1853, already mentioned, he had hardly ventured to travel; so that this journey to Lancashire was proof that in some respects his health had improved. Indeed he was then, and during the year following, much better; and continued so till the beginning of the ensuing spring of 1859. When Lent came on, he would observe the fast strictly; though justly exempted from any obligation to fast, on account of his age and infirmities. When entreated not to attempt to fast, he said that he wished to do what he could, because there were several at the parlour table who were unable to observe the fast, and he was unwilling to appear to set the example himself. But he soon found that it was too much for him to attempt, and sunk under it; so that he was obliged to give up fasting altogether. He officiated at the high altar, and gave the ashes on Ash Wednesday. He also conducted the devotion of the Stations on the Friday following. This was the last public function that he performed in the chapel, except that on the feast of the Assumption of our Blessed Lady, he sung an early Mass for the few students who were assembled at the college.

After the First Sunday of Lent, in the middle of March, he became very unwell. He was obliged to keep his room, and soon after was confined to his bed: indeed he was so ill, that it was feared he would never rise from his bed again. During this time he received the Holy Communion almost every day, which was administered to him by the worthy Vice-President, Canon Bagnall. He suffered with the greatest patience, and most exemplary resignation. What seemed to afflict him most, was that he was unable to attend the usual Meditations in the chapel, as he had always done most punctually. He feared that his absence might cause disedification: the very same apprehension which the writer remembers to have been felt by the illustrious Bishop Milner; who when staying at Oscott, and unable from infirmity to rise early enough for the hour of Meditation, which was halfpast six, very humbly begged pardon when he came down, for the disedification which might have been caused by his not appearing earlier, informing us that he could not get any sleep till morning. So it was now with poor DR. WEEDALL, and he had the same delicacy of conscience as his great master and model. He often desired the servant to ask Canon Bagnall to come to his room, as he went down to the chapel, as he wished to speak to him; and it was always to express how sorry he was that he could not attend himself, and to request him to explain to the ecclesiastics the reason of his absence. He was so particular on this point, that when better in health, he never absented himself from the Meditation, though he would have been amply justified if he had done so; for owing to his habitual complaint, he never had a good night's rest. He was disturbed nearly every half hour of the night, and often could get but little sleep till perhaps four o'clock; and often said that when the servant came to call him soon after five, he felt then that he could sleep. Nevertheless he invariably got up, that he might be present in the chapel with the rest at the Meditation.

Dr. WEEDALL partially rallied from this illness; but he had but little relish for food, and his stomach often would not retain it; which is generally the final result of the peculiar malady under which he had suffered more or less through life, but especially for the last six years. The third Provincial Council of Westminster was held at St. Mary's College, as usual, in July; but Dr. WEEDALL felt unequal to attending it, and went to Malvern, in hopes of receiving benefit to his health. He staid there but a short time, and derived very little benefit. When he returned to the college, his stomach was in a state of great debility, so that he could hardly retain any food. It was evident that the stomach had lost its tone and power, and that his dissolution could not be averted by any human means. He kept on, however, as well as he could, at his usual duties; but with much suffering, and many interruptions. The writer received a short note from him, dated October 21st, only sixteen days before his death, in which he said that he was quite unequal to any correspondence, and begged his friend's prayers.

Having so long taught others how to live, he was now to teach them by his own example how to die. The evening was come, and the faithful labourer was to be called to receive his hire. At the end of October he became much worse. A clerical friend paid him a visit on All Saints Day, and found him extremely distressed by constant vomiting, and suffering from fever and thirst. By his own desire, his friend read to him the Epistle and Gospel of the festival, and he remarked: "What a beautiful and impressive Mass it is to day!" On his friend's remarking to him that he hoped he would soon be of that glorious band, for he must now say: "*Cursum consummavi—fidem servavi*," he stopped him, and said, bursting into tears: "Ah! would that I could say the remainder; "*in reliquo reposita est mihi corona justitiæ*." His friend could not proceed for some moments, for the burst of emotion with which DR. WEEDALL was affected: he was deeply moved himself, and could say but little on that occasion. On Saturday, November 3rd, the venerable man received the Holy Viaticum; and on the Sunday morning, Extreme Unction; both administered to him by Canon Bagnall. About half-past twelve in the day, he was seized with violent cramps and spasms, so that he was thought to be at the point of death, and Canon Bagnall gave him the Last Blessing, and read the Recommendation of a Departing Soul. From that time till nearly five o'clock he was not perfectly conscious. The clerical friend before mentioned came to see him again on that evening. He found him in constant convulsions, but perfectly conscious and able to speak, though with difficulty. This good priest began to recite the *Miserere* Psalm, intending to say it all through himself; but DR. WEEDALL took up each alternate verse, and as his articulation was much impeded, he took particular care to finish every word, and every verse, with the greatest accuracy. When afterwards his friend began those words of St. Paul, "*Quis me separabit a charitate Christi?*" Dr. WEEDALL went on with them, finishing off the whole verse in the midst of his convulsions, adding: "I think it is something like that, is it not?" Then his friend began some other ejaculations, but he said, interrupting him: "Say for me that one you said from St. Paul last time." He did so: "*Cursum consummavi, fidem servavi, etc.,*" and when it was ended, he stopped and dwelt upon it with evident delight.

He suffered greatly and constantly from thirst, and when offered some iced water, he said, "Don't you think it too great a luxury?" and he would not finish the draught. That pious priest observed in the narrative with which he favoured the writer, and from which he has been enabled to give these edifying particulars,—that "he preferred the thought of the *haustus æternæ vitæ* to refreshing his poor body in its last necessity," and that "many things had been utterred by him in a similar strain at other times, indicating the unvarying consistent goodness of this holy man." It was thought that he could not survive beyond the next day. He held out however during Monday, and Canon Bagnall sat up with him during that his last night. After midnight he lost all consciousness, and calmly expired at four o'clock in the morning on the 7th of November, having completed his 71st year on the 6th of the previous September, and spent forty-three years of his life at Oscott.

Thus did this holy man consummate his course: but he had not *run in vain, nor laboured in vain.*[*] A better eulogy could not be penned with reference to him than that which appeared in the *Weekly Register*, with the well-known signature of "Father Thomas." "One of the best, kindest, humblest of men has gone away from us. He was all his life the same, pious, quiet, bland, ever with a smile on his lips, and ready to do any kind thing for every one. To make others happy was his only ambition, peace and charity at any price, forbearance and indulgence, and all that the word meekness signifies, were eminently his. Dr. Weedall made Oscott what it was in the most prosperous days of that college, and under his rule it lost in latter time none of its eminence. There was a solidity in Dr. Weedall, that did not show out on all occasions; but it was there, and when required, was forthcoming. His was a mind that you could reason with, and although a superior, the lowest in the college had nothing to apprehend from Dr. Weedall's position. He would patiently hear and calmly argue the case, without impetuosity or imperiousness. Dr. Weedall was a superior man; his mind and heart never ambitioned the tawdry nothings, the vain distinctions of this hollow world, nor the high levels. The good, humble, and learned Dr. Weedall saw through, and over all these unsubstantialities, and cared for them nothing. God speed his spirit, for it was a meek and humble one, and pure as snow." This is the spontaneous

[*] Phil. ii., 16.

testimony of a priest of sound judgment, and long experience of men; and it is the more valuable as coming from one totally unconnected with the College of Oscott, or the diocese of Birmingham.

Dr. Weedall had piously desired to be buried in the habit of the third order of Mount Carmel, of which he was a member, and of course his wish was obeyed. The funeral took place on Friday, November 11th, and was conducted with great and becoming solemnity. The Bishop of Birmingham sung the High Mass of *Requiem*. The Bishops of Shrewsbury and Northampton were present in the choir; Monsignor Searle, as representative of the Cardinal Archbishop; the Cathedral Chapter of Birmingham, and about forty other priests. The coffin bore the following inscription :—

Rmus. Dnus. Henricus Weedall, S.T.D.
Præl. Domest. SS. D. N.
Præpositus Cap. Birminghamien.
Hujus Collegii Rector.
Pie. Obiit Die VII. Novembris.
A.D. 1859. Ætat Suæ 72.
R. I. P.

When the procession passed out from the entrance hall of the college, along the terrace, and round the outside of the chapel, with nearly a hundred, including students, walking in surplices, followed by the Canons of the Chapter of Birmingham, and the three Bishops immediately before the coffin, the spectacle was quite overpowering. The weather unfortunately was bitterly cold, and felt severely in that elevated situation. The coffin was finally deposited in a recess in the crypt, immediately above that which holds the remains of the first who was laid there, the Rev. William Foley.

The funeral Sermon was preached after the High Mass by the Very Rev. Dr. Newman, of the Oratory. His text was from the first Psalm:—*He shall be like a tree which is planted near the running waters, which shall bring forth its fruit in due season. And his leaf shall not fall off; and all whatsoever he shall do shall prosper.* Dr. Newman felt deeply, as he acknowledged in the sermon, that he "was not the person who had any right, or" as he humbly said, "any power to refer back to the history of Catholicism in these parts,....not even," he added, "in his own personal character can I worthily describe the man whom I so much loved and so much admired;....for I have never lived nor worked with him,....I have never witnessed his daily life, and am unable, except in that external aspect which is presented to a stranger, to record his virtues and his good works." Nevertheless, all who know Dr. Newman will know that nothing from him can fail to be excellent; and with all his disadvantages, thus humbly avowed, he delivered a very beautiful, and highly interesting discourse, tracing the leading points in the life, and seizing the main features of the character of the deceased prelate, with astonishing discernment and correctness. The Sermon was published at the request of all present, Bishops, Clergy, and Gentry. Canon McDonnell, so long connected with Oscott and Birmingham, had, by request, penned a short memoir of DR. WEEDALL for the information of Dr. Newman; but by some mistake, it did not reach him in time for the composition of his Sermon, for which it would have been very valuable. He has, however, availed himself of it in several interesting notes in the published Discourse.

After the funeral obsequies, a meeting was held in the library, with the Bishop in the chair, to consider in what way the memory of the departed president could be best honoured and perpetuated. The Bishop proposed the erection of a chantry attached to the college chapel, to be designated "*The* WEEDALL *Chantry.*" This was unanimously approved, and a subscription was at once begun to defray the expense, which Canon McDonnell claimed the honour of heading with his name, as the oldest friend of DR. WEEDALL present, having known him fifty-seven years. A Committee was finally chosen to procure subscriptions, and promote the laudable object of erecting this appropriate and beneficial memorial, where Masses may be continually offered for the soul of the departed.

A memorial in the temple of the Lord. And they that are far off shall come, and shall build in the temple of the Lord.[*]

The just shall be in everlasting remembrance: he shall not fear the evil hearing.[†]

The memory of him shall not depart away, and his name shall be in request from generation to generation.[‡]

[*] ZACH. VI., 14, 15.   [†] PS. CXI., 7.   [‡] ECCLUS. XXXIX., 13.

CHAPTER XX.

Dr. Weedall's Personal Appearance, Physical Qualities, and Habits—Mental Qualities—Tastes—Love of Reading—Neglect of Correspondence—His Cheerfulness and Wit—His Qualities as President—Instances of Benevolence—His Talents and Peculiarities as a Preacher—His Great Virtues—Conclusion.

THE foregoing pages have placed before the reader the history of HENRY WEEDALL from his childhood to his grave,—that grave which he entered *in abundance, as a heap of wheat is brought in in its season. Behold this is even so as we have searched out: and now thou hast heard it, consider it thoroughly in thy mind.** It has been searched out by his old and devoted friend, who had had the happiness to know him for fifty-six years. And now that the reader has perused it, he has assuredly found much for him to *consider thoroughly in his mind*. It only remains for the writer to sum up the qualities, physical and mental, which characterised this eminent man; and this he will proceed to do, at the hazard of some repetitions, to the best of his ability.

To speak first of DR. WEEDALL's personal appearance, formation, and bodily frame. He was very

* Job v., 26, 27.

low in stature, hardly measuring five feet two inches: but he was not slightly made. The defect was in the lower limbs, which were disproportionately short, giving him a diminutive appearance; but he was so well formed otherwise, that when he was seated at table, his short stature would not be suspected. His bust was very fine: his head large, and with all the developments that would delight a phrenologist. He had a broad and noble forehead, and though his lips were a little too full and prominent, it was manifestly the prominency of eloquence. His eyes, though the torture of his life, and always a sad barrier to his pursuit of study, presented no outward indications of weakness, except that they were often unusually moist and glistening. But they had a bland, cheerful, and benevolent look, and were large, and very expressive. They could not bear much light; and if he walked out in the snow, he suffered great pain from its dazzling whiteness, and could not at all endure it in the sunshine. His complexion was pale and transparent; but his countenance extremely pleasing and prepossessing, and his address always kind and cordial. None of his friends will forget the warm shake with both hands, with which he was wont to greet them, nor the rich tone of his hearty, "How do you *do?*" with the emphasis strongly laid upon the last word.

Though diminutive in stature, he was strong, and particularly active; and with all his chronic ailments, he contrived always to keep about, and attend the best he could to every duty of his position.

That he attained the advanced age of seventy-one, is sufficient proof that he had radically a good constitution, and he never was much troubled with coughs or colds. His habits were hardy, and he abhorred any luxurious indulgences. He made plentiful use of cold water, washing his eyes and head in it several times every day, both in winter and summer. He was rather particular in his toilet; and often rallied by his friends for his copious establishment of water jugs, sponges, brushes, and other appendages of the dressing table. But the state of his head and eyes required very frequent ablutions, and this gave him the habit of attending so much to personal neatness. This care extended naturally to his dress, in which he was always very particular. Care and economy were constantly observed by him in a remarkable degree. Indeed he was fussy and fidgetty in this respect; and full of precautions and contrivances which others would never imagine. When cassocks began to be worn at the old College, he calculated that the friction of the knees would be seriously detrimental to his drapery, and so had knee caps made of an inferior fabric, which he would carefully tie on whenever he resumed his cassock, on coming in from his walks abroad. If he had any nice article of furniture, such as an ornamental fire screen, he would cover it with a case, and rather endure day by day the unsightliness of a holland covering, than expose a handsome piece of furniture to premature disfigurement; thus practically losing all enjoyment of what he professed so much to value. He kept a large supply of clothes by him, and frequently changed his habiliments in the day, before the use of cassocks became general. One Sunday morning at Oscott he came down in a fine new coat, well made and nicely adjusted. Bishop Milner was staying at the college, as he so often did, and could not help noticing DR. WEEDALL's fine coat, and good-naturedly indulging in a little banter, said: "What a fine coat you have got, MR. UDALL!* You look quite smart to day." To which the little man cleverly replied: "Why, my lord, great men, like your lordship, have higher recommendations; but we little men must make the most of ourselves, even by the cut of a coat." The answer exceedingly amused the good, kind-hearted Bishop, who was always very fond of DR. WEEDALL, and well knew his worth.

His room, his library, and all about him, was always neatly arranged, and indicative of good taste. His habits, as already observed, were ever active and industrious, and his pursuits always in accordance with his vocation and position in the College. As a youth he excelled in most games, and in after life he would do everything well that he had undertaken. He often observed that if any thing was worth doing at all, it was worth doing well; and with reference to books, he used to say, that any book that deserved to be read once, would

* Bishop Milner often called him *Udall:* alleging that this ought to be is name, as it was a genuine old English name, and that of a distinguished old controversial writer.

be worth reading a second time. As his eyes could bear so little reading, it was wonderful what a knowledge of books he managed to acquire. It was remarkable too how readily he learned from others reading to him, and how well he could keep his attention to such reading. If he chanced, however, to be distracted, he would invariably request to have the passage which had escaped him read over again, sometimes indeed to the trial and annoyance of his reader.

His handwriting, like his every other performance, was particularly neat, regular, and graceful. His writing in early life was evidently formed upon the examples of his first masters at Sedgley Park, good old Mr. Harbut, and Rev. Joseph Birch, especially of the latter, as is apparent in some Theological Essays found among his papers, where the handwriting was as yet unfixed, and not equal to that which every one so much admired in his subsequent course. He was always, however, a good writer; and when at Sedgley Park he was famous for flourishing swans, eagles, pens, and other figures, which he would readily do for others also, when requested. He had much taste for pictures, but no talent for drawing; which it is remarkable that very few of the clergy have. Indeed he once asked the writer, whom he found drawing, some questions about the mode of representing sloping ground and other objects in landscape, which proved that he had no idea even of the simplest drawing. Yet he had a keen perception of all that was picturesque and beautiful, whether in nature or art; he had a fine ear for music, and a clear melodious bass voice; and he sung correctly, and with great feeling and expression: but he never played on any instrument, and once expressed surprise how any one could play treble and bass together, from written music, and without looking at the keys of the piano; this being, as he said, a fourfold operation, which would perplex him exceedingly.

He was, like many others, quite carried away by the enthusiasm for Gothic architecture and mediæval decoration, which was so much the rage at the time when he was building the New College. He was a steady patron of Pugin, and eulogised him highly in his funeral orations on Bishop Walsh, and the Earl of Shrewsbury. But his studies were directed in every way that was at all within his reach; and it seemed as if the disqualifications which he suffered from the sad nervous affection of his eyes and head only made him more anxious and assiduous in cultivating every branch of learning in his power. He was always seen with books about him, or carried under his arm, or actually under perusal. He rarely came down to meals without bringing to the table some book, which he would seize the first chance of getting some one to read to him. His memory was excellent, even wonderful; and to this happy retentive faculty was doubtless owing his astonishing store of knowledge of almost every kind. He acquired it with more difficulty than others, and retained it on that account more satisfactorily than the generality of students.

One fault his friends had always to complain of, that he was a bad epistolary correspondent. It is, as St. Basil beautifully observes, a great comfort to those who cannot meet together, to correspond by letters. "Magnum Deus præbuit solatium his qui coram congredi non possunt, colloquium per litteras."* St. Basil was not the only one among the holy Fathers who felt the value of punctual writing, and knew how to rebuke tardy correspondents. "I am not ashamed," says St. Jerome, "of the importunity with which I have frequently obtruded my letters, while you were silent, that I might deserve an answer."† It certainly betrays great selfishness, and a great want of friendship, to neglect writing to those friends who are known to attach much value to letters, and derive great solace from them. Dr. Johnson has well said: "To let friendship die away by negligence and silence is certainly not wise. It is voluntarily to throw away one of the greatest comforts of this weary pilgrimage; of which when it is, as it must be, taken finally away, he that travels on alone, will wonder how his esteem could be so little."‡ In Dr. Weedall's case there was certainly no indifference to the value of friendship, nor the least idea of letting it die away; but he was ever dilatory, and ever complaining of the multitude of his occupations, as his

---

* S. Basil. *Epist.* ccxx., *Al.* ccxcix.

† Non me pœnitet impudentiæ, qua tacentibus vobis, epistolas meas frequenter ingessi, ut rescriptum mererer.—St. Hieron. *Ep.* lxxxii., ad *Marcell. et Anaps.*

‡ Boswell's Johnson, iv., ch. v.

excuse for not writing. Thus he would say, that he had not been able to write "from the inexorable pressure of letter writing and *College Discipline and Police*," which had prevented him from reading as well as writing:—Dublin Reviews, Ramblers, Callista, &c., all remaining on his table uncut and unread. But, unfortunately for his defence, he was reminded that it was just the same when he had no college business, and no heavy mission to attend to. It was in fact his habit, and wherever he might have been, he would have been the same. He never could be enticed into regular correspondence.

In the course of this biography, allusion has been often made to Dr. Weedall's cheerfulness and general good spirits amidst all his ailments. His familiar conversation was always sprightly and agreeable. He dearly loved a joke, and his laugh was hearty and contagious. No one told an anecdote better, though they might relate it in less time, for he was rather long over a story. It was well said of him, by an old friend—"His manner is elegant, his substance ingenious. Wit sparkles over his sentences, as rapid as the coruscations of the Northern Lights."* The misfortune is, that like those meteors, wit dazzles for the moment, and expires; so that nothing is so difficult to recall as the sparkling effusions of wit. Thus though the writer has been delighted with so many bright flashes from Dr. Weedall, he can fetch up scarcely any in addition to those already recorded in the foregoing

* Canon McDonnell.

pages. He must beg the reader to consider the few following specimens which he can remember as by no means fairly representing the bright powers which DR. WEEDALL brought into play continually. When he used to attend certain Philosophical Lectures in Birmingham, going from Oscott for the purpose, on one occasion it was a very rainy evening. An Unitarian minister who knew him, and used to attend the same course, said to him : " I see you don't mind the weather," " No," he replied, " I come, *weather* or no." When the writer of these pages was his pupil, and the class had just been explaining Horace's ode,

> " Beatus ille qui procul negotiis,
> *Ut prisca gens mortalium, etc.*"

it happened that the chair on which Professor WEEDALL was seated broke down under him; when taking up the broken chair he pleasantly alluded to its age and antique construction, by saying: "I think this is rather *ut prisca gens mortalium.*"

Once when a question was discussing as to precedence between a Vicar General and a Provost, one present, who happened to hold both offices, observed that he should find it difficult to walk *before* himself. DR. WEEDALL directly said: "Not more so, than to walk *after* yourself."

Upon a friend's remarking, as they walked down the college garden, what an excellent succession crop there was of beans, DR. WEEDALL said: " O yes, *fuimus*, we have *been*." One morning at breakfast, he observed one of the company taking an unusual quantity of dry toast, and proceeding to butter it, and thought to give him a hint, by saying: "Perhaps Mr. F. all the company may not like their toast buttered." The other, however, who was always ready, and quite a match for him, answered, "All that I am buttering for, do." When some one was ill, and it was observed in answer to an enquiry after his health, that he was but "So, so." Dr. Weedall said: "I suppose you mean, '*sic, sic.*'" He always enjoyed a pleasant chat at night; and however late it was, and however drowsy he felt, he would at once cheer up and encourage a prolonged parley at such a time: and then was the witching hour when he brought out his stores of puns and pleasantry, and indulged most richly in wit and anecdote.

These, however, were but the sparks which flew off from a mind radiant and brilliant, with powers of the highest order. His conversation was always agreeable and instructive, remarkable for great shrewdness of perception, soundness of judgment, solidity, and fairness of reasoning. When speaking on any grave subject, his manner was slow and sententious: he chose the very words to produce the greatest effect, and uttered them with strong emphasis and powerful expression. His abilities were brought out conspicuously in his important office of college president. It occasionally happened, as it must ever happen in such establishments, that he had to address the students collectively upon some breach of discipline, or some objectionable practices which had crept in amongst them. On such occasions his command of language and forcible inculcation of their duties were very striking. But not less so was the paternal solicitude and kindness, with which he always blended and tempered his correction.

On one occasion, he came upon two church students quite unexpectedly in the playroom, who, during study time were enjoying some merriment of a noisy character. But when he saw them performing some very ludicrous antics, wholly unconscious of his presence, he only said, with a smile of great good nature: "Well, if you did want to amuse yourselves, you need not make a noise to disturb the whole house."

No one could have more equably held the balance between severity and indulgence; and no superior was more generally loved, as well as respected. He knew how to encourage talent, and also to discard discreditable idleness. When he was once remonstrated with, and charged with requiring optimism, he smartly replied that he did not seek to secure *optimism*, but to exclude *pessimism*.

But a thousand instances are known of his great kindness and consideration for those under his care. He once sent for a boy to his room, who was fond of fishing. He said to him: "I hear you are rather fond of fishing, is it so?" "Yes, Sir," said the boy, "I am fond of it." "And what do you bait with?" "Some times with worms." "Is not that cruel? How would you like a hook big enough for you, to be thrust through your body, and yourself plunged into the water, and a fish a good deal bigger than yourself coming and biting at you? I will give you a shilling, if you won't bait with worms."

When the same boy grew up, and became a divine and cantor, he asked the Doctor's leave to go to the Musical Festival in Birmingham, as he had never heard the "Messiah" thus sung, and thought it would help his musical taste, as well as prove a great enjoyment. DR. WEEDALL said, that as a young divine he thought it would be an inconvenient precedent and example, and asked him to deny himself the enjoyment. The young man said he would do as the Doctor wished, and would think no more of it. The next morning, DR. WEEDALL came quietly and unexpectedly into the young divine's room, closed the door, and gently said: " I have been thinking over your request to go to the Festival. I will permit you to go. And should another young divine wish to follow your example, and plead the precedent, he need not have leave, unless he have the same office. But is it not expensive?" " Yes, Sir, I suppose the ticket will be a sovereign." "That," rejoined the Doctor, "is a great deal for a young divine to pay." Then, producing a sovereign, he said: "Will you buy a ticket, and allow me to present it to you?"

With talents such as DR. WEEDALL possessed, he would undoubtedly have attained excellence as a poet, but beyond the few pieces already spoken of in the foregoing pages, he wrote no poetry.

Besides sermons indeed he wrote very few pieces of any kind, but his compositions were remarkably correct and elegant. He was an excellent reader, but rather apt to make his public reading too long. At one time he was accustomed to read a lecture to the students every morning after Mass, before they left the chapel. He read from Gobinet's *Instruction of Youth*, an admirable book, containing perhaps the very best course of spiritual reading for most persons. But he read an unreasonably long time, forgetting that the attention of young persons particularly cannot be secured beyond a moderate space. It happened that Bishop Milner was present on one occasion, it being the day of the Midsummer Exhibition, at which he came, as usual, to preside. It was customary for his lordship, on the morning of that day, after Mass, to examine the students in catechism and in religious knowledge in general. So after Mass, Dr. WEEDALL did not give his usual reading, but all waited for the Bishop to turn round and begin his examination. Dr. Milner, however, never thought of the matter, but quietly sat down in his faldstool, and composed himself to listen to Dr. WEEDALL'S customary lecture. After a considerable pause, as no one came forward, the prefect gave the usual signal for the boys to depart, and the chapel was soon cleared. At breakfast, some one said to the Bishop: "Why, my lord, you sadly disappointed us all: we expected you to examine in catechism as usual." To which he replied: "Why did not some one tell me? I never thought about it. I was expecting to hear a *long* lecture from MR. WEEDALL on Confession, or Matrimony."

Though DR. WEEDALL excelled in almost every thing that he undertook, preaching was evidently his grand distinguishing talent. His sermons were composed with great attention, and polished again and again with untiring labour. This however was productive of some unfortunate results. Having by compositions so elaborate at first, acquired a certain high standing as a preacher, he felt, as he used to acknowledge, as if he must always keep up the same reputation. Also, when he attempted to speak extempore, he would say something sufficiently intelligible, and then refine and refine it away, till one could hardly tell what he really meant. When he composed a regular sermon, he wrote, or dictated, the first draught readily, and generally made it such as would satisfy most critics; but he seemed never satisfied himself. Several of his sermons were written out twice, or even three times, with copious alterations and improvements. His style was ornate and elegant, but the structure not always in accordance with the strict rules of grammar and composition. He seemed often carried away too much by his subject to stop to arrange all by rule; and thus his sentences were frequently overloaded and lengthened, till their balance was partly lost, and their effect somewhat weakened. Again, he often paid little attention to punctuation, employing a dash where he ought to have placed a stop, the practice of too many slovenly and half educated writers, though assuredly he was neither. The defect in his case arose from the rapid and impetuous flow of his ideas, which would hardly bear subjection to rules of composition. Sometimes, on the other hand, he would put a full stop, and then go on with another sentence without any verb, which ought properly to have been the completion of the sentence preceding, and been attached to it. But these after all were only small spots on a sun of dazzling splendour. His sermons were the outpourings of genius, strong, rich and eloquent to a startling degree. They were singularly beautiful as compositions, and contained a powerful theology, on which was grounded what was most edifying and instructive. He attained assuredly the two great ends of Christian oratory, to convince and persuade. The reader has read several specimens in the course of this work, mostly taken from his published discourses. These, however, were not his best; and it is to be hoped that his friends and admirers will encourage the publication of all his Sermons. He had no great stock, not much above fifty; and when it is remembered what pain it cost him to write, it is only wonderful that he composed so many.

His delivery was as elegant as his compositions. When he spoke extempore indeed, his habitual desire of excellence made him often dissatisfied with his language, so that he sometimes repeated and hesitated painfully. But this was the case in his extemporaneous effusions only. His prepared sermons were carefully committed to memory; and the memory that could retain those long and elaborate compositions, was itself wonderful. Yet in those palmy days of his preaching,—which the writer so well remembers,—he delivered his written sermons with perfect ease and without hesitation: all seemed to flow spontaneously, and all was perfectly natural and apparently unstudied.

In his latter years, however, he found it impossible to learn his sermons by heart, and when he gave a written discourse, was accustomed to read it. Towards the end of his career, he generally preached extempore. He often had in his hand, partly concealed by a handkerchief, a slip of paper, on which he had noted the leading paragraphs and texts, to aid his memory in the delivery; but he was rarely observed to have recourse to it. Once he got out completely; but without showing any embarrassment, he honestly avowed it in these words: "Having unfortunately lost the thread of my discourse, I will proceed to another part of the subject;" and so went on and finished with perfect self possession.

His pronunciation of every word was clear and distinct; so that, though he never spoke loud, he was always heard well, and listened to attentively; his voice was mellow and deep toned; his attitude dignified and commanding. He usually preached from the altar step: but there were no tossings about, no tricks of oratory, no antics to surprise, no coming forward, or stepping backward, no pointing to the sky, or lowering hands to the earth. Leaving all the mountebank gesticulations in which too many preachers indulge, his action was simple, natural, and graceful. The expression of his countenance was enough: he needed no studied gestures, or artificial postures, to impress his audience, and seldom had recourse to any extraordinary action. Once in a most moving sermon on Good Friday his voice faltered, and he covered his eyes with his hands, as he uttered in tender accents: "Come, my fellow sinners, come to Calvary, come to the cross!" On that great day his sermon was always very pathetic, and bespoke the most ardent love of his crucified Redeemer; and he used to explain the ceremony of kissing the cross in a striking and satisfactory manner, quite his own. The great feature of his delivery was the earnest and emphatic manner with which he uttered his finely constructed sentences. He laid strong accent on most of the syllables, and made many words emphatic, but particularly certain rather favourite and sonorous words, such as "propounded," "calculated," "commensurate," and similar expressions. He was heard with rivetted attention, and when he was expected to preach, every one was glad, and anticipated both pleasure and spiritual profit.

The only drawback to his utility as a preacher, was the great length of his sermons. He never took in the sage maxim: "*the more said the less retained.*" Nearly every one of his sermons might have made two of sufficient length. Though he did so much good, he would have benefitted others even more, saved himself much painful exertion to little purpose, and prevented much impatience and grave inconvenience to his audience, if he had limited himself to a reasonable length. He forgot that if his fountain could flow for ever, his hearers could not hold for ever; and even *his* sermons, eloquent and touching as they were, sometimes tired out the patience of many before they were concluded. In the middle portion of them, too, he was apt to philosophise in a manner rather dry and didactic; which, if continued long, is very trying to the hearer's powers of attention. Still, though it has been considered right in a work like this to show the shade as well as the light of these compositions, they were all masterly productions, noble emanations of a clear head and a warm heart, the radiations of genius, the effusions of religious ardour, the discourses of talent absolutely unrivalled, and moving exhortations of most pure and tender piety.

Dr. Weedall indeed was a truly pious man. He had learned to practise first himself what he taught to others; which, as St. Bernard assures us, gives real force to the preacher's words: "Dabis voci tuæ vocem virtutis, si quod suades, tibi prius cognoscereris persuasisse."* His soul was pure, and his life spotless. With all his talents he had no pride, no love of distinction, no ambition. He was unmindful of injury, and a stranger to resentment. He was mixed up in one instance with others in a certain expression of disapprobation of the conduct

---

* Thou wilt give to thy voice a voice of power, if what thou inculcatest to others, thou art known to have become first convinced of thyself.—S. Bern., *Serm. V. in Cantic.*

a brother priest; but he quickly sought occasions of pursuing him with friendly salutations, and substantial proofs of charity and friendship, which dissipated every remnant of unpleasant feeling. There was a period in his life, as these pages have shown, when he had much to suffer; but never was he heard to speak of his trials, or to reflect upon any who might have occasioned them: and if Bishop Ullathorne could truly say of him that he never made an enemy, it may be proclaimed with equal truth that he never appeared to think that any one had acted injuriously towards him. When certain friends were observing to him the strong indications of hostility which one party in particular showed towards him, he merely said: "Well, I know it takes two to get up a quarrel, and I will not be one." He was ever kind, benevolent, and full of holy charity. His love of God and religion was manifest in the devotion with which he said Mass, and officiated in every function of the sacred ministry, as well as in the recollection and profound respect with which he always appeared in the house of God, and the devout attention with which he was accustomed to pray, and join in every religious exercise. He was the judicious tutor and trainer of youth, the guide and instructor of ecclesiastics, the educator of priests, nay even, as his Bishop declared, the father of Bishops, for under him were brought up three Bishops, Drs. Willson, of Hobarton; Mostyn, of Abydos; and Browne, of Shrewsbury.

But he is gone, he has been taken from us; and as the same Bishop so well expressed it: *God blessed his work, and now he has taken the workman!*

" On earth we've lost, in heaven we've gained a friend!"

Like the prophet of Israel, he was carried up in fire,—in the flames of his own ardent charity. Though his humility shrunk from presuming upon it, we can have no doubt that there was *laid up for him a crown of justice, which the Lord the just Judge* was ready to *render to him.** And as to us, whom he has left still " banished sons of Eve," still " groaning and weeping in this valley of tears," let us look to his great example, and strive for his glorious reward.

> " The spell is broken! never more
> Can mortal life again seem gay;
> No future ever can restore
> The perished and the passed away!"†

Still let us learn some useful moral from our desolation, and " As we daily see our friends die around us, we that are left must cling closer, and if we can do nothing more, at least pray for one another: and remember, that as others die we must die too, and prepare ourselves diligently for the last great trial."‡

But we that live, bless the Lord, from this time, now and for ever.||

* 2 Tim. iv., 8.   † Moir.   ‡ Johnson. || Ps. cxiii.

The End.

www.ingramcontent.com/pod-product-compliance
Lightning Source LLC
Chambersburg PA
CBHW030740230426
43667CB00007B/783